FREE TRADE
— IN THE —
BERMUDA TRIANGLE

...and Other Tales of Counterglobalization

BRETT NEILSON

T0337902

University of Minnesota Press

Minneapolis

London

An earlier version of chapter 1 was previously published as "Deterritorializing the Bermuda Triangle: Popular Geography and the Myths of Globalization," *Space and Culture — the Journal* 6 (2000): 48–62; reprinted by permission. An earlier version of chapter 3 was previously published as "Unmapping the Golden Triangle; or, the World on Drugs," *Passages: Interdisciplinary Journal of Global Studies* 2 (2000): 159–85; reprinted by permission. An earlier version of chapter 4 was previously published as "Inside Shangri-La/Outside Globalization: Remapping Orientalist Visions of Tibet," *Communal/Plural: Journal of Transnational and Crosscultural Studies* 8 (2000): 95–112; reprinted by permission of Taylor & Francis and the Research Centre in Intercommunal Studies.

Published by the University of Minnesota Press
111 Third Avenue South, Suite 290
Minneapolis, MN 55401-2520
http://www.upress.umn.edu

Library of Congress Cataloging-in-Publication Data

Neilson, Brett.
    Free trade in the Bermuda Triangle . . . and other tales of counterglobalization /
Brett Neilson.
        p.   cm.
    Includes bibliographical references and index.
    ISBN 0-8166-3871-3 (HC : alk. paper) – ISBN 0-8166-3872-1 (PB : alk. paper)
    1. Capitalism. 2. Globalization. 3. Popular culture. I. Title.
HB501 .N367 2003
337– dc22

                                                                                2003014541

Printed in the United States of America on acid-free paper

The University of Minnesota is an equal-opportunity educator and employer.

12 11 10 09 08 07 06 05 04   10 9 8 7 6 5 4 3 2 1

A Lisa e Marcello

Contents

Acknowledgments   ix

Introduction
Popular Geography and the Myths of Globalization   xi
    From the Popular to the Multitude   xx
    Resistance Comes First   xxv

One
Where the Information Crashes: Adrift in the Bermuda Triangle   1
    Where Is the Bermuda Triangle?   4
    From Disaster to Irony (and Back Again)   20
    Periodizing the Bermuda Triangle   31
    Wild Globalization   38

Two
Transnational Transylvania, Europe's Monstrous Other   53
    The Undead Question   56
    Dracula Lives   69
    Monstrous Geography   82
    Circulate, Circulate   90

Three
Unmapping the Golden Triangle; or, The World on Drugs   102
    Wonderland of Opium   105
    Mapping the Unmappable   120
    Dirty Laundry   126
    Trainspotting   136
    The World on Drugs   139
    Drug Wars   143

Four

Outside Shangri-La: The Lost Horizon of Tibet   **152**

The Hollywood-Lhasa Axis   154

Searching for the Outside   161

Tibetology and Orientalism   165

New Age Politics   174

Free Tibet and Shambhala   183

Mysticism and Ideology   191

Conclusion

Counterworlds: Toward an Alternative Economy of Global Space   **199**

Works Cited   **211**

Filmography   **228**

Index   **231**

Acknowledgments

This book was written in fits and starts over a period of five years. During this time I worked in the English and Comparative Literature program at Murdoch University and in the School of Humanities at the University of Western Sydney, where I was also a member of the Centre for Cultural Research. There are many people to thank for the support and exchange of ideas they offered.

My interest in space, culture, and globalization began as a graduate student at Yale University. The teaching of and discussions with a number of people contributed to the early fermentation of ideas for the book, and I note in particular Jennifer Wicke, Sara Suleri-Goodyear, John Guillory, Peter Brooks, Nico Israel, and Thad Ziolkowski.

The project gained impetus through presentations and seminars at various institutions: the University of Tampere, Università di Bologna, the University of Melbourne, the University of Western Sydney, and Università di Milano. Thanks to the audiences on all of those occasions for valuable feedback. I would especially like to acknowledge Vita Fortunati and Simon During for their early words of encouragement.

At Murdoch University I found an environment conducive to writing and research. Colleagues who offered advice and support include Vijay Mishra, Jenny de Reuck, and Kateryna Longley. Special thanks are owed Horst Ruthrof for his unswerving commitment to fostering research among younger colleagues. A Murdoch University SHRAF grant allowed me to spend two weeks at the Central Institute for Higher Tibetan Studies in Sarnath, India, in late 1998. Thanks to the staff at the library of that institute for help in compiling research materials for the Shangri-La chapter of this book.

The bulk of writing for the book was completed after my move to the University of Western Sydney in mid-1999. I thank my colleagues at the Centre for Cultural Research for creating a stimulating and dynamic environment in which to think, feel, and work. Ien Ang and Zoë Sofoulis have offered invaluable encouragement. Thanks also to Gar Jones and Peter Hutchings for help in obtaining financial support that assisted with the completion of the manuscript. Matthew Glozier provided helpful research assistance, particularly with the compilation of the filmography.

Chapters 1, 3, and 4 of this book consist of substantially revised and expanded journal articles that appeared in *Space and Culture, Passages,* and *Communal/Plural,* respectively. Thanks to the editors of these journals for permission to reprint sections from the earlier articles. I am also indebted to the readers who acted as anonymous referees for these publications. Their comments aided in the process of converting the project into a book and shaping my overall thought about popular geography and globalization.

Several people read sections of the manuscript and offered insightful comments. Thanks to Nico Israel, Fiona Nicoll, Bob Hodge, and Geert Lovink, as well as to anonymous reviewers for the University of Minnesota Press. Megan Neilson provided generous help with proofreading. Thanks also to Richard Morrison of the University of Minnesota Press for his belief in the project, patience, and support in seeing the work through to print.

Last but most important I wish to thank Elisabetta Magnani, who lived with the daily grind of my facing the blank computer screen. Lisa read every word I wrote and offered continual criticism and encouragement. Without her support this book would not have been written.

Introduction

Popular Geography and the Myths of Globalization

> In a word, the free trade system hastens the social revolution.
> It is in this revolutionary sense alone, gentlemen, that I vote in
> favor of free trade.
>
> — Karl Marx, "On the Question of Free Trade"

In December 1970, Bruce Gernon, a twenty-nine-year-old pilot with about six hundred hours of flying experience, took off from Andros Island, the largest in the Bahamas, in a Beechcraft Bonanza A36. His destination was Palm Beach, Florida, but as he approached the island of Bimini, he encountered an unusual elliptical cloud. Trying to soar above it, Gernon noticed that the formation was rising with him. Before he knew it, the cloud had encompassed his craft, forming a giant doughnut hole. With little choice but to gun the plane toward an opening, he plunged at full speed into a tunnel of cloud, approaching a cylindrical hole that was becoming progressively smaller. The walls of the tunnel shone luminous white, and small puffs of cloud were clearly visible revolving clockwise around the central shaft. At the critical moment, the Bonanza's wing tips touched the wall on either side. For a few seconds, Gernon floated as if in zero gravity before emerging into a greenish haze. Although none of the navigational instruments were functioning, Miami radar control soon made contact, reporting a small plane flying west toward the city. Gernon felt sure this was another aircraft, since according to his flight time, the Bonanza should still have been over Bimini. But then, huge slits began to appear in the haze, suddenly opening like Venetian blinds to reveal Miami Beach stretching below. Upon landing, it became clear that the plane had completed a seventy-five minute flight in less than forty-five minutes, covering a distance of two hundred fifty miles rather than the regular two hundred. Gernon had evidently been caught in some sort of antigravity trap or mysterious warp, having been subject to inexplicable displacements in both space and time.

Fraught with the innuendo of an anxious masculinity, stories like this are a familiar feature of popular culture. Part local gossip and part commercial fantasy, they embody fears, desires, hopes, and just plain wonder. But unlike the freak events they report, these narratives rarely occur in isolation. Gernon's tale forms part of a larger cultural formation, namely, the complex array of books, films, television programs, newspaper articles, magazines, Internet sites, and other items of material culture that perpetuate the myth of the Bermuda Triangle. As recounted in Charles Berlitz's *Without a Trace* (1977), Gernon's story is inseparable from dozens of related tales involving phenomena such as time travel, disappearing ships and planes, spinning compass needles, alternative energy sources, interrupted radio messages, UFOs, and the lost continent of Atlantis. One fascinating aspect of these narratives is their tendency to collocate, articulating anomaly to anomaly as if in the fabrication of some vast conspiracy theory. Slowly but surely, the links fall into place, fashioning a larger cultural mythography. On one level, this exists simply to thrill and titillate, but on another level it engages some of the most pressing issues of the day: the growing intensity of transnational flows, the fracturing of homogeneous empty time, the instability of geographical boundaries, the prevalence of risk, the fragility of the world environment. Moreover, this mythography becomes associated with a particular area of the earth's surface, suggesting an alternative means of mapping the world, dissociated from the dominant geographical paradigms of the nation-state, the economic region, and the global/local marketing nexus.

Clearly the Bermuda Triangle is not the only popular mythography to attract such unruly cartographic practices. *Free Trade in the Bermuda Triangle* joins an investigation of this mysterious zone to the consideration of three other popular geographic formations: Transylvania, the Golden Triangle, and Shangri-La. Like the Bermuda Triangle, these anomalous spaces have a strong resonance with the complexities of contemporary global culture. Exploring issues such as postsocialist nationalism, the global drug trade, and the Chinese occupation of Tibet, the book takes a heterodox approach to globalization. Unlike most works on this topic, which prove remarkably sober, it combines serious political economic investigation with gleeful analyses of popular realities, drawing both on materials cutting-edge and banal, theoretical and downright middlebrow.

If the Bermuda Triangle is a kind of paranormal free trade zone, the site of unexplained disappearances and disrupted flows, Transylvania is a space of spectacular technological renderings, the mist-covered demesne of the vampire, beyond conventional knowledge and register. In *Nosferatu* (1922), F. W. Murnau's despairing classic of German expressionist cinema, the passage of the unsuspecting visitor into this forgotten land is marked by a stunning visual inversion. Black reverses for white, as the film tickles past the lamp in negative, staging the encounter with the vampire on the jagged edges of the possible. Suddenly the landscapes no longer look like realistic captures, but are possessed with a strange visual quality that lends a something's-wrong dimension to the scene. Murnau's secular magic is redolent with a fascinated anguish that poses the vampire as an archetypal threat to the status quo, undefined by nature and passing as a symbol for almost every imaginable other: the proletariat, the Jew, the homosexual, the Nazi, the colonial subject, the hysterical woman. *Nosferatu* is a film about networks of contagion and contamination, which are at once networks of secret and subversive communication, ethereal lines of interaction and dependency, transfer and substitution, rooted in the latest technologies and generating alternative vectors of kinship and affect. Little wonder that even as Murnau appropriated the plotline of Bram Stoker's *Dracula* (1983 [1897]), changing the character names and locations, he refused to compromise on the vampire's lair, transporting crew, actors, and equipment to Slovakia in a maniacal and ultimately bankrupting attempt to gain location shots that would resemble the mythical Transylvania.

Perched between Romania and Hungary, Transylvania is a long-established borderland, a place in which the international boundaries shifted four times during the twentieth century. Historically an outpost of the Roman and Hapsburg empires, this land-beyond-the-forest has for centuries supplied an imagined buffer between Europe and its various others: Persians, Ottomans, Russians, Roma. Even today, when the province forms part of postsocialist Romania, this border mentality persists, inscribed in geopolitical decisions made thousands of miles away, such as the October 2002 announcement that Hungary but not Romania would enter the European Union. Cut out from the circuits of free trade but nonetheless eager to open itself to transnational flows of goods and money, Transylvania is a space in-between, an indeterminate zone whose resistance to easy geographical classification makes it the perfect site to locate a sinister vampiric brood. Murnau, as much as Stoker, was obsessed by the threat posed by this uncertain otherness to the rationality of power. In a scene cut from the final version of *Nosferatu,* the vampire, now transported to the German city where he has invested in real estate, is attacked by a thief and stabbed in the heart. Instead of blood, gold coins fall to the ground. This substitutability of money for blood not only points to the biological metaphor that underlies the economic notion of circulation but also suggests that the vampire's perverse rituals of predation provide a means of reflecting on capitalist modes of exchange. If contemporary cultures of circulation are created and animated by the forms that flow through them, then Transylvania remains a site for rethinking the workings of global capitalism. This historical borderland is a postsocialist terror park in which the operations of capital are perverted and estranged, flashed up in negative as the monster's suffering suggests an alternative potentiality of being, filtered through new communicative and biological technologies.

Without doubt the vampire's thirst for blood is an addiction, a yearning without end that erases the borders between need and desire. Unable to enjoy a natural death, the revenant lives for centuries, condemned to vegetate in the *longue durée* by an insatiable hunger punctuated only briefly by moments of delirious satisfaction. In the contemporary world, this dynamic of unsatisfied longing becomes generalized and dispersed: markets that can only sustain themselves with a constant absorption of capital, workers who cannot extract themselves from the demands of corporate life, technologies that claim a never-ending supply of fossil fuels. Everywhere the vampire's affliction asserts itself with a druglike insistence. No surprise that late capitalist societies are increasingly dependent on intoxicants and pharmaceuticals, constantly redefining the lifework of the citizen on the confines of neurochemistry. Paxil, Prozac, Zoloft: the names alone evoke the shifting norms of sociality under corporate psychopharmacology. Not to mention the panoply of drugs that alter the ways we age, reproduce, and perform on the sports field and in the bedroom. At stake is nothing less than a new biopolitics of what the human should or should not be. On the one hand, this is marked by a moral imperative to ingest substances that extend life or normalize social interactions. On the other, it generates harsh edicts against drugs that deliver excessive forms of pleasure, escape, or privation. Of the latter, the opiates are only the most prevalent and profitable, encircling the world in a series of illicit flows that not only elude state security systems but also trouble the mechanisms of global capitalist control.

Welcome to the Hall of Opium. Set in Golden Triangle Park, on a hillside near a bend in the Mekong River where Laos, Burma, and Thailand meet, this new attraction aims to hook some of the million tourists who trek annually to northern Thailand to visit the mythical Golden Triangle. The world's largest opium-producing area, alongside central Asia's Golden Crescent, which briefly topped production in the late 1990s, the Golden Triangle spills across national boundaries, encompassing parts of Thailand, Laos, Burma, and China. But it is the Thai sections of the Triangle that have enjoyed the tourist boom, attracting travelers and adventurers from around the world, drawn by the exoticism and danger of the opium industry. The Hall of Opium caters to these fantasies, guiding visitors through a multimedia tour that begins in an underground tunnel and passes through a range of displays before finishing in a gift store and café, where guests can feast on poppy-seed bagels and other opium-related snacks. The First 5,000 Years, the Dark and Bright Hallway, From West to East, Prohibition/Crime/Wars, the Gallery of Excuses/Gallery of Victims, the Hall of Reflection: these are some of the exhibits that tourists visit as they wind their way through the museum, encountering representations of the horrors of addiction and the medical benefits of opium, as well as quotes from famous heroin users — Lenny Bruce, "I'll die young, but it's like kissing God." At the height of the Vietnam War, the Thai areas of the Golden Triangle were off-limits, rattled by dangerous militia activity and dotted with opium poppy fields cultivated by indigenous tribes such as the Lahu, the Meo, and the Lisu. Today these same groups inhabit squalid refugee camps, engage in cottage industries, or play host to ethnotouristic hill tribe treks, performing the rituals of opium consumption for gaping backpackers who are often keen to sample the narcotic. Meanwhile, across the border in Burma (or Myanmar as it is now known), the cultivation of the poppy continues apace.

The world's largest opium-producing nation, outpacing Afghanistan in 2001, Burma is a hotbed of ethnic insurgency. Militias such as the pro-Rangoon United Wa State Army face off against resistance movements like the Shan State Army, clashing also with the Thai military in skirmishes that flash across the border. Those sections of the Golden Triangle controlled by the pro-Rangoon forces are outlaw zones, prodigious in the production of opium and now diversifying into the manufacture of methamphetamines. Chinese tourists cross the border to visit casinos and transvestite shows, while hidden laboratories refine the world's purest and most coveted heroin, the fine powder known as China White. Smuggled across hill paths into Thailand, China, and India, and from there to the cities of the advanced capitalist world, the profits generated by this substance are huge, a model of free trade gone wild, regulated only by the cumbersome apparatus of nation-state law enforcement agencies. If the attempt to interdict drug flows has been one of the primary means by which nation-states have made themselves over as more flexible and less territorial entities, collapsing internal police and external military activities, the global drug trade has only expanded under current capitalist conditions. In particular, the business of money laundering thrives in deregulated financial markets, giving rise to movements of money that confuse traders and regulators, destabilizing the networks of risk management and digital control that undergird global capitalism. The link between money laundering and financial crises is by now established for the downward run on the Thai currency that prompted the Asian economic meltdown of 1997. Nonetheless, tourists continue to stream through the Golden Triangle, searching for that elusive taste of paradise, the deadening promise of opium that captivates addicts, travelers, and profiteers alike.

This dream of a highland Asian paradise is inseparable from another inveterate myth of popular geography, perhaps the most fanciful of all. Travel brochures for the Golden Triangle often describe the area as a hidden Shangri-La, juxtaposing glossy photos of hill tribe people with lurid prose praising the area's natural beauty. These images trade off an antique fantasy of escape and tranquility, associated preeminently with the mountain valleys of Tibet. With roots in the Tibetan Buddhist mythography of Shambhala, describing a hidden city accessible only to those with the correct spiritual disposition, the Shangri-La myth finds its most popular incarnation in James Hilton's novel *Lost Horizon* (1933), subsequently incorporated into Hollywood's celluloid canon by Frank Capra (1937). Capra's *Lost Horizon* is a masterpiece of Great Depression camp, the story of a gung-ho British diplomat abducted into an ersatz mountain paradise where compliant Orientals tend on foppish overanxious whites. After the curving Chinese-style credits, the film opens with a series of title cards that flip over like the pages of a book: "In these days of wars and rumors of wars — haven't you ever dreamed of a place where there was peace and security, where living was not a lasting struggle but a lasting delight?" From the start, Shangri-La is a fantasy of security in an ever more unstable world, a vision of quietude won at the price of exclusion and border control. Life in this metaphysical gated community passes pleasantly, and, like vampires, the inhabitants refuse to age, accumulating spiritual merit in a boom economy paradoxically based on humility, monasticism, and moderation.

Capra shot his film on a Hollywood back lot, but to give the final cut a taste of the Tibetan highlands he sent a crew to the Ojai Valley north of Los Angeles to grab a few shots of its spectacular mountain views. Perhaps this marks the beginning of the Shangri-La myth's tendency to migrate since, from that time on, the town of Ojai has advertised itself as a spiritual paradise. In 1946, Aldous Huxley established the Happy Valley School there, along with spiritual leader Jiddu Krishnamurti, whose presence over the years served as a magnet for hippies and artists. During the 1970s, Ojai figured in utopian fantasies of quite a different stamp, providing the setting for the television thrillers *The Six Million Dollar Man* and *The Bionic Woman,* adolescent premonitions of contemporary biotechnology. Today the town is a New Age haven, playing host to organizations with names like Church of the Tzaddi, Life Divine Center, Yogaversity, Vortex Institute, and Satha Yai Baba . . . all topped off with a thin layer of celebrity, added by the presence of half-forgotten personalities like Larry Hagman. One sweep of the camera, and the landscape is permanently altered, marked by the almost contagious spread of the Shangri-La ethos. Not only Ojai but also Franklin D. Roosevelt's Maryland hideaway (now known as Camp David) attracts the name of Shangri-La. Let alone the bevy of shopping malls, restaurants, hotels, and tourist resorts that carry the label. Amid this proliferation, the security implications of the term remain intact. Named for the Singaporean hotel in which it is held, the Shangri-La Dialogue is an annual Asia security conference where defense ministers like Australia's Robert Hill and the Philippines' Angelo Reyes rub shoulders with the likes of U.S. Deputy Secretary of Defense and Iraq hawk Paul Wolfowitz.

Nonproliferation challenges, military transparency, asymmetric threats, strategic encirclement, zero-sum security: the language that Wolfowitz and company throw around in the Island Ballroom of the Shangri-La Hotel aims at the maintenance of sovereign police control over the Asia-Pacific, keeping the region as open as possible to the free flows of global production. Centered as they are on Sino-American relations, these discussions have important implications for the geographical area most often associated with Shangri-La — Tibet. Since the Chinese invasion of 1959 and the fleeing of the Dalai Lama, Tibet has been a site of ethnocide, a place far removed from the blissful close of the happy valley. But Tibetan exiles and activists, drawing on their own religious traditions, continue to promote the myth of Shangri-La, partly because it attracts the support of Western sympathizers. As the Dalai Lama makes the Hollywood A-list, appearing at photo ops with Harrison Ford and Richard Gere, well-heeled activists lobby Washington to pressure China about human rights in Tibet. Despite the popularity of such demands, they are frequently brushed aside, not least because excessive pressure on this front would endanger U.S. interests in opening Chinese markets to free trade. Similarly, Chinese military officials like Major-General Zhan Maohai, Beijing's delegate at the Shangri-La Dialogue, condition support for U.S. military operations in the Asia-Pacific on noninterference with the one-China policy, which rejects the independence claims of Tibet. Caught in the crossfire of these economic and strategic agreements, Tibet counters by mythologizing itself (and allowing itself to be mythologized) as an untouched sanctuary, a space outside of globalization, immune to flows of people, money, and goods, and thus capable of providing an alternative to the dominant global regimes of commerce and power.

But what is the possibility of a space outside of globalization? The word "globalization" implies an unfolding toward totality, a full encompassing of the earth's surface that leaves nothing excluded, no place unmapped or beyond the reach of capital. From Bali beach clubs to medieval Carpathian towns, Bahaman islands to Moscow theaters, everywhere is a potential tourist resort, a potential target, and a potential market. As Sloterdijk (2001) explains, the totalizing mythography of globalization is born from the enterprise of colonial exploration, the gradual filling of the white spaces on the map. No longer the ancient sphere of cosmic perfection, the globe has become the stalking ground of merchants and geographers, the fallen mythographers of the contemporary age. Now the world has no outside, unless it is the dark frontier of the extraterrestrial itself, that vast surrounding emptiness from which it is possible to observe the planet as a whole. No wonder popular dreams of an outside to globalization frequently center on terrestrial spaces supposedly touched by the extraterrestrial, familiar parts of the earth's surface that suggest alternative forms of ordering. Whether zones of unexplained disappearances, sites of necromancy, areas marked by the druglike distortion of reality, or hidden demesnes of spiritual beneficence, these spaces partake of an otherworldliness that is decidedly of this world. Possessed with the power to generate alternative visions of the globe, they are nonetheless grounded, mapped out on the earth's surface and susceptible to the contingencies of physical and human geography: natural disasters, sunny afternoons, the claims of sovereign power, the vicissitudes of capital. At stake is not an externality that appeals to a divine or transcendental power, but the opening of a horizon, the registration of possibilities that remain immanent within the multitudinous forms of life on earth. In this sense, the view from above, the sublime image of the planet surrounded by the swirling gases of the atmosphere, attests not a celestial vision but merely the technical advances in astronautics and telecommunications. Girded by satellites, the orbiting relay stations of planetary information and defense networks, the world has become nothing so much as the spinning logo that graces the credits of the evening news.

A simple given fact produced in singular historical circumstances, the currently unfolding globalization of space and time is neither the manifestation of an eternal truth nor an inevitable necessity. Equally, however, there is no going back, no return to a preglobalized world in which the borders of the national and international remain intact. To assert that one is against globalization, antiglobalization, is no less problematic than claiming that globalization is somehow predestined and unavoidable. Far from closing down possibilities for revolutionary transformation, the process of globalization opens them up. The increased interconnectedness of the world provokes a crisis in the human appropriation of terrestrial space, pointing to alternatives that arise from within the heart of the global capitalist system itself. To write of counterglobalization is neither to partake in atemporal ethical judgments nor to launch merely contingent attacks against existing forms of economic administration. Rather it is to question the very articulation of globalization to capitalism, to search for alternative forms of transnational connectivity that resist subordination to the imperatives of the market and the state. The Bermuda Triangle, Transylvania, the Golden Triangle, Shangri-La: the four sites of investigation are at one level popular locales that generate counterhegemonic readings of globalization and, at another level, echoes of this same globalizing system. As such, they offer partly compromised grounds on which to reimagine the production of space at the present historical conjuncture. *Free Trade in the Bermuda Triangle* charts these popular geographical sites in a multidimensional perspective, examining their formation and transformations, their virtual and actual topographies, their implications for the politics of race and gender, their transmission through cultural technologies, and their reformulations of space and time. In so doing, the book seeks a language and imagery with which to represent a range of global futures that move through and beyond the capitalist imaginary.

From the Popular to the Multitude

One of the hallmarks of contemporary globalization studies has been a turn from temporal-historical to spatial modes of analysis. Following Lefebvre (1991), for whom space is a constitutive, historically produced dimension of social practices, globalization theorists have understood the currently unfolding transformation of the world-system as a dynamic reconfiguration of spatial relations according to a new flexible logic of capital accumulation. In particular, they have asked how transnational flows of goods, people, and information have configured new geographical entities and modes of cultural belonging. *Free Trade in the Bermuda Triangle* adds to the growing literature on these topics. But because it points to transnational practices that question the inevitability of contemporary modes of capitalist exploitation, it makes a significant departure from much work on culture and globalization. By studying popular mythographies that generate alternative mappings of the earth's surface, the book aims to rethink the economy of global space. As such, it makes a positive intervention in a field that is often content to describe the world as it is, drawing on popular belief, superstition, and feeling to challenge the seemingly unshakable myth of capitalism's global dominance.

In facing this task, the book brings together two important areas of contemporary cultural analysis, the study of popular culture and the study of transnational cultural processes. By examining large-scale geographical spaces mapped out in popular culture, it becomes possible to question many of the shibboleths that have come to dominate these fields. Doubtless, there are other ways of mapping the changing geographical contexts of the current global order. After all, the rapid fluctuation of world borders over the past fifteen years has led to a remapping of the earth's surface, whether through the emergence of new territorial states such as Uzbekistan or Slovakia, the formation of free trade blocs such as NAFTA and the European Union, or the reunion of divided territories such as East and West Germany. This official redrawing of boundaries has accompanied new patterns of economic and cultural exchange that intersect the processes of capitalist globalization in complex ways. For instance, the fragmentation of the former socialist bloc has resulted in the appearance of new nation-states, which struggle for integration into regional and global economies while also exhibiting forms of cultural and political nationalism that seek to limit the dislocating effects of global capitalism. There can be no doubt that nationalism remains a powerful means of organizing the affective dimension of human belonging, whether instituted from above by means of state-orchestrated nation building or constructed from below as in subaltern struggles. But nationalism is clearly not the only way of imagining human communality.

The technologies and institutions that produce national feeling now exist increasingly and massively on the transnational scale. Bounded territories give way to networks of flow as technologies, people, ideologies, financial systems, and media messages become unfixed from the territorial container of the nation-state. Today globalization researchers deploy notions such as deterritorialization (Deleuze and Guattari 1983), glocalization (Robertson 1995), the space of flows (Castells 1996), transnational-scapes (Appadurai 1996), and the global/local nexus (Wilson and Dissanayake 1996) to describe the spatial reorganization of world capitalism at both the sub- and suprastate scales. But these transnational geographical classifications, however useful in a technical sense, fail to capture the popular energies that attach themselves to the nation-state — for instance, in the context of international sporting events such as the soccer World Cup or the Olympic Games. They remain abstractions, the building blocks of a postnational cartography that, while perfectly valid as theoretical instruments, are unlikely to become rallying points for popular emotion or identification.

Defenders of the nation-state do not fail to recognize this. Anderson (1991) represents the absence of genuine feeling or action on the transnational scale as the absence of anything outside the nation worth dying for. "Who," he famously asks, "is willing to die for Comecon or the EEC?" (53). By this argument the nation is the repository of popular emotion, while transnational loyalties reflect rational calculation and detachment, an irresponsible withdrawal from the constituency in which one can perform the most meaningful political action. But in a world where political and economic power is increasingly manifest at the transnational scale, nation-state politics have limited capacity to shift the structural imbalances of the contemporary global order. One of the principal challenges of a critical transnationalism that seeks to contest dominant forms of globalization is to train popular energies toward the appropriation of the spaces of capitalist accumulation. As Robbins (1999) argues, this requires recognition of the way in which popular allegiances stretch across national borders, a remapping of the world that charts the complex interactions between popular feeling and global processes. The following explorations of popular geography are exercises in this regard.

While I do not suggest that people are (or should be) prepared to die for geographical entities like the Bermuda Triangle, Transylvania, the Golden Triangle, and Shangri-La, these popular geographical spaces register the circulation of vernacular sensibilities at the transnational level. Moreover, the production of these spaces involves the mobilization of popular desires that inflect global capitalism so as to reveal its internal limits and instabilities. In exposing these limits and instabilities, *Free Trade in the Bermuda Triangle* engages the utopian dimension of popular culture (Jameson 1979), interrogating the status of utopian thought in a postutopian world, a world in which it seems, as Walter Benjamin (1982) once quipped, that capitalism will die no natural death.

Over the past three decades, the analysis of popular culture has become a prominent field of critical intellectual inquiry. This is largely because the consumer-driven capitalism of late modernity has meant that a vast proportion of the planet's population, both in the wealthy capitalist world and the poor nations, experiences a more or less constant exposure to popular cultural representations and practices. Not only is popular culture increasingly visible as an economic force (a central feature of the new global information economy), but it also serves as a powerful means of education and socialization, as one of the primary ways in which people make sense of themselves, their lives, and the world. As such, it is something more than a representation of, or a fantasy about, the real world. Rather, popular culture is a significant part of material reality, since it effectively shapes the possibilities for our existence on both the representational and affective levels.

Roughly speaking, studies of popular culture can be divided into two approaches: the Frankfurt School denunciation of the culture industry as mass deception (Adorno and Horkheimer 1979) and the various studies of pleasure and resistance that came to the fore in the 1980s (Chambers 1986; Fiske 1989; Hebdige 1979; Radway 1984). Typically, these ways of studying popular culture are placed at loggerheads, the former condemning popular texts as degraded products of the capitalist system (the ideological sublimation of labor's constraints) and the latter discovering popular resistance in the practices of interpretation and appropriation that oppressed and/or marginalized groups bring to these texts. What remains implicit in both approaches is a tendency to understand society as structured according to a primary opposition between the dominant and the dominated, the hegemonic bloc and the subaltern, or the ruling classes and the people. Unfortunately, such a binary division of the social does not always sit easily with an emphasis on micropolitical struggles (Laclau and Mouffe 1985), leading either to a homogenization of the diverse elements that make up the popular (the masses in the Frankfurt School nomenclature) or to an insufficient appreciation of the way in which the pleasures of the popular articulate to wider political positions. Why, it must be asked, are certain forms of popular empowerment not always effective as resistance, and why do certain practices of resistance fail to produce challenges to structures of power?

These were the questions that critics of popular culture grappled with as they attempted to explain the popular conservatism of the Reagan-Thatcher years. The rise of what Hall (1988) calls authoritarian populism drew attention to the complex relations between popular culture and the state. Not only did the new conservative formations in the United States and the United Kingdom mobilize the struggles of popular culture to gain control of the state, but they did so in a way that won the support of class factions that clearly had interests to oppose them. This prompted a renewed interest in what Gramsci (1988) called the national-popular and the way it could be deployed to subordinate popular emotions to state-interests at precisely the moment when, as postcolonial theorists argued, increased cultural migrancy was eroding the hyphen between the nation and the state. Critics of popular culture were forced to confront the pitfalls of their own enterprise, reassessing the perils of an intellectual practice that sought to deliver a critique of dominant social practices in the name of the popular, often approaching the people as the textually designated emblem of the critic's own activity (Morris 1990).

By the mid-1990s, when globalization theorists had begun to explore the possibilities for thinking and feeling beyond the nation, much work in popular cultural studies still remained bound by the parameters of the state, seeking to reclaim governmental structures in the name of a popular nationalism. One symptom of this, as noted by Ang and Stratton (1996), was the tendency to divide the field into different nation-state traditions: British cultural studies, U.S. cultural studies, Taiwanese cultural studies, and so forth. In some cases, scholars who had built their careers on the analysis of popular cultural forms (Bennett and Woollacott 1987) began to advocate an explicit collaboration with state apparatuses, a cultural policy movement (T. Bennett 1992). One pair of authors went so far as to alter the title of Raymond Williams's foundation text of cultural studies, *Culture and Society* (1958), naming their study of cultural politics and governmentality, in explicit contrast, *Culture and the State* (Lloyd and Thomas 1998). As the 1990s pressed on, it was no surprise to find a critic like Beverley (1997) declaring that the only way for cultural studies to sustain its recuperative gesture of solidarity with oppressed groups was to explore the conditions of possibility for a different kind of state — a people-state driven by the democratic, egalitarian, and multicultural character of its citizenry. It is tempting to suggest that the populism of cultural studies has always provided an alibi for the state. But such a position only reinforces the perception that popular emotion and affect stop short at the national borders.

The current work is written with the conviction that there exist important forms of popular investment that operate beyond the boundaries of the national-popular and that, consequently, hold a more complex relationship to the state. By exploring the production of popular geographical spaces that undermine the territorial and extraterritorial imperatives of the nation-state, the book shifts the debate surrounding popular representation and affect away from the question of national belonging and identification. To this extent, the agency it identifies with the popular might better be attributed to the political subject that Hardt and Negri (2000) name the multitude. Studies of popular culture that seek to recruit the agency of the people against the hegemony of the state assume that the people supply the originary basis of the nation. By contrast, Hardt and Negri claim, "*the modern conception of the people is in fact a product of the nation-state*, and survives only within its specific ideological context" (102). Unlike the people, which is always identical with itself, the multitude is "a fluid and amorphous plane of singularities, given to perpetual differentiation and bearing an indistinct, inclusive relation to those outside it" (103). Furthermore, the multitude supplies the constitutive power that fuels the global capitalist enterprise, the living labor that the forces of capital must constantly harness and suppress in order to operate smoothly. Hardt and Negri write that the movements of the multitude "cannot be completely subjugated to the laws of capitalist accumulation — at every moment they overflow and shatter the bounds of measure.... A new geography is established by the multitude as the productive flows of bodies establish new rivers and ports" (397). *Free Trade in the Bermuda Triangle* maps an important aspect of this new geography.

The book differs from parallel studies that chart the displacements of travel (Kaplan 1996), the multiple paths of postcolonial diaspora (Joseph 1999), or the discrepant cosmopolitanisms of servants, slaves, and other subaltern actors (Clifford 1997). Much of this work on globalization-from-below intersects my concerns, describing the production of what Brah (1996) calls diaspora space, but the resulting cartographies of dispersion and global interconnectedness fail to attract the popular investment that distinguishes geographical formations like the Bermuda Triangle, Transylvania, the Golden Triangle, and Shangri-La. One of my central concerns is to join the study of pleasure (particularly in its political aspects) to the study of globalization. The question of pleasure has been a key preoccupation in a number of fields of cultural research, including film studies, queer theory, and the Lacan-inspired philosophy of Žižek. Works in these areas tend to build on psychoanalytic notions of desire, and their rhetorical-theoretical efficacy often rests on a performance of pleasure that animates the critical text itself — what Barthes (1975) famously called *le plaisir du texte*. By contrast, much of the work on globalization is deadly sober, and rightly so, given the increasing polarities of wealth and poverty that mark the contemporary world.

Resistance Comes First

It is no exaggeration to claim that most globalization theory derives its conceptual apparatus from Marx's critique of political economy and its need-based notions of volition and agency. While the postcolonial politics of difference insinuates itself into more culturally inflected approaches to globalization, the specter of Marx is never quite absent. *Free Trade in the Bermuda Triangle* is no exception. The project takes impetus from Marx's essay "On the Question of Free Trade" (1848), originally delivered as a public speech before the Democratic Association of Brussels. In this piece, Marx excoriates the supporters of free trade for celebrating the freedom of capital to crush the worker. But his criticism of free trade does not constitute an acceptance of protectionism, which he understands as a means of consolidating bourgeois power in a single nation-state and defending the interests of workers in the rich countries against those in the poorer areas of the world. Ultimately, Marx pronounces in favor of free trade insofar as it breaks up old nationalities and exacerbates the struggle between capital and labor. This ambivalent enthusiasm for the transformative powers of capitalism provides an appropriate backdrop for the present study, even if the current system of global capitalism differs significantly from the state-centered system of Marx's time.

Today global capitalism no longer structures itself around the demands of nation-states, but nation-states structure themselves according to the demands of capital. Transnational firms coordinate production between and across national territories, pulling out if conditions are unfavorable and deliberately playing jurisdictions off against each other in search of the cheapest and most efficient labor. This means that global chains of production and consumption are in constant flux, subject to the continuous interactions between competition, differential gaps in the conditions of profitability, social conflicts, and the mobility of capital. Nonetheless, Marx's basic insights concerning the tendency of capital to develop on the global scale inform much of the current political economic work on globalization. World-systems theorists like Wallerstein (1979) and Arrighi (1994) base their understanding of global capitalism on a historically oriented analysis of cycles, trends, and long-run structural features of the world economy. Similarly, thinkers like Harvey (1989) and Amin (1997) attribute the current round of globalization to the systemic crises of capitalism beginning in the 1970s, the latter advocating the delinking of developing national economies from the global system. In this discursive realm, the question of desire is remote and, indeed, often seems a problematic that distracts from more urgent issues such as hunger, uneven development, the international division of labor, AIDS, or the degradation of the world environment.

But the question of desire is central to these issues, particularly if one considers the way they revolve about the biological existence of human beings. As is well known, Foucault (1978) introduced the term "biopolitics" to describe the way in which power, from the dawn of the modern era, began to produce subjects whose very politics were at stake in their natural bodies. As transformed by thinkers like Agamben (1998) and Hardt and Negri (2000), the concept of biopolitics describes the field of contestation specific to a new mode of power that functions not simply by exerting disciplinary control over the subject but by reaching down to control the production and reproduction of life itself. This paradigm of power, which develops as modernity opens toward the postmodern, involves the production and manipulation of desire, whether in relation to struggles over nature and the environment, the politics of the body, the construction of race and gender, or the control of networks of language and communication. As Deleuze and Guattari (1983) write, there "is no such thing as the social production of reality on the one hand, and a desiring-production that is mere fantasy on the other.... [D]esire produces reality, or stated another way, desiring-production is the same thing as social production" (28–30). By this argument, it is impossible to attribute a special form of existence to desire, a mental or psychic reality, that is distinct from the material reality of social production. *The (social) production of desire is necessarily linked to the (social) production of space.* This is especially clear in the case of the global networks of media and communication, which not only produce, stimulate, and manipulate human affects but also map out spatial topographies, whether defined by the patterns of transmission and reception (such as television satellite footprints), virtual cartographies (such as the firewalls and proxies of the Internet), or the plotting of popular geographies (such as the ones under consideration in this book).

Communication is undeniably one of the central elements that establish the relations of production under global capitalism, but the productive capacities it marshals cannot be completely subordinated to biopolitical control. This is because communication is an interactive process in which the decentralized locus of command confronts the power of all those who contribute to the production and exchange of information. Production, in this context, refers not only to the manufacture and supply of media content and communicative technologies but also to the processes by which audiences construct meaning and make affective investments in the messages they receive. In the contemporary media environment, an important form of resistance is the production of alternative sources of information: community radio, independent media Web sites, zines, and so forth. Another form of resistance is the underground production and circulation of pirated CDs, videos, DVDs, and software programs, which dominate markets in many parts of the world and have driven corporate giants like Microsoft and Hollywood's Motion Picture Association to vigorously enforce their intellectual property rights. But resistance is equally manifest in the resources of irony, anger, and selectivity that overlapping and internally differentiated audiences bring to the consumption of media texts. Such popular agency must always be balanced against the continued capacity of the global media to act as instruments of command, resolving conflicts and managing potentially disruptive hopes and demands. As Stuart Hall (1996) argues, the resistance generated by audience response is complex, susceptible to incorporation, and without guarantees. Nonetheless, it constitutes a desiring-production that creates new social networks, forms of community, and spaces of contestation.

It is not a question of whether media producers or audiences assume a sovereign position in relation to each other. Senders and receivers become linked, constituting a single productive mechanism. Indeed, as in the case of the new information technologies, they are often indistinguishable. These actors occupy a space in which the practices of everyday life are traversed by flows of information and affect, flows that are in turn subordinated to relations of property and exploitation. Under these conditions, resistance cannot take the form of a dialectical negation of existing powers, a countering that forever struggles to escape from the presuppositions of the system it challenges. The *counter* in counterglobalization signals not an afterthought or pipedream, an imperative to reimagine the planet that assumes the preexisting hegemony of the nation-state or the dominance of capital. Rather, the desiring-production at work in such counterglobalization abides by the Deleuzian maxim: *"Resistance comes first"* (Deleuze 1988, 89). With this seemingly paradoxical affirmation, Deleuze argues that resistance acts against the conditions of its contrariety. That is to say, resistance is not simply a negative response to a dominant force or situation, a hopeless attempt to realize that which could be or might have been. Rather, resistance *is*. Its force of countering precedes that which it counters, insofar as every force doubles and is doubled by another force that destabilizes and opposes it. In this way, the popular geographies I study are not merely negative recapitulations of the global capitalist system that produces and sustains them. They precede the dominant cartographies of global capitalism insofar as they expose their modes of constitution and methods of operation. These anomalous spaces exist in their own right, imposing their singularity by means of duplicitous strategies that destabilize global capitalism from within. They are spaces of feeling and passion that are at the same time registers of a living counterpower — a counterpower that capitalism can only ever hope to reign in but never completely subsume.

Another way of describing this real-production of desire, space, and society is to say that it is imagined. Adapting Anderson's (1991) account of communal imagining to the transnational sphere, Appadurai (1996) argues that "the work of the imagination . . . is neither purely emancipatory or purely disciplined but is a space of contestation in which individuals and groups seek to annex the global into their own practices of the modern" (4). For Appadurai, the imagination is "a collective social fact" that has "become a part of the quotidian mental life of ordinary people" (5). While the imagination performs the work of symbolic artificiality, it does so by means of real material conduits that, like the global networks of electronic mediation and mass migration, interact across large and irregular transnational terrains. No longer can the imagination be equated with fantasy or contemplation, since it is now central to all forms of agency and acts as a key component of the new global order. Thus understood, the imagination is the primary faculty at work in the desiring-production that generates the popular geographies examined in this book. These spaces are charted within the circuits of global media transmission, but they are also articulated on another level after having been received and recirculated by audiences, themselves given to movement and heterogeneity. Each site comes into being through an interaction of readers and texts, effects and contexts, which constructs a popular mythography that becomes associated with a particular part of the earth's surface. No matter how fantastic or implausible these mythographies may prove, the geographical spaces they encompass remain material and tangible, subject to the variations of the environment, the ravages of capital, and the territorial claims of states as much as other terrestrial sites. It makes no sense to classify these constructs either as real or imagined spaces. Rather they are what Soja (1996) calls real-and-imagined domains, which by their very nature unsettle the distinction between the social and the symbolic, the real and the imagined, the bodily and the cultural.

Each of these anomalous spaces embodies a desire for the unknown, the intangible, the thing, place, and/or experience that cannot be explained by global capitalism. In the case of the Bermuda Triangle, this falls into the category of the paranormal. For Transylvania, it is associated with the supernatural, the uncanny divide between the living and the dead. The Golden Triangle produces such perplexity in the form of intoxication, the immediate rush and prolonged withdrawal of drugs from the human body. Shangri-La is built upon the protocols of mysticism and the occult, often in a New Age vein. But while such outlandish connections lend these spaces an aura of unbelievability, they do nothing to sever their connection to the earth. Each site is a kind of ground zero where the dreams of global capital meet the flesh and dust of everyday life. The results are always unpredictable, provisional, and given to excess. In a certain sense, they are also ungrounded, removed from any certainty that might limit the irresolution and contingency that constitute political practice. This is why the sites under investigation generate opportunities for contestation, struggle, and subversion. Nobody can rightly claim that these popular geographies exist in isolation from the processes of capitalist globalization. But nor can anyone convincingly assert that they are entirely subordinated to these same processes. *Free Trade in the Bermuda Triangle* explores the space between complicity and intervention, seeking alternative ways to understand the links between the spatial constitution of society, the workings of capitalist accumulation, and the shifting geographies of globalization.

While it is possible to produce maps of the Bermuda Triangle, Transylvania, the Golden Triangle, and Shangri-La, there is no uniform protocol that allows them to be charted on a common surface, as if they found their foundations in a pregiven order or generated homogeneous, teleological visions of the future. Not only are the texts that construct these mythographies in continued and variegated production (often in highly ephemeral media like everyday conversation or e-mail messages), but they also span a range of visual and narrative technologies. Each of these technologies deploys different techniques of mapmaking, and the spaces delineated in any one medium are often inconsistent with those charted in the others. Furthermore, the passage of these texts around the world is itself complex. They reach discrepant shifting audiences, eliciting divergent affective responses, and their transit intersects in unpredictable ways with other types of transnational movements: financial, ideological, technological, and demographic. Under these conditions, there is no way to produce a definitive map of any of the topographies in question. Each of these popular geographical spaces has a prehistory that precedes the current era of globalization, but at the same time each is subject to constant processes of recontextualization and remapping. This is why they provide such fertile grounds for reimagining the production of global space in the contemporary world.

The following chapters approach the work of mapmaking as a process of linkage, joining physical space, memory, and desire to forge a complex non-Euclidean geometry of the new global forms of uncertainty. Moving beyond both the fixed grids of latitudes and longitudes of power relations and the fluid exchanges of free-floating meaning, the resulting maps are open and connectable in all their dimensions, susceptible to reworking by individuals, groups, and social formations. Rather than pretending to transparently chart an empirical reality, they present themselves as temporary mechanisms for proceeding from one point to the next. Each time a new connection is established, the structure of the entire system is rewritten. Thus one might venture that the Bermuda Triangle swallows global flows, while Shangri-La shuts them out. Or note that the Golden Triangle pumps out flows, distributing drugs around the world, while Transylvania, like the vampire, drains and weakens them. But these symmetries are always makeshift and changeable. They cannot be called upon to connect these irregular spaces into each other like jigsaw-puzzle pieces or the interlinked spatial constructs of area studies: northern Africa, the Middle East, Central America, and so forth. The popular geographies under investigation are not discrete territories that fit together to form a coherent world-picture. Rather, they overlap and mismatch in their terrestrial coverage, producing disjunctive patterns that constellate into particular events and social forms in multiple nonnational contexts.

As provisional attempts to map intersections between popular feeling and transnational processes, these popular geographies delineate a terrain in which quotidian energies become linked to spatial formations that question the inevitability of belonging to a fixed or determined *topos*, to a nation, an identity, or a people. But this terrain is not necessarily bound by utopian horizons. Rather it remains caught in the immanence of desire, finding its only possible point of orientation in the vertigo that makes the inside and the outside of the contemporary global system appear, for all practical purposes, indistinguishable. What are the possibilities for imagining social betterment in a postutopian age? How might assertions of radical openness, difference, and potentiality be pinned to real conditions in which the construction of alternatives becomes something more than an upbeat device of closure or just another appeal to the imagination? In confronting these questions, *Free Trade in the Bermuda Triangle* pursues a strategy that brings together the reimagination of global space, the living forces of counterglobalization, and the popular energies marshaled by transnational networks of communication. At stake is not simply a remapping of the world in the image of the popular but the affirmation of an alternative terrain of critique, a terrain on which the real-and-imagined conditions of a passage beyond capitalism begin to take shape.

One

Where the Information Crashes: Adrift in the Bermuda Triangle

It would be surprising if those people for whom the flow of money and goods represents reality did not also believe in influxes and effects of another nature.

— Peter Sloterdijk, *Die letzte Kugel* (The last sphere)

A pilot reports a strange haze enveloping his plane before disappearing forever. A freighter steams in placid waters and is never seen again. A pleasure yacht sails past without a soul on board. A pilot calls for help after encountering an unidentified flying object and then vanishes without a trace. Tales like these are standard fare of the Bermuda Triangle mystery. But despite its reputation for unexplained disappearances, this anomalous area in the western Atlantic has never been definitively mapped. First named by Vincent Gaddis in *Argosy* magazine of February 1964, the Triangle is generally supposed to be cornered by Miami, Puerto Rico, and Bermuda. While the name has stuck, enthusiasts of the myth, including Gaddis (1975) himself, have regretted this act of mapping, since the idea of a triangle implies boundaries that contain the mysterious phenomena reputed to occur within. Successive cartographers have stretched the area in every possible way: north, south, east, west, up to the skies, down to the ocean depths, around the world, beyond the earth's atmosphere, and into dimensions yet unknown. What type of space is the Bermuda Triangle? And what is the relevance of its unstable geography for understanding the forces that fuel the current global reorganization of space and time?

Not accidentally does the initial wave of cultural production on the Bermuda Triangle occur in the early 1970s, following the first oil shock and the accompanying crises of Fordist capitalism. Best-selling books like Richard Winer's *The Devil's Triangle* (1974) and Charles Berlitz's *The Bermuda Triangle* (1974) tap into an imminent sense of catastrophe and uncertainty, taking their place alongside

Hollywood disaster films such as *Airport* (1970), *The Poseidon Adventure* (1972), *Earthquake* (1974), and *The Towering Inferno* (1974). Common to these works is a pronounced anxiety regarding the continued legitimacy of time-tested economic and cultural practices amid unpredictable and often spectacular changes. Huge oil tankers are swallowed by the ocean, passenger airliners swerve mysteriously from their course, massive skyscrapers burn to the ground, entire cities are rent by the force of the earth — the imagery is that of apocalypse and revelation, complete with sens-surround and Charlton Heston he-man antics. But these overreaching paranoid fantasies cast their shadows upon the real, supplying the ideological coordinates for confronting more insidious and invisible transformations that interrupt the certainties of life in every homely pleasantville. The collapse of the Bretton-Woods monetary system, the soaring price of fossil fuels, stagflation, rising unemployment, increased flows of migrants and asylum seekers — these are the symptoms that usher in a new phase of capitalism, calling to an end the postwar boom. For thinkers like Mandel (1975), Harvey (1989), and Jameson (1991), the early 1970s mark the collapse of mass-production capitalism and its correlate system of economic nationalism. Salient features of this transition include the flow of capital and technologies to the world's wealthiest nations, the deregulation of financial markets, the emergence of global cities, the burgeoning of transnational corporations, and the increasingly transnational reach of culture and communication. The Bermuda Triangle finds its genesis amid these changes. With its fluctuating borders and uncertain geographical positioning, it suggests a flexible, nonnational charting of global space appropriate for a reorganized capitalism defined less by territoriality than by flow.

But nothing is as it seems in the Triangle of death. As the system of global capitalism takes hold, displacing the Soviet system of state socialism and engendering new practices of circulation and exchange, it becomes discontent with the mere domination of the physical world. New fantasies and ideological mechanisms propel capital toward an imagined overcoming of the metaphysical dimensions of space and time. Magical notions such as that of unlimited power through disembodied mobility or of a global market hooked up by immaterial money that flashes around the world many times a minute — these are the fantasies regularly projected as capitalism's new wave sweeps the globe. The vision is one of uninterrupted flow, smooth space, and the obligatory opening of markets. But the Bermuda Triangle suggests quite a different production of space and time. In this popular geographic zone, flows of transport and communication go astray; ships founder, airplanes vanish, information crashes, navigational instruments malfunction, and time itself refuses to travel in a straight line. Disjunction, delay, and chaos rule the day. Not only does the Triangle attract multiple inconsistent mappings, but, by disrupting transnational flows, it also questions the fantasy of a borderless world open to the unhindered circulation of people, money, technologies, and commodities.

Apart from being a site of intense shipping and tourist activity, the Bermuda Triangle is also an area of heavy refugee transit — as Haitian and Cuban asylum seekers attempt to cross the Florida Straits. As such it is a space invested with complex racial anxieties, which interact in complicated ways with fantasies of engulfment and detainment that carry charged sexual connotations. Interrogating the processes of space-time production in this anomalous zone requires an engagement with the collective imaginings that construct the area as a site of mysterious and unexplained phenomena. No matter how outlandish and speculative these imaginings may prove, Bermuda Triangle narratives articulate popular desires that produce the real as a particular configuration of space and time. This chapter engages these popular desires, examining their intersection with and divergence from the desiring-productions that constitute the spatial imaginary of global capitalism.

Despite its mysterious properties, the Bermuda Triangle does not give rise to uncompromised modes of counterglobalization. The popular mythographies that construct this space produce densely ambivalent meanings and effects. Not only do the significatory and affective regimes at stake have no straightforward relation to the processes of late capitalist accumulation, but they also have complex and contradictory relations to other forms of hegemonic exploitation; for instance, patriarchal gender domination or the patterns of racial oppression that mark the histories of the Caribbean and the Atlantic. Nonetheless, the time-space dislocations of the Triangle delineate a makeshift ground upon which to rethink the workings of contemporary capitalism and their entanglement with dominant constructions of race and gender. In particular, these displacements suggest the possibility of moving beyond two apparently opposed approaches to globalization: Marxist theories that posit the division of the world according to center/periphery relations and poststructuralist theories that highlight the disruptive temporal dynamics of cultural hybridization.

My analysis of the Bermuda Triangle draws on Deleuze and Guattari's understanding of globalization as a dynamic of deterritorialization and reterritorialization. I contend that the Triangle's plural mappings represent attempts to contain or reterritorialize the processes of deterritorialization unleashed by the increasing deregulation of transnational flows in global capitalism. In other words, the shifting borders of this amorphous zone register unsuccessful efforts to control or triangulate the transnational circulation of commodities, ideologies, information, technologies, and people. Deleuze and Guattari (1983, 258) explain that capitalism requires the forces of reterritorialization to "prevent the decoded flows from breaking loose at all the edges of the social axiomatic." For them, the attempt to reterritorialize the flows unleashed by capital is tantamount to the exercise of control over the body and the maintenance of dominant race and gender hierarchies. Understood in this way, the uncertain geography of the Bermuda Triangle reflects not only the internal disequilibrium of the global capitalist system but also the fragility of the corporeal economies that legitimate practices of patriarchal and white race privilege. I suggest that the Triangle's unsettled boundaries register the possibility of what might be called wild globalization — an alternative economy of global space in which transnational flows become detached from the axiomatic of capital. In this anomalous zone, it is as if capital had relinquished its control over transnational processes or as if chaotic forces had overpowered capitalist rationality, pushing it to a limit where it can no longer be restrained by the regulatory regimes that oversee its routine survival.

Where Is the Bermuda Triangle?

Gaddis's initial mapping of the Triangle as cornered by Miami, Bermuda, and Puerto Rico is controversial, as subsequent commentators quickly expand these boundaries. One widely disseminated alternative represents the area as a trapezium stretching up the U.S. coast as far as New Jersey and encompassing the greater Caribbean islands. Richard Winer, who first develops this view of the Triangle in *The Devil's Triangle* (1974), quips that the first four letters of the word trapezium more than adequately describe the area's mysterious properties. Another version charted by Alan Viliers in *Posted Missing* (1974) has the Triangle extending between Key West, Chesapeake Bay, and Bermuda, a mapping designed to encompass a supposed area of disappearances off the U.S. Navy base at Norfolk, Virginia. Charles Berlitz, in his bestselling *The Bermuda Triangle* (1974), stretches the area to include

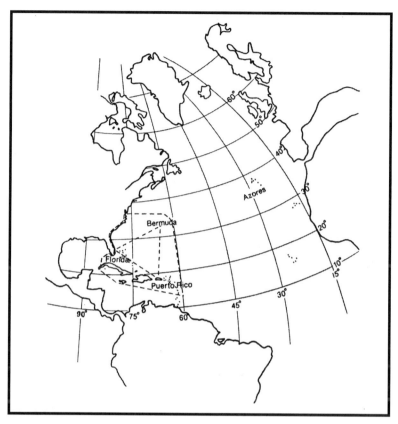

Map contrasting the central Bermuda Triangle with the larger version of Richard Winer. From Lawrence Kusche, *The Bermuda Triangle Mystery — Solved* (Amherst, N.Y.: Prometheus Books, 1986, 1995), 4. Reprinted by permission of the publisher.

the Sargasso Sea, the legendary graveyard of lost ships in the mid-western Atlantic. His version of the Triangle extends between Miami, Bermuda, and an indeterminate point off the northeast coast of Latin America. Similarly, John Godwin, who, in *This Baffling World* (1968), refers to the area as the Hoodoo Sea, charts a quadrangle of strange disappearances cornered by Miami, Puerto Rico, Bermuda, and Norfolk. But it is John Wallace Spencer who offers the most extensive early mapping of the Triangle in *Limbo of the Lost* (1969), the first book-length study of the mystery. Expanding the area to encompass the entire Caribbean basin and the Sargasso Sea, Spencer extends this mysterious zone east as far as the Azores Islands, a point closer to Europe than to the Florida peninsula and its surrounding islands.

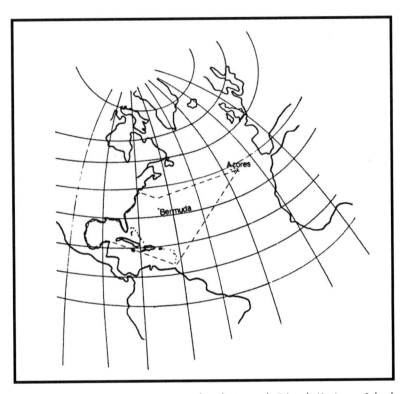

The limbo of the lost. From Lawrence Kusche, *The Bermuda Triangle Mystery — Solved* (Amherst, N.Y.: Prometheus Books, 1986, 1995), 15. Reprinted by permission of the publisher.

These mappings of the Triangle from the 1960s and 1970s provide the basis on which later cartographers build. Perhaps the most extensive contemporary resource on the mystery is the bermuda-triangle.org Web site, compiled by Gian J. Quasar, a Californian historian, avionics enthusiast, and consultant for cable television stations like The Discovery Channel and The History Channel. Quasar describes his site as presenting "up-to-date, in-depth research on the mystery of the Bermuda Triangle . . . including incidents that have happened in the last twenty years." Adding some seventy disappearances, over thirty-five of which have supposedly occurred since 1980, the Internet resource revitalizes the mystery for the twenty-first century, encouraging skepticism about the supernatural explanations advanced in the 1970s while refusing to "equate the natural with the conventional as many debunkers do." On a page titled "Sea of Expanding Shapes," Quasar superimposes the maps of Berlitz, Winer, and Spencer to create a ready index of the areas encompassed by competing versions of the Triangle. He also includes a map that traces lines between Miami, Puerto Rico, Norfolk, and Bermuda to chart what he calls "The Sea of the Four Triangles" — a kite shaped area that corresponds more or less to Godwin's Hoodoo Sea. Another of Quasar's maps deploys an animated graphics file to switch rapidly between four versions of the Triangle, providing the viewer with a dynamic register of the area's unstable geography. These cartographies abandon the hope of locating the Triangle in a fixed spatial domain, attempting rather to locate the unlocatable, to track as best they can the area's unpredictable displacements of space and time.

At one level, these remappings are reactions to the myth's disbelievers, who dismiss the esoteric theories evoked to explain vanishings in the Bermuda Triangle by claiming that many of the supposed disappearances have occurred outside the area as traditionally mapped. Spencer and Berlitz, for instance, enlarge the Triangle to include the Sargasso Sea, citing figures such as Christopher Columbus, who reported strange lights and unusual compass movements in the area, to add historical credibility to their allegations. Similarly, Viliers and Winer stretch the area to encompass a host of possible disappearance sites that fall outside the central Triangle, including the area off Norfolk and the conjectured vanishing point of Flight 19 — the Triangle's most celebrated mystery, involving the disappearance in December 1945 of five U.S. Navy Avenger bombers and the Martin Mariner flying boat sent to rescue them. In the 1975 article where he expresses regret at his initial act of mapping, Gaddis explains that "these marine mysteries take place all around a shapeless area in the Caribbean Sea and out into the Atlantic Ocean, including part of the Sargasso Sea" (3). But despite this constant redrawing of boundaries, the Triangle's shifting location cannot be traced in a ready series of debates and cross-references, contained in a coherently structured collection of books, films, and other documents. Proponents of the myth base their claims on oral narratives and inductive reasoning, taking almost any reported abnormality in the western Atlantic as evidence for their case. By contrast, their detractors stress critical thinking, deductive reasoning, and patient archival research.

Typical of the mystery's opponents is Lawrence Kusche, a former librarian at Arizona State University, whose *The Bermuda Triangle Mystery — Solved* (1975; reprinted in 1986 and 1995) represents years of meticulous research into the Triangle's most reputed disappearances. Making constant reference to meteorological and insurance records, Kusche seeks logical explanations for the incidents he studies. A telling sign of his investigative technique is the assertion, as reported by Ebon (1975), that he had nothing to gain by traveling to the area to conduct research. Kusche's aversion to fieldwork contrasts the techniques of the myth's enthusiasts, who rely on eyewitness accounts, letters, and interviews, as well as the inevitable flights and diving expeditions to search for wrecks, magnetic anomalies, underwater formations, vanishing islands, and the like.

In *Without a Trace* (1977, 73), Berlitz ridicules Kusche for his refusal to visit the area, suggesting it provides "a refreshing comment on investigative techniques which would immeasurably simplify the work of detectives, police, research investigators, and explorers throughout the world." These debates parallel and mimic disputes about ethnographic authority in the academic world: for instance, the ongoing controversy surrounding Claude Lévi-Strauss's reluctance to conduct fieldwork, apart from the investigations in Brazil recorded in *Tristes Tropiques* (1976). But despite Kusche's assertion that the Bermuda Triangle is a "manufactured mystery" (277), his work does nothing to diminish the area's reputation. Perhaps this is because his investigations, like those of his more esoteric adversaries, are carried out not in the annals of science or the jargon of government reports but in the discourses of popular culture. Kusche explains that he "like everyone else" enjoys "a good mystery" (277), and the cover art and pricing of his book suggest that he seeks a similar audience to writers who promote the legend. Whether elaborated from a skeptical or celebratory standpoint, the Bermuda Triangle myth clearly inhabits the sphere of popular culture, carrying with it the densely overlaid ideological and utopian meanings typical of this type of popular construct.

Consider again the competing versions of the Triangle. As first described by Gaddis, the area is delimited by Puerto Rico, Bermuda, and Miami. In this provisional mapping the Triangle backs on to South Florida, encompassing an expanse of ocean firmly contained within the U.S. sphere of influence. One way of understanding the Bermuda Triangle phenomenon is to associate it with other forms of Floridiana: beach culture, *Gentle Ben,* pastel-and-neon architecture, Carnival cruise ships, retirement homes and golf courses, theme parks and tourist traps of every kind. Indeed for a state that began its life with a series of shadowy real estate deals and today boasts a voting population of which over 70 percent was born elsewhere, the shifting boundaries of the Triangle provide an appropriate register of a larger cultural transience. There is something about farfetched stories of disappearance and intrigue played out against the luxury background of yachting and aviation communities that reflects the steamy underside of Florida's no-state-tax cornucopia — whether in the clandestine dealings of underworld figures like Meyer Lansky or the more mundane shoddiness discovered by Ross (1999) behind the gingerbread facades of up-market dwellings in the Disney town of Celebration. It is not just that Florida abounds with simulations, suggesting that the constitutive inauthenticity of Bermuda Triangle narratives somehow arises spontaneously from its shores, but that these simulations seem to foreshadow the future of the United States as a whole. As Paterniti (2002) writes, Florida is "a state where everything seems to happen first — or somehow in the extreme, . . . a microcosm of America [that] has come to reflect the psyche of America itself." But to approach the Bermuda Triangle simply as a reflection of U.S. national obsessions, even as peculiarly refracted through Florida's multicultural prism, is not yet to ask how these obsessions inscribe themselves on the geographical space encompassed by this mysterious zone. If, over the past century, U.S. constitutionalism has exhibited an expansive tendency that issues in the decentered networks and unbounded terrains of contemporary globalism, the space encompassed by Gaddis's initial mapping of the Triangle seems entrapped by an older form of imperialism — one marked by a history of territorial conquest, pillage, genocide, colonization, and slavery.

Apart from Miami, a complex urban hub that organizes diverse cultures in dynamic patterns of intersection and segregation, Gaddis's Triangle corners on two island groups that remain subjugated by regimes of territorial imperialism. Ever since 1612, three years after the English ship *Sea Venture* was trapped in a hurricane and wrecked on the surrounding reefs, the island of Bermuda has been a British possession. Quickly populated with African slaves, the colony emerged as an important military base and survived partly by trading sea salt until the late nineteenth century, when it began to attract winter tourists from the U.S. east coast. Today Bermuda remains one of fourteen British overseas territories, retaining Queen Elizabeth II as its head of state after voting in 1995 to remain a member of the British Commonwealth. Similarly, Puerto Rico is an unincorporated U.S. territory. The world's oldest colony, never having been independent since the Spanish occupation of 1508, the island's indigenous Taíno population was largely extinguished or put to work on sugar and coffee plantations alongside African slaves. The U.S. presence on Puerto Rico, which dates to the Spanish American War of 1898, is based in a legacy of racially rooted imperialism, forcing the island's inhabitants to take their place in a nation that neither wants them nor wants to let them go.

This older style imperialism also pertains on the islands that fall inside Gaddis's initial version of the Triangle. Although an independent nation since 1973, the Bahamas remain a member of the British Commonwealth. And the Turks and Caicos Islands, like Bermuda, are a British overseas territory. Both of these small western Atlantic nations have a complex history of imperialism, slavery, piracy, and slaughter. In the case of the Bahamas, the archipelago also served as a refuge for British loyalists who fled the North American colonies in the wake of the War of Independence. Today the economic revenue of these island nations derives primarily from tourism, particularly from the United States, and from their role as offshore banking centers. Gaddis's mapping of the Bermuda Triangle thus reinforces the myth's articulation to the recreational activities of a white leisure class. With its continuing imperial topographies, it suggests the displacement of this group's anxieties on to a region where many are likely to visit or perhaps deposit their funds — a part of the world firmly surveyed by the white tourist gaze if not subject to a territorial imperialism that appears quite untimely in the era of network societies, just-in-time wars, and transnational capitalism.

Gaddis's initial projection of the Triangle east from Miami seems almost deliberately to dissociate the mystery from the larger Caribbean islands to the south and from the complex demographic flows that have made South Florida's largest city a crucible of multicultural politics. Granted the inclusion of Puerto Rico raises the prospect of racial fears associated with the Puerto Rican communities who inhabit mainland U.S. cities. But unlike, say, Cuba and Haiti, Puerto Rico remains formally subjugated by U.S. economic and geopolitical powers. There are two important registers of this. First is the continued construction of the island as a tourist paradise — *la isla encantada,* the home of Bacardi rum, secluded rainforests, and palm-lined beaches. Second is the use of adjacent Vieques Island for U.S. Navy weapons testing and target practice. Ever since 1941 when the U.S. Navy forcibly expropriated the bulk of the island's territory, Vieques has been a site for military training exercises and experimentation with new weapons. The island is one of a select set of twenty-one U.S.-owned weapons testing facilities known as the Major Range and Testing Facility Bases. While operated and maintained primarily for Department of Defense test and evaluation missions, these facilities are also available to commercial users on a reimbursable basis. Under this arrangement, the United States has rented out Vieques to corporations like General Electric, which established a missile plant on the island in 1969, and Raytheon Aerospace, which has used the facility to test systems such as the Phalanx Block AB-1, a computerized rapid-fire canon that shoots depleted uranium shells. The eastern part of the island is by now highly toxic, littered with bomb fragments, unexploded ammunition, and scrap iron targets that have decomposed, releasing chemicals such as TNT, RDX, and Tetryl into the drinking water. Not surprisingly the impact on the island's population has been devastating, including massive cancer rates and the appearance of many rare and serious diseases. Since 1964, when a group of residents blocked the expansion of the Navy base along the island's south coast, Vieques has hosted an organized resistance movement. With the deadly bombing in 1999 of a civilian night watchman, this movement gained momentum, resulting in a massive campaign that eventually forced the U.S. government to promise to cease weapons testing on the island by 2003. But this decision signaled more an effort to capture the mainland Puerto Rican vote (those on the territory itself have no representation in Congress) than to release the colony from over a century of U.S. domination.

Significantly, Vieques Island features prominently in Bermuda Triangle geography. Travel writer Andrea Diehl (2000) claims that the precise point where the Triangle hits land is Puerto Diablo, on the island's northeast coast. The site is not far from the U.S. Naval operations tower in Camp Garcia, where eleven protesters, including the African American activist Al Sharpton, were arrested in May 2001. This is by far the most noxious part of the island, a section of the earth that boasts more craters per square mile than the moon, having been bombarded with multiple toxins, including Agent Orange and napalm. Puerto Diablo also faces north toward the Puerto Rico Trench, a huge underwater fissure over five miles deep and two hundred and twenty miles long. This ocean trench, which is the deepest in the Atlantic, is also an area of reputed magnetic faults. Some have even suggested it as a possible disappearance site for the six planes and twenty-seven personnel that went missing with Flight 19 in 1945. In any case, the association of this section of the Triangle with military training and weapons testing activities reflects the myth's more general entanglement with the U.S. armed forces.

Apart from Flight 19, there are some twenty-four recorded military disappearances in the Triangle, perhaps most famously the cases of the USS *Cyclops,* a massive 522-foot collier that vanished in 1918, and of two massive KC-135 jet Stratotankers, which disappeared during a regular refueling mission in 1963. The Bermuda Triangle myth is strongly articulated to a discursive formation that both celebrates and questions the power of the U.S. military. Thus while the mystery's enthusiasts routinely launch attacks upon military secrecy, they fetishistically embrace the sophistication of U.S. military technology, constantly pointing to minutiae that distinguish one vanished craft from another. They also make much of the occasional references to the mystery in official military documents: for example, the U.S. Navy fact sheet that describes the Triangle as "an imaginary area . . . noted for a high incidence of unexplained losses of ships, small boats, and aircraft" (quoted in Berlitz 1974, 10). Surely it is no accident that those mappings of the Triangle that extend up the U.S. coast (Godwin's Hoodoo Sea or Quasar's Sea of Four Triangles) identify Norfolk, Virginia, site of the world's largest naval base, as the area's northernmost point. These extended versions of the Triangle, which reach toward the geographical centers of U.S. political and economic power, Washington, D.C., and New York City, suggest more is at stake in the mystery than the power of the military alone. As if in a mystical translation of Florida's reputed capacity to reflect the future of the United States as a whole, these mappings imply that the Triangle exerts a surreptitious influence on the nation's economic and political fortunes. One possible register of this is the furor that followed the presidential election of November 2000, when the malfunction of voting technologies in South Florida's Dade, Broward, and Palm Beach counties resulted in a juridical-media battle that eventually subjected the nation, and the world at large, to a rerun of the Bush presidency.

One in a line of bizarre South Florida events, the Bush victory was followed within a year by a series of malicious incidents with dire consequences for Washington and New York City. Not only did Florida's flight schools train the pilots that executed the September 2001 attacks on the Pentagon and the World Trade Center, but Mohamed Atta, one of the chief planners and perpetrators of the assaults, inquired about crop dusters at Belle Glade municipal airport, rented cars at Pompano Beach, worked out in a Delray Beach gym, and passed himself off as a pilot in a Hollywood bar before embarking on his mission. In the weeks after the event, television commentators began to speak of a Florida curse, borrowing the rhetoric of the Bermuda Triangle mystery to colorfully describe the news emanating from the state. Then came the first reports of the deadly anthrax attack on the offices of American Media in Lantana, near Boca Raton. Oddly enough, the anthrax had been delivered in a love letter addressed to the Latina actress and singer Jennifer Lopez. More strangely, this letter had been mailed to the publishers of tabloid newspapers such as the *National Enquirer* and *Weekly World News,* champions of the Bermuda Triangle mystery since the early 1970s. Not only had the state governed by the president's own brother, Jeb Bush, harbored terrorists, but it had also emerged as a site for new forms of biohazard. Whatever the complexities surrounding these as yet unconnected events, their dual effects did nothing to diminish the reputation of South Florida as the source of an alien menace — a perception reinforced by Bermuda Triangle maps that stretch north toward Washington and New York City.

These connotations of the mystery are offset by those versions of the Triangle, such as Winer's Devil's Sea, which reach south from Miami, encompassing the Caribbean Sea and Gulf of Mexico. Here the pull is not toward the sovereign centers of U.S. political and economic power but toward the decentered arc of the Caribbean. Unlike the islands in the central Triangle, many of which remain subordinated to imperial regimes more proper to the modern era than to contemporary globality, nations like Cuba and Haiti have complex (and differing) anticolonial histories. Recent writings on the Caribbean abound with metaphors of chaos, fragmentation, uprootedness, and disruption. For Benítez-Rojo (1993, 9), the Caribbean is "not just a multiethnic sea or group of islands divided by different languages" but "a cultural meta-archipelago without center and without limits." Hall (1995, 4–5) argues that it is "impossible to locate in the Caribbean an origin for its peoples" due to the "dislocations of conquest, colonization and slavery...and the distortions of living in a world culturally dependent and dominated from some center outside where the majority of people lived." He also suggests that these dislocations are "important for counteridentities, providing sources on which the important movements of decolonization, of independence, of nationalist consciousness in the region have been founded." Brennan (1997) takes the syncopated rhythms of Cuban salsa music to symbolize the region's anticolonial struggles. He notes that these emblematic beats are produced in a context inhospitable to capitalist reproduction, registering the production of popular pleasures under socialist governance. Versions of the Triangle that encompass the Caribbean draw the Florida peninsula into this complex diasporic matrix.

It is as if the cultural tug of these islands counters the sovereign pull of Washington and New York City, highlighting the historical role of the peninsula in the region's destiny and the need to understand contemporary forms of transculturation in Florida as an ongoing part of the Caribbean diaspora.

Such a view of the area's diasporic flows is complicated by national regimes of territoriality that draw lines in the treacherous waters separating Florida from the greater Caribbean islands; fixed borders that, unlike the shifting boundaries of the Triangle, are subject to constant nation-state surveillance. As demonstrated by the March 1996 incident in which Cuban forces shot down two light aircraft belonging to the Miami-based exile group Brothers to the Rescue, which purportedly searches for distressed rafters, the positioning of craft with respect to these national boundaries is crucial for their physical (and political) survival. More routinely, U.S. authorities survey these waters to interdict the passage of refugees from Cuba and Haiti. It is not unreasonable to suggest that disappearance narratives that involve this section of the Triangle allegorize the racial and economic anxieties associated with the movement of asylum seekers. Certainly many incidents in the Florida Straits do not involve refugee craft. But episodes like the vanishing of the *Jamanic K,* a 357-ton freighter that went missing between Cape Haitien and Miami in March 1995, suggest the imperiling of flows in this area, pointing to dangers that refugee vessels, like all other craft, must confront.

There have been two major influxes of asylum seekers to South Florida. First, in the years 1977–81, came the arrival of sixty thousand Haitians in commercial craft and homemade rafts. To these can be added the Marielitos — 125 thousand Cubans (many of them convicted criminals and homosexuals) who left at Castro's instigation and were shipped to Miami on vessels chartered by the exile population, many of whom believed they were ferrying relatives across the straits. Then following the 1991 coup in Haiti came another wave of asylum seekers, over thirty thousand in 1992. Many of these people were processed via the U.S. Navy base at Guantánamo Bay, leased from Cuba, but this practice ceased in May 1992 when the U.S. Coast Guard began to return their vessels to Haiti in direct violation of UN directives, a Bush policy continued by Clinton despite election promises to the contrary. Of those Haitians detained at Guantánamo, some 275 had their applications for asylum stalled on the basis that they were HIV-positive, turning the Guantánamo base into the world's first prison camp for HIV-positive people. Caught in a state of legal limbo,

these detainees remained housed in makeshift wooden barracks surrounded by barbed wire until June 1993 when Camp Bunkeley, as the
HIV prison was known, was closed due to a federal court action by
mainland AIDS activists. No sooner had this episode been resolved
than a new wave of boat people set out from Cuba. Their numbers
peaked in August 1994 when Castro threatened another Mariel and
eighteen thousand refugees were returned to Guantánamo. After that,
the United States agreed to accept more immigrants through legal
channels in exchange for Cuba preventing rafters from leaving its waters. But this arrangement ceased in 1996 with the Brothers to the
Rescue shooting.

In 1999 there occurred an incident involving Cuban refugees that
attracted marvelous explanations of the type reserved for Bermuda
Triangle disappearances. On 25 November a six-year-old boy, Elián
González, was found floating in an inflated car tire inner tube off the
Fort Lauderdale coast. One of three survivors from the capsize of a
makeshift refugee vessel, the child, who had lost his mother during
the passage, became the object of a custody battle that had everything
to do with international politics, *patria*, and the representation of ethnicity. Installed in the Miami home of his relative Lázaro González,
Elián emerged as the star of a seven-month media spectacle that eventually saw his seizure by federal agents in April 2000 and return to
Cuba with his father the following June. For many in Miami's Cuban
community the boy's repatriation was unthinkable, as it signaled U.S.
acquiescence with a regime they hold to be totalitarian and in violation of human rights. Part and parcel of the struggle over Elían was
the mythologization of the boy's survival ordeal. Rumor had it that
dolphins had protected him from sharks and nudged him back into
the inner tube when he was unconscious. There were reports that
Elían had reached toward an angel floating above as he was rescued.
Once lodged with his Miami relatives, the six-year-old attracted sight-
ings of the Virgin Mary, one in the mirror of his bedroom, another
in the window of a nearby bank. Some claimed that Elían was the
personification of Eleggua, an Afro-Cuban voodoo deity represented
by a mischievous child. While these popular mythographies intersect
religious beliefs that occupy quite a different discursive register than
the renegade theories used to explain Bermuda Triangle incidents, they
contribute to the area's overall association with supernatural or metaphysical forces. Moreover, they articulate the mysterious properties of
the Triangle (or at least those versions of it that encompass the Caribbean) to refugee movements, suggesting that stories about vanishings

in this area embody mainstream U.S. fears about the permeability of national borders and the imperfect exclusion of aliens.

It is no secret that these anxieties have escalated in the wake of the September 2001 events in Washington and New York City, resulting in stringent new measures of surveillance and border control. But these attacks, with their South Florida and anthrax synchronicities, have also impacted upon the Caribbean with the establishment at Guantánamo Bay of the lyrically named Camp X-Ray — a prison camp for the detainment of alleged Al Qaeda and Taliban fighters captured during the U.S.-led coalition's war in Afghanistan. Guantánamo Bay has always occupied an important position in Bermuda Triangle geography, having served as a training base for U.S. Navy pilots during World War II. In *Gold Wings, Blue Sea* (1980), former Navy aviator Rosario Rausa relates the tale of two Douglas A-1 Skyraiders that strayed off course due to the unexplained malfunctioning of radio and navigation equipment during a flight from Vieques Island to Guantánamo Bay — a story embellished with fears of flying into Cuban airspace. Recalling this episode some forty years later, Rausa's fellow pilot Jim Reid (2001) elaborates: "In retrospect, we may have been beyond the so-called Bermuda Triangle, but I sure felt . . . that its dark and mysterious ways played with us that day." Doubtless the checkered history of the U.S. Navy base at Guantánamo Bay lends the site an air of danger and secrecy. Established in 1898 at the end of the Spanish-American War, leased from Cuba in 1903, a forward post in the Cold War (when Castro planted the surrounding area with cactus to discourage defections), and an HIV and detention camp in the 1990s, Guantánamo rests for legal purposes within Cuba, meaning that it can be used by the U.S. military to conduct activities that would be constitutionally unlawful if carried out on national territory.

This becomes clear with the designation of the Al Qaeda and Taliban fighters held at Camp X-Ray as unlawful combatants, neither enemy soldiers nor common criminals but agents of a moral evil held in a permanent state of exception, outside the rule of law both national and international. For Agamben (1998), such a suspension of the law is the prerogative of the sovereign. Following the German political theorist Carl Schmitt, he identifies the sovereign as the person or the power that, by declaring a state of emergency, can legitimately conduct actions outside the law. Blindfolded, gagged, and shackled in iron cages, the detainees at Camp X-Ray are the immediate objects of such command, which in effect declares a global state of emergency, the war against terror. If the attacks on the Pentagon and World Trade

Center demonstrate that the world's most powerful nation is no longer sovereign, unable to protect itself from nineteen men armed with box-cutters, the lockdown of detainees at Camp X-Ray represents only the most oppressive face of a more globally extensive sovereignty. This sovereignty, which identifies an invisible transnational network as its enemy, marshals military, economic, and communicative powers to pursue actions that are either wholly deniable or justifiable within the rhetoric of the just war — a war waged with food parcels as much as night-vision glasses, unmanned spy planes, and daisy-cutter bombs. Significantly, those maps of the Bermuda Triangle that extend up the U.S. coast and down into the Caribbean link the sites of the September 11 attacks with the Guantánamo camp, as if to suggest that U.S. sovereign power has been dragged south, where it assumes the most brutal and retributive of forms.

But the expansion of the Bermuda Triangle does not stop on the doorstep of the Caribbean. More extensive versions of the Triangle, such as Spencer's Limbo of the Lost, stretch eastward into the Atlantic, reaching toward Europe, Africa, and Latin America. If those versions of the Triangle that encompass the Caribbean islands reflect U.S. nationalist fears about border security and the illegal passage of aliens, these larger projections of the area imply that similar anxieties are operative at the transatlantic scale. It is no secret that the moral panic surrounding the transit of asylum seekers and economic migrants to North America and western Europe is out of step with global capitalist imperatives, particularly those that fuel the economies of wealthy capitalist nations with low-cost unskilled labor. But while the economic dominance and demographic balance of the advanced capitalist powers cannot be sustained without the productive capacities of the south, there is a continued projection of dread and uncertainty from the North Atlantic states toward the impoverished nations of Africa, the Middle East, and Latin America. One mark of this is the sense of insecurity and danger registered by large-scale versions of the Bermuda Triangle that separate North America and western Europe from the continental landmasses to the south.

Perhaps the most extensive existing map of the Bermuda Triangle appears on a Web site administered by Tobias Gibson (1995). Gibson's map contrasts Gaddis's central Triangle with Winer's Devil's Sea and what he claims is the actual area where unexplained incidents have occurred. The latter is a huge quadrangle that extends up the U.S. coast to Maine, traverses the Atlantic at fifty degrees of latitude, bisects the British Isles (passing through Stone Henge), reaches down past the coast of Africa to encompass Brazil and Central America, and then hugs the Gulf of Mexico back to South Florida. The near hemispheric dimensions of this map suggest that the Bermuda Triangle myth derives its meaning from the complex transcultural history of the North Atlantic. From this perspective, the Triangle's dangers would be engendered by Europe's commerce with the Americas, infused with the blood of the African slave trade and perpetuated in the tectonic politics of the new world order.

Since the publication of Paul Gilroy's *The Black Atlantic* (1993), there has been much attention to the shaping of current forms of Atlantic transnationalism by the trauma of slavery and the subsequent three-point movement of black bodies, minds, and cultures between Africa, the Americas, and Europe. While the preeminent institutions of North Atlantic globalism (NATO, the World Bank, the New York Stock Exchange, the European Union) effectively paper over the terror of the slaves' middle passage, there occasionally occur events that return this horror to the surface. In *City on the Edge* (1993, 51), a study of the complex ethnic transformations of Miami, sociologists Alejandro Portes and Alex Stepick report that media representations of "shirtless black refugees huddled aboard barely seaworthy craft" evoke "images buried deep in the American collective mind" — images of the slave ships that carried African laborers to the Americas in the past. If, as I suggest, the transatlantic mapping of the Bermuda Triangle indicates that the mystery embodies anxieties associated with these historical and contemporary passages, there is reason to understand the myth as a means of at once concealing and revealing the violent underside of North Atlantic capitalist hegemony.

That these modes of anxiety are articulated to paranormal theories and various forms of weird science should not be used to dismiss them out of hand. It is less the detail or the bizarre unbelievable content of Bermuda Triangle stories that is important than the fact of their production and existence. As Dean (1998, 166) argues of alien abduction narratives, they testify "to what for many is the predominant sense of contemporary reality: insecurity." The perception that borders have been moved or violated is not an insensible response to a world in which we confront an overload of information, and the boundaries between black and white, national and foreign, real and imaginary are forever shifting and blurring. Pointing out that U.S. politics have always consisted of boundary maintenance, Dean suggests that this is why, when we hear and can't possibly believe fantastic stories about UFO visitations or disappearing ships and planes, we feel reassured.

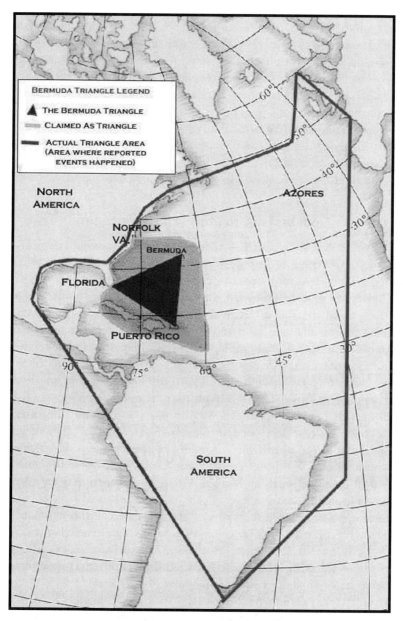

The Bermuda Triangle mapped by Tobias Gibson. Reprinted by permission of Tobias Gibson.

The Bermuda Triangle mystery cannot be conceived in separation from the violation of borders, and, for this reason, an understanding of its meanings and effects cannot be achieved by studying its individual mappings alone. These cartographies are the mere husks of the Triangle, contingent attempts to stay its fluctuating boundaries. Any account of the area's complex articulation to global capitalism must begin with a consideration of its uncertain geography, since this provides the (ever-shifting) parameters within which such connections are made and unmade. Not surprisingly these connections are historically shaped, giving rise to the multiform meanings and interpretations the mystery has attracted over time, from those marked by mistrust and paranoia to those redolent with irony and disbelief.

From Disaster to Irony (and Back Again)

Tarzan, Zorro, Dr. Kildare — these are among the popular cultural heroes introduced to the world by *Argosy* magazine. First published in 1894 by telegraph-operator-cum-publishing-entrepreneur Frank Munsey, *Argosy* spearheaded the pulp publishing revolution, outselling and outlasting all its rivals. Munsey's publishing strategy was a revolution in mass industrial production, capitalizing on North America's growing immigrant population, increasing literacy rates, and expanding mail delivery service (Goodstone 1970). One of the few pulps to survive World War II, *Argosy* became a slick in 1943, changing its focus to men's adventure. By 1964 when Vincent Gaddis's article "The Mystery of the Deadly Bermuda Triangle" appeared, the magazine had developed an interest in unexplained phenomena. Under the direction of Ivan T. Sanderson, science editor and former proprietor of a New Jersey roadside zoo, *Argosy* had begun to publish articles on topics such as Bigfoot, lunar monuments, and the Minnesota Iceman. Gaddis's piece, which was the most successful of these, drew upon previous discussions of strange nautical and aeronautical disappearances such as George X. Sand's *Fate* magazine article "Sea Mystery at Our Back Door" (1952) and Dale Titler's *Wings of Mystery* (1962). The article attracted dozens of letters describing mysterious happenings in the triangular area (Miami, Puerto Rico, Bermuda) that Gaddis had named the Bermuda Triangle. By August 1968, the reputation of this anomalous zone had been sufficiently established for *Argosy* to run a cover story titled "The Spreading Mystery of the Bermuda Triangle." In the meantime, Gaddis had published a chapter on the phenomenon in his *Invisible Horizons*

(1965), and from there, the story had been picked up and recycled by mainstream magazines, including *National Geographic* and *Playboy*. Spencer's *Limbo of the Lost* (1969) built on this growing web of articles and chapters, expanding the area as far north as New Jersey and southwest across the Caribbean. But it was not until the early 1970s, in the wake of the energy crisis and the shift away from mass production capitalism, that the myth assumed a powerful grip on the popular imagination. Significantly, in 1972 as the Bermuda Triangle story exploded with a wave of best-selling books, B-movies, and television shows, *Argosy* closed shop. Its parent company, Popular Publications, once the world's largest pulp publisher, found its techniques of mass distribution unsuited to a new era of more flexible cultural technologies in which media like cable television and the VCR were taking over.

A brief examination of the myth's infectious spread through 1970s information networks reveals continual cross-hatching between media, genres, languages, and technologies. Chief among the popular books published in this period were Adi-Kent Thomas Jeffrey's *The Bermuda Triangle* (1973), Richard Winer's *The Devil's Triangle* (1974), Charles Berlitz's *The Bermuda Triangle* (1974), Warren Smith's *Triangle of the Lost* (1975), and Alan Landsburg's *Secrets of the Bermuda Triangle* (1978). There also appeared countless articles in newspapers and magazines from *Catholic Digest* to the *National Enquirer*. Some of the most popular magazine articles to appear in the first half of the decade, including pieces by Gaddis and Sanderson, were repackaged and remarketed in Martin Ebon's edited volume *The Riddle of the Bermuda Triangle* (1975). As the decade wore on, the stories were recycled for children's books like Jim Collins's *The Bermuda Triangle* (1977) and Ian Thorne's *The Bermuda Triangle (Search for the Unknown)* (1978). But most important for the myth's expanding notoriety was its reworking in B-movies and television documentaries: William A. Graham's *Beyond the Bermuda Triangle* (1975), René Cardona Jr.'s *The Bermuda Triangle* (1978), Donald Brittain's *Secrets of the Bermuda Triangle* (1978), and Richard Friedenberg's *The Bermuda Triangle* (1979). Almost all of these cultural artifacts were produced in North America, but they circulated in global markets. By the mid-1970s, there had appeared translations of Bermuda Triangle books in languages as diverse as Danish and Japanese. There also existed original works in languages other than English, including Alejandro Vignati's *El triângulo mortal de las Bermudas* (1975), Jean Prachan's *Le triangle des Bermudes*

(1978), and Frans Grosfeld's *Het mysterie van de Bermuda driehoek* (1976). Furthermore, the myth sparked extensive production in material culture, including items such as T-shirts, board games, and pinball machines. In *Without a Trace* (1977), the follow-up to his best-selling *The Bermuda Triangle,* Charles Berlitz reproduced a bumper sticker from Turkey to demonstrate the extent of the mystery's transnational dissemination. By the end of the 1970s, the myth had clearly established itself as one of the great enigmas of the contemporary age.

Why the sudden explosion of interest in the Bermuda Triangle? The emphasis on strange disappearances and inexplicable disasters suggests that the myth struck a chord with audiences anxious about the cultural and economic transformations of the 1970s, whether in race and gender relations or the sphere of structural economic change. Vanishing ships and planes, lagging clocks, weird space-time disturbances — these are the stuff of popular mystery and intrigue. But they also reflect actual changes that accompanied the shift to post-Fordist capitalism, exposing people to new risks and reconfiguring the space-time arrangement of the world. In particular, the scenario of interrupted or disappearing flows implies the presence of an agency that sabotages capitalism's routine functioning, subjecting it to unpredictable space-time displacements, contesting its dominant modes of symbolic representation, and disrupting familiar practices of production, exchange, and consumption. Understood in this way, the mystery would appear to manifest the fears of the dominant sectors of U.S. society regarding the decline of established methods of capitalist accumulation. At stake in the Triangle's mapping is an understanding of the emergence of post-Fordist capitalism as the dawning of a new age of global uncertainty and precariousness. But despite this preponderance of paranoid significations, the myth also carries utopian implications, which are particularly evident in relation to environmental and energy-supply issues.

Perhaps the most extraordinary explanation for the mysterious Bermuda Triangle disappearances offered in the 1970s involves electromagnetic disturbances produced by energy-generating crystals, supposedly deployed by the inhabitants of the sunken continent of Atlantis and subsequently lost in the Tongue of the Ocean, a huge underwater canyon near the Bahamas. As elaborated by Berlitz (1974), this theory finds confirmation in the 1968 discovery by Dr. J. Manson Valentine of an underwater arrangement of rectangular stones off the Bahaman island of Bimini, the so-called Bimini Road. Berlitz hypothesizes that this strange underwater formation is the remains of an ancient Atlantean aeronautical landing strip, once exposed to land. He claims that Edgar Cayce, the famous sleeping prophet who died in Virginia in 1945, foresaw the discovery of this irregular collection of stones. During one of his readings or trance-induced dictations, Cayce spoke of advanced air- and seacraft, supposedly piloted by the inhabitants of Atlantis and powered by a crystalline energy source similar in operation to present-day laser beams. Extending these prophetic observations and drawing conjectural evidence from archaeological and geophysical research, Berlitz proposes that the Bermuda Triangle disappearances are benevolent UFO kidnappings by ancient time travelers from Atlantis. These visitors from the past seek to ascertain the extent of human technological progress to save the contemporary world from the catastrophe that destroyed Atlantis, the submergence of the continents due to global warming.

This prehistoric-eco-extraterrestrial fantasy resonates clearly with the increased awareness of energy-resource limitations and environmental deficits sparked by the oil shortage of the 1970s. Berlitz (1974, 185) directly mentions the prospect of global warming, writing "it is evident that Earth and its populations are in increasingly greater danger of planet-wide ruin and destruction." But the catastrophic aspects of his theory, which link to disaster movie paranoias, are tempered by the postulation of a greater intelligence that guides humankind through the crises of capitalism and its related environmental impacts. If Berlitz's primary message is one of trepidation and uncertainty, he also offsets the disorienting effects of capitalist transformation with the suggestion of a benevolent, protective agency. One reading of the Cayce-Atlantis-Bimini hypothesis is that it licenses wealthy capitalist societies to continue on their course of overaccumulation and fossil-fuel burning. If an ancient or extraterrestrial force provides a safeguard against environmental and economic catastrophe, there is no need to drastically alter existing patterns of production, exchange, and consumption. These practices can continue despite the telltale signs of atmospheric warming and the increasing dislocation of people, cultures, and livelihoods on a global scale.

In a different way, the Reagan-Kemp and Thatcher administrations that came to power in the 1980s offered a version of this same promise. Invoking the mythologies of the free market rather than those of the paranormal (although one must recall Nancy Reagan's engagement with astrology), these governmental regimes sought to alleviate the anxieties of capitalist transformation by means of tax cuts, deregulation, privatization, and the obligatory opening of markets. The consequent abatement of economic foreboding and environmental apprehension led to a diminution of cultural production of the Bermuda Triangle type. In the United States, however, these anxieties made an uncanny return in the form of the 1986 *Challenger* space shuttle explosion, an accident that significantly occurred in the Bermuda Triangle area at Cape Canaveral on Florida's Atlantic coast. As Lavery (1992) argues, the *Challenger* disaster exposed the faultlines in the Reagan military-entertainment complex, questioning the ideological notions for which the space shuttle had come to stand: scientific progress, manifest destiny in space, the superiority of a U.S.-centered transnationalism to the ailing socialist bloc, and so forth. Nonetheless, the overwhelming cultural and political currents of the Reagan-Thatcher era worked to gloss over the contradictions of capitalist globalization. This remained the case at least until the Black Monday crash of October 1987. The market fall opened a fissure of uncertainty that the first Bush administration would seek to resolve in the media simulations of the Gulf War — significantly, a struggle over the supply of fossil fuels. But in the Reagan-Thatcher context, the production of works on the Bermuda Triangle underwent a downturn. While there appeared texts such as David Group's *The Evidence for the Bermuda Triangle* (1984) and David Jungclaus's *City Beneath the Bermuda Triangle* (1985), the popular energies surrounding the myth failed to match those of the previous decade in both enthusiasm and sheer bulk.

Not until the 1990s, when the collapse of the socialist bloc enabled the imagination of a truly global marketplace, did a second wave of production occur. Among the books that appeared in this period were John Wallace Spencer's *The Bermuda Triangle — UFO Connection* (1991), Fletcher McGhee's *The Bermuda Triangle Subdued* (1998), Terrance Alexi's *Through the Vortex: Escape from the Bermuda Triangle* (2000), and Greg Donegan's *Atlantis: The Bermuda Triangle* (2000). Once again, there was a round of children's publications, including Brian Innes's *The Bermuda Triangle* (1999) and Chris Oxlade's *The Mystery of the Bermuda Triangle* (1999), as well as novelty items such as Justin Schmid's role-playing game, *The Bermuda Triangle* (1998). Also prominent in these years were television movies and documentaries, among them John Simmon's *Equinox: The Bermuda Triangle* (1993), Doug Campbell's *The UFO Diaries: The Bermuda Triangle/Area 51* (1995), John Wilcox's *The Bermuda Triangle: Secrets Revealed* (1996), Ian Toynton's *The Bermuda Triangle* (1996), Scott P. Levy's *Beneath the Bermuda Triangle*

(1998), Norberto Barba's *Lost in the Bermuda Triangle* (1998), and Chris Carter's *Triangle* (1998), an episode for the television series *The X-Files*. The 1990s also saw an unprecedented expansion of computer networking, and, not surprisingly, the Internet emerged as an important medium for the dissemination of material on the Bermuda Triangle. A Web site titled *Dreamscapes* (2001), which bills itself as "the biggest database on the internet for Links to Mysteries all over the world," lists over 170 Bermuda Triangle sites. The most comprehensive of these is Quasar's bermuda-triangle.org site, but there is by now an incredible variety of Internet resources dealing with the mystery, including educational sites, sites hosted by skeptics, UFO sites, and those devoted to various forms of alternative science.

More is at stake in this second coming of the Bermuda Triangle myth than the celebrated capacity of popular culture to cannibalize itself, recycling images from its own vast storehouse. If by the 1990s the anxieties associated with the first oil shock appeared to have subsided, the systemic crises of capitalism initiated in the 1970s were by no means resolved. What had changed was the ideological situation. The new mobility of capital, particularly in its speculative forms, continued to displace working populations on a worldwide scale, gathering ever-greater numbers into the proletariat and often fueling defensive nationalism. But the dominant classes imagined this ongoing subsumption of society by capital as a seemingly endless wave of economic expansion. In the relatively worry-free Clinton years of dot.com mania, there emerged a belief that capitalism had outpaced its cyclical busts, giving rise to an unprecedented period of growth, what the new technology magazine *Wired* dubbed "the long boom" (Schwartz and Leyden 1997). By this view, the unpredictable and chaotic behavior of transnational capital was no longer perceived as a threat. Rather it was understood as an opportunity, ready to be seized by those with the requisite skills and information-wealth to surf the ever-changing currents of global capital — those in the right place at the right time to establish ever more specialized niches within the world market. If this fantasy was tested by the Asian meltdown of 1997 and the dot.gone crash of April 2000, the resulting shocks were insufficient to demotivate the narrative of capital's global triumph. Just the right tax cut or interest rate adjustment promised to jump-start the flagging world economy, guarding against radical modifications in behavior or expectations. Consequently, the ideological coordinates that underlie the dream of unending speculative opportunity remained intact. As Jameson (1997, 263) explains, the capitalist imaginary produced "a new cultural realm or dimension that is independent of the former real world." It was not a matter, as in the modern (or even romantic) period, of culture withdrawing into the supposedly autonomous space of art, but of culture suffusing and colonizing the real world, leaving no outside in terms of which it might be found to lack.

As remapped in the post–Cold War era, the Bermuda Triangle exists in such a new cultural realm, a space where the virtual becomes (or, more accurately, is produced as) the real. In this domain, capital appears not only to have become unshackled from the limits of the physical world, most notably its dependence upon nonrenewable resources, but also to have transcended the regulating mechanisms of an older geographically bound market. Equally in this space, movements of capital appear disorganized and chaotic, such that they cannot be controlled or mastered but only ever monitored, and that imperfectly. Thus the obsession with market data — streamed across news tickers, transmitted to cell phones, never out of reach of the crafty speculator who at any instant may need to act to maximize return or avert disaster. In the Bermuda Triangle, this lack of control reaches fever pitch as flows of transport and communication become haywire, difficult to track, and impossible to explain. Here an agency greater than (or other to) capital appears to control the world's destiny, sucking those in the wrong place at the wrong time into oblivion or some sort of parallel universe. But far from suggesting a scenario of fear and paranoia, capitalism never abandons the dream of harnessing this unknown agency, welcoming it into the fold as a new (and renewable) energy source that might continue the spiral of profit and exploitation. This is why, in the current historical context, the Bermuda Triangle attracts the resources of irony above those of terror.

Clearly the Bermuda Triangle myth has a flexibility that allows its reproduction in a number of global capitalist contexts. Due to this adaptability, the popular needs, desires, and fantasies played out in any particular disappearance narrative can differ wildly, depending on the time and place of enunciation, the details of the event in question, and the identities of the storyteller and audience. One reason for the myth's longevity is the opportunities it offers for articulating anxieties about capitalism and globalization to any number of related (or unrelated) popular fantasies. These include fears and desires associated with race (particularly as regards demographic flows from the Caribbean and Latin America toward the United States), gender (predominantly the masculine fear of engulfment by the maternal-feminine), and the environment (especially the scenario of global warming).

In this regard, it is significant that cultural production on the Bermuda Triangle is almost entirely of U.S. provenance, and does not arise from any of the complex island cultures that lie within the area's fluctuating boundaries. Berlitz (1977) lists a Haitian refugee vessel that disappeared in the Old Bahama Channel in July 1973 among the vanishings he catalogs. But he also notes that the vast majority of incidents involve leisure craft, presumably manned by the wealthy white class factions that most frequently participate in such recreational activities. This preponderance of wealthy white victims is even more noticeable in recent accounts of the Triangle, which fail to mention the thousands of Cuban and Haitian refugees who have perished in the Florida Straits. In the Question and Answer section of the bermuda-triangle.org site, Quasar explains that such incidents do not count as vanishings since the disappearance of a "dilapidated Cuban or Haitian boat, overcrowded with dozens of people, suggests some very prosaic causes, such as sudden foundering, plunging, or capsizing." For a disappearance to appear in the Triangle's litany, it "must not have any immediate, acceptable answer" such as the flimsiness of the vessel or unfavorable weather conditions. Nonetheless, the focus of Bermuda Triangle narratives on wealthy, white, and predominantly male victims suggests that the myth embodies a primary concern with the fate of the most powerful sectors of U.S. society amid changing demographic patterns, gender regimes, and rising economic uncertainty. The loss of familiar bearings creates a feeling of vertigo or disorientation, and, not surprisingly, the resulting anxiety is projected south, where phallic-shaped Florida meets the decentered and chaotic cultural currents of the Caribbean.

Not accidentally does this enigmatic zone acquire an unbreakable association with the triangle, a geometrical form that carries a strong morphological link with the female pubic area. It is tempting to offer a psychoanalytic reading of the Bermuda Triangle mystery, rehearsing familiar Freudian themes such as desire as lack, femininity as the absence of the phallus, fear of castration, and male anxiety at the prospect of engulfment. These are well-worn motifs, not simply in popular culture but in Euro-American cultural production as such. Doubtless, there is scope for understanding the Bermuda Triangle as a maternal maelstrom that swallows unsuspecting pilots and sailors. Certainly this reading accords the details of the Triangle's most celebrated mystery, the case of Flight 19, which involved the disappearance of twenty-seven U.S. marines. Such a psychoanalytic understanding of the Triangle as a metaphorically

U.S. Coast Guard intercepts Haitian asylum seekers. Reprinted by permission of the *Tampa Tribune* and John R. Stanmeyer.

feminine space might also corroborate the arguments of feminist geographers (Massey 1994; Rose 1996), who claim that imagined or conceived space is gendered as feminine, while real, concrete, or scientifically verifiable space carries the connotation of masculinity. By this view, the efforts of skeptics to debunk the myth through rational scientific investigation would represent an attempt to impose clearly defined masculine boundaries over a radically open feminine terrain that encourages rather than suppresses difference. Such a gender-based argument supplies valuable insight into the masculine anxieties at stake in the mystery and their articulation to dominant race and class positions. But it must carefully be distinguished from the view by which feminine space is passive and unintelligent, offering an unlimited source of supply for the powering of male actions and fantasies.

I have already commented on how the Bermuda Triangle myth intersects the historical shock of the 1970s oil crisis and prospect of resourcelessness that looms over the planet in its wake. Clearly a complex nexus of fears and desires articulates the myth's monstrous feminine aspects (the threat of engulfment and disappearance) to the fantasy of the Triangle as a container of renewable energy resources (ancient power-generating crystals and the like). These dual scenarios of nurture/smothering and provision/plunder imply the construction of feminine space as a facilitating, maternal environment that is the matrix of an unlimited and threatening containment. The Triangle is at once the repository for countless lost vessels and the container of an endless energy supply, waiting to be tapped by those with the technical know-how to harness it (and perhaps already being utilized by a superhuman or extraterrestrial intelligence). As Sofia (2000) points out, such container technologies, traditionally coded as feminine, tend to be understood as passive and unintelligent. By contrast, active, masculine, or phallic technologies (such as ships or planes) are coded as smart and machinelike, although they too are containers of a certain type. What is glossed over in this male/female, dynamic/static typology is the active, machinelike function performed by spaces of containment, even if, like the Triangle, they prove to be leaky or ineffective containers. Holding and supply are not simply the passively inhering properties of dumb or inert spaces but are themselves forms of action and intelligence. The unbound, feminine space of the Bermuda Triangle thus should not be set against the strictly delineated and mappable qualities of masculine space so as to cast it as a passive, facilitating/engulfing domain that embodies all the fantasies of the maternal-feminine. Insofar as it is a feminine space, the Triangle is also a smart space — the locus of an agency that disjoins transnational flows, performing this task with an intelligence that exceeds and scrambles capitalist rationality.

These disjunctive operations suggest that the Triangle accords neither the Oedipal code of psychoanalysis nor the correlate understanding of desire as lack. While the fear of engulfment is doubtless an anxiety associated with the disappearances in this area, the Triangle in no way regulates the flows that transverse its boundaries, submitting them to a process of coding or rechanneling that strictly separates masculine and feminine spaces. Like the Oedipal Triangle that, in Deleuze and Guattari's (1983) account, is broken apart by the decoded flows of capitalism, the Bermuda Triangle constantly dissolves itself, questioning the territorial imperatives that call it into being. For Deleuze and Guattari, the "Oedipal triangle is the personal and private territoriality that corresponds to all of capitalism's efforts at social reterritorialization" (266). In other words, the familial structures of Oedipal subjection and subjectification are firmly embedded as a necessary foundation for capitalist accumulation and patriarchal domination. But while "the Oedipus complex inserts desire into triangulation," it also "prohibits desire from satisfying itself with the terms of the triangulation" (79). This is why, under global capitalism, flows of desire constantly supersede the Triangle's boundaries, breaking it apart with "the irresistible pressure of lava or the invincible oozing of water" (67).

If, as Deleuze and Guattari argue, "desiring-machines are in social machines and nowhere else" (302), such a transgression is at once a dismantling of the gender polarities of psychoanalysis and an overriding of capitalism's devices of reterritorialization. The same might be said of Gaddis's assertion that the Bermuda Triangle cannot contain the mysterious phenomena reputed to occur within its boundaries. Not only does Gaddis's claim question the identification of the area as a passive castrated space (the site of purely masculine anxieties), but it also challenges the dominant liberal-democratic consensus by which the instabilities of the capitalist world-system can be overcome by regulation, whether imposed by the state or interstate organizations. The most salient geographical feature of the Bermuda Triangle is its susceptibility to plural mappings. At stake in this popular mythography is a chaotic production of space, unpredictably mutating across unstable territorial limits. This displacement of boundaries involves not an accelerated version of the way in which official political and economic borders move, but a mode of deterritorialization that contests causal-linear models of historical and social change. In other words, the Bermuda Triangle upsets not only the predominant view of space as an abstract and empty container but also the correlate understanding of time as a homogeneous and unidirectional process of becoming.

Periodizing the Bermuda Triangle

At the end of a 1996 television documentary, *The Bermuda Triangle: Secrets Revealed,* the narrator, Richard Crenna, declares that while the anomalies of the area are perhaps inexplicable, there will always be a Bermuda Triangle. Such projections of the myth into the future are as endemic to the end of narratives about the Bermuda Triangle as claims for the mystery's archaism are to their beginnings. Like acts of national imagining that seek to hide their modernity by proclaiming their antiquity, stories about the Bermuda Triangle often repeat tales about Columbus's encounter with the Sargasso Sea or claims for the area's dangers as documented by Phoenician and Carthaginian seafarers. Not surprisingly the mystery's proponents can cite dozens of disappearances from the nineteenth and early twentieth centuries, including the enigmatical case of the *Mary Celeste,* the famous U.S. brigantine found drifting without a crew in 1872. Among the most notorious early disappearances are the USS *Pickering,* which vanished on a voyage from Guadaloupe to Delaware in 1800, the *Rosalie,* the first recorded merchant disappearance in 1840, the *Spray,* a world-circumnavigating yacht mysteriously lost off Miami in 1909, and the *Carroll A. Deering,* a schooner found abandoned near Cape Hatteras in 1921. Berlitz (1977) lists some sixty-one disappearances prior to 1945, a catalog to which Quasar adds another seven unexplained losses. But despite this impressive litany, most commentators agree that there has been an escalation of vanishings since the end of World War II. Indeed, December 1945 marks the most extraordinary incident to have occurred in the Triangle, the disappearance of Flight 19 — an event that boasts pride of place in all the books, films, and Web sites, and still commands an annual memorial service at the Hollywood–Fort Lauderdale airport.

The popular cultural production surrounding Flight 19 is profuse. The incident not only provides the background story for films such as Steven Spielberg's *Close Encounters of the Third Kind* (1977) but also inspires numerous research expeditions, most recently a search in the Okefenokee Swamp led by Gian Quasar and documented by The History Channel. Apart from these exploration missions (some of which involve advanced technologies such as satellite photography and underwater robotic vehicles), there is the annual military pageant organized by the Naval Air Station Fort Lauderdale Historical Association. The ceremony features vintage aircraft (including Avenger bombers of the type that disappeared) and a commemorative mural signed in 1992 by the first George Bush, who trained as a Navy pilot at the station during World War II. Apparently Bush encountered the painter, Bob Jenny, at an Oval Office meeting and was sufficiently moved by the description of the work to put his signature to the mural during his next visit to South Florida.

The articulation of Bermuda Triangle mystery to U.S. military nostalgia is complex. At one level, it suggests the myth can be understood as a manifestation of U.S. Cold War paranoia. This interpretation has its merits, given the claims for the escalation of vanishings after 1945. Not only does the mystery find its genesis in the mid-1960s in the wake of the Cuban missile crisis, but the two major waves of popular interest coincide with important events in Cold War history: the energy crisis and détente in the 1970s and the fall of the socialist bloc in late 1980s/early 1990s. Such a reading can also explain the myth's persistence into the 1990s, given the tendency of U.S. popular culture to sustain Cold War themes and modes of representation: for example, the 1995 Miami-based film *Fair Game* in which William Baldwin and Cindy Crawford save the world from a Russian nuclear submarine based in Cuba. Indeed the proximity/inclusion of Cuba to/in the Bermuda Triangle has prompted much speculation over the years. Berlitz (1974) reports that, at the time of its disappearance in 1963, many attributed the loss of the *Marine Sulphur Queen,* a huge 425-foot freighter, to confiscation or capture by the Cubans. But if such Cold War paranoia has surrounded the Bermuda Triangle phenomenon, the more prevalent explanations have been far more outlandish.

It is not my intention to dredge up all the paranormal, prehistoric, and extraterrestrial theories floated to explain the mysterious disappearances in the Bermuda Triangle. Suffice it to say that most of these theories understand the area to be plagued by what Ross (1991) calls strange weather. Numerous meteorological oddities have been invoked to explain the vanishings, including wind shear, wake turbulence, freak tidal waves, falling asteroids, and underwater methane spouts. At the more far-out end of the spectrum, there are speculations involving electromagnetic anomalies (the Triangle is traversed by the so-called Agonic Line along which compasses point to true north and magnetic north at the same time), sea monsters, gravity sinks, and UFO kidnappings. Explanations of this kind cut across the myth's Flight 19–Cold War–Bush family axis in a quite different way than the celebratory theatrics of the Fort Lauderdale veterans. By attributing disappearances to extraterrestrial or supernatural agencies, these hypotheses undercut military secrecy and governmental assurances of security. The possibility that aliens or other mysterious actors might be involved in the vanishings makes the military (and other state agencies) appear weak and evasive, as if involved in a vast cover-up of their inability to protect national subjects.

As Dean (1998) argues, the much-commented-upon parallel between space aliens and non–U.S. citizen aliens (formalized in the 1997 film *Men in Black*) implies that abduction narratives articulate cultural anxieties around otherness, especially when they involve stories about abortion, DNA extraction, and hybrid reproduction. Given the Bermuda Triangle's positioning in a zone of intense refugee and drug transit, it is possible to suggest that the myth maps out a kind of nonnational space that destabilizes the disciplinary power exercised by nation-state authorities such as governments and military forces. Furthermore, abduction theories such as Berlitz's Cayce-Bimini-Atlantis narrative embody anxieties about global warming and ecological degradation, implicitly questioning the environmental impact of military activities that, as the weapons testing on Vieques Island attests, are massively devastating. These aspects of the myth work against its reduction to a simple allegory of Cold War paranoia. Such a periodization of the mystery is thwarted not only by the ambivalent politics of its parascientific and ecotopic aspects but also by a corresponding problematization of assumptions regarding time and history.

The ancient Atlantean version of the story embodies a temporal paradox insofar as it involves visitors from the past who come to save the world from its future. But such temporal anomalies are endemic to the Bermuda Triangle mystery, even at the level of individual disappearance narratives. Consider the case of the *Star Tiger,* a British South American Tudor IV passenger plane that disappeared during a flight from the Azores to Bermuda on 29 January 1948. Wolfe (1975) reports that radio operators up and down the U.S. east coast received signals tapping out the message "s-t-a-r t-i-g-e-r" in Morse code five days later. A similar incident involves a National Airlines flight that was reputedly lost on radar for ten minutes as it approached Miami.

Upon arrival, the pilots reported that they had flown through a haze, and when they checked their watches, they were ten minutes slow, as were the plane's chronometer and the timepieces of the passengers. Similarly Berlitz (1977) narrates the story, mentioned earlier, of Bruce Gernon, a licensed pilot who encountered a strange cylindrical cloud over the Bahama Banks during a flight from Andros Island to Palm Beach in December 1970. Among the most famous Bermuda Triangle cases, Gernon claims that his journey resulted in a dramatic time-space shift, involving the loss of half an hour and the coverage of an extra fifty miles. Narratives of this type lead the mystery's enthusiasts to speculate that the Triangle exists as some sort of time-trap, exhibiting the theoretical curvature of space and time described by Einstein and possibly allowing aliens to enter through a portal or warp.

Berlitz (1974) elaborates upon this notion of time-space curvature by recounting the details of the so-called Philadelphia Experiment, a World War II research exercise in which the U.S. Navy purportedly made a large ship disappear by surrounding it with a powerful electromagnetic field. Subsequent commentators enlarge upon this fringe science. Quasar, who remains skeptical about the theories of Berlitz and his informants, cites the work of John Hutchinson, a Vancouver-based researcher who claims to have discovered alternative energy sources using methods developed by the early-twentieth-century radio pioneer Nikola Tesla. Hutchinson's experiments involve Tesla coils, rotating filaments that receive pulses of electricity so that their generation of energy continually increases due to the resulting resonance. Using this technology, Hutchinson claims to tap into "zero point energy," creating a space-time disruption that releases small amounts of energy from the vast reservoir contained at a subatomic level. Apart from imagining miraculous solutions to energy supply and environmental problems (on a par with Berlitz's 1970s fantasy of energy-generating crystals), he enumerates a series of incredible effects that follow from his experiments: levitating tennis balls, smashing mirrors, water spontaneously swirling in containers, lights suddenly appearing and vanishing. Hutchinson's work also supplies the basis for recent Bermuda Triangle narratives such as Norberto Barba's 1998 telemovie *Lost in the Bermuda Triangle*. The film recounts the story of a Chicago banker who discovers his missing wife on a vanished island after financing a fringe scientist to break through a time-space continuum using rotating Tesla coils. Only two weeks have passed, but the wife, who cannot leave the island because she was pregnant and suffering from terminal cancer at the time of her disappearance, presents the banker with a six-year-old son, who returns to the other side of the time-warp with his father.

By this scenario, the Bermuda Triangle is an area in which time does not always travel in a straight line, but unpredictably breaks away from the main flow, carrying with it whatever might be in the area at the moment. Quite apart from implying that missing vessels may have been transported to the past or future (or to a parallel world), this hypothesis frustrates established notions of temporal duration that lend themselves to the act of historical periodization. If time cannot be assumed to move at a uniform pace and in a single direction, it becomes impossible to identify periods or blocks of time that give the impression of a historical totalization, a seamless web of phenomena that express a consistent worldview or unified set of structural categories.

In "History and the Social Sciences: The *Longue Durée*" (1980, 49), Braudel argues that historical periods "can be recorded only in relation to the uniform time of historians, which can stand as a general measure of all these phenomena, and not in relation to the multiform time of social reality, which can stand only as the individual measure of each of these phenomena separately." For Braudel, no event can put "the historian beyond the bounds of the world's time, beyond historical time," which is "so imperious because it is irreversible, and because it flows at the very rhythm of the earth's rotation" (48). In the case of the Bermuda Triangle, however, it is precisely this neat correlation between the earth's rotation and the steady flow of historical time that tales of space-time dislocation call into doubt. By raising the prospect of unexplained geophysical or extraterrestrial disturbances, these narratives question the understanding of history as a linear succession of periods, stages, or moments. As Jameson (1981, 28) explains, "individual period formulations always secretly imply or project narratives or stories — narrative representations — of the historical sequence in which such individual periods take their place and from which they derive their significance." Such period formulations tend to privilege a particular element within a totality, treating it as a master code that explicates the features of the whole. They also imply the existence of deeper interpretive allegories by which historical events are rewritten in terms of implicit master narratives: providential schemes (such as those of Hegel or Marx), catastrophic visions (such as that of Spengler), or cyclical histories (such as those of Vico, Braudel, or more recently Giovanni Arrighi). The space-time properties of the Bermuda Triangle repudiate such grand narratives and their twin categories of narrative closure and historical subjectivity. This leaves the Triangle without a utopian horizon, embodying an interrupted or delayed temporal flow that unsettles sequential narratives and disables the identification of discrete historical periods. In this way, the myth questions the model of historical time that underlies its reading as a Cold War allegory or indeed as a supererogatory effect of any particular historical event.

In questioning totalizing historiographical schemes, the Bermuda Triangle mystery performs a popular translation of complex theoretical notions such as Walter Benjamin's *Jetztzeit* or Homi Bhabha's postcolonial time lag. In his "Theses on the Philosophy of History" (1969), Benjamin shifts the focus of historiography away from totalizing narrative forms by declaring the revolutionary potential of an interruptive or messianic time. He directs his argument against the idea of historical progress (or what he calls historicism) understood as the functional replacement within modernity of the homogeneous empty time established by tradition. Benjamin's critique of modernity's time-consciousness exerts strong influence on poststructuralist thinkers like Derrida, whose understanding of the linguistic sign as a disruptive temporal structure also implies a critique of modernity's mythology of progress. Transferred to the debate about globalization, this deconstructive emphasis on the rhetoric of temporality contrasts Marxist theories that emphasize the production and politics of space. In *The Location of Culture* (1994), for instance, Bhabha brings a deconstructive reading of Benjamin's *Jetztzeit* to the study of the power differentials of modern imperialism. Bhabha self-consciously casts his argument against "the more 'spatial' traditions of some aspects of postmodern theory" (244). For him, the temporal discontinuities that separate the metropolis from colonies that will not and cannot catch up produce a time lag that fractures the *"contemporaneous reality"* supposedly implied by the postmodernist fascination with mapping (244). Significantly, this theoretical division between disruptive temporality and socially produced space also appears in the founding text of contemporary spatial theory, Henri Lefebvre's *The Production of Space* (1991). Lefebvre accuses poststructuralist thinkers of "promoting the basic sophistry whereby the philosophico-epistemological notion of space is fetishized and the mental realm comes to envelop the social and physical ones" (5). But the Bermuda Triangle myth suggests a intertwining of these rival theoretical strands since it produces a space that at once disrupts the sequential passage of time and, as

Berlitz (1974, 195) observes, maintains a real-material presence "on the familiar territory of our planet."

Like Bhabha's (1994, 219) third space, the Bermuda Triangle is "continually, *contingently,* 'opening out,' remaking the boundaries" to produce a time in which "the past is not originary, where the present is not simply transitory." But it is also a socially produced space since, as Lefebvre (1991, 402) writes, it "cannot be resolved into abstractions and...consists neither in a collection of things in space nor in an aggregate of occupied places." By giving a material grounding, however contingent or temporary, to poststructuralist notions of disjunctive temporality, the myth rescues Bhabha's postcolonial time lag from a purely formalist reading. Osborne (1995, 199) worries that Bhabha's trope of displaced repetition threatens to elide the social referent, reinstating "original difference across its supposed temporal rupture in a...purely constructed form." But the Bermuda Triangle performs such radical temporal disruptions while maintaining an unstable positioning on the earth's surface.

Another way of explaining this is to refer to Giorgio Agamben's reading of Benjamin on *Jetztzeit* or messianic time. Agamben (1999, 168) explains that one of the paradoxes of Benjamin's argument is that "another world and another time must make themselves felt in this world and time." Messianic time can neither simply cancel out historical time nor be perfectly homogeneous with history: "the two times must instead accompany each other according to modalities that cannot be reduced to a dual logic (this world/the other world)" (168). In the context of the Bermuda Triangle, Agamben's argument suggests that the area's anomalous space-time dislocations do not license a parallel world scenario that attributes the disjunction of transnational flows to a supernatural or mystically produced space with no intrinsic connection to the physical geography of the western Atlantic. These real and imagined spaces cannot be separated by the binary logic "this world/the other world" since they are inextricably fused by a desiring-production that produces the real as the imagined and vice versa.

Clearly the Bermuda Triangle's uncertain placement generates temporal irregularities that problematize the myth's periodization as a Cold War allegory (or for that matter as an allegory of any other periodized historical phenomenon: the African slave trade, post-Mariel refugee movements, the rise of North Atlantic global hegemony, NATO, and the World Bank). But this does not mean that the area's mysterious properties can be explained solely in terms of its geographical positioning. For while the Triangle is inscribed on the planet's surface, it resists definitive location, giving rise to multiple inconsistent mappings. As J. H. Miller (1995) argues of the imagined spaces mapped out in literary and philosophical texts, this popular geographical formation creates atopical disturbances in the production of space, exposing the unmappable topographies that lurk within every cartographic projection. But it is not a purely discursive construct or what Lefebvre (1991) would call a representational space, a space lived exclusively through its association with symbols and signs. Unlike the unmappable loci identified by poststructuralist thinkers in literary and philosophical texts, the Bermuda Triangle is at once concrete and abstract, material and metaphorical, real and imagined. It is a version of what Soja (1996) calls real-and-imagined space, a space that has an actuality other than the abstract signs and real things it attempts to contain but, at the same time, cannot be reduced to empirically manifest or scientifically verifiable materiality. This dual capacity of the Bermuda Triangle, its ability to encompass both poststructuralist theories of temporal difference and Marxist notions of socially produced space, makes it a potent locus for rethinking the workings of capitalist globalization.

Wild Globalization

Consider the following phrases. I am a citizen of the Bermuda Triangle. A treaty signed in 1997 permits free trade in the Bermuda Triangle. My grandmother took a holiday in the Bermuda Triangle. My flight passed through the Bermuda Triangle. Of these, only the final two are plausible, and the second to last barely so. Clearly the Bermuda Triangle is not a nation or an economic region, or some other kind of territory defined by the social and economic operations of capitalism. Yet as a renowned tourist area, the world's busiest shipping lane, a site of refugee transport, and a heavy zone of drug trafficking, it might properly be identified as a space of flows. I use this term in a different sense to that applied by Castells (1989) to the informational city, since the Triangle is not a demographic or technological hub that generates and regulates transnational movements of commodities, information, people, and capital. The space of the Bermuda Triangle is defined not by what it contains or even by what passes through it, but by what it consumes, traps, or detains, be that aircraft, refugees, or time itself.

In this sense, the Bermuda Triangle might better be called a space of broken flows, since it performs radical space-time dislocations in practices of communication and transport, repeatedly disrupting the cartographic techniques that seek to constitute it as a readily mappable territory. The idea of flow has been crucial to studies of globalization, but it remains poorly understood, as if it involved the continuous and direct transit of materials from one place to another. While the concept has precedents extending back to Heraclitus, it finds its most powerful modern enunciation in the philosophy of Henri Bergson, who identifies it with the lived quality of time's passing, the heterogeneous flux of bodily intensities and experience. At least it is from Bergson that Deleuze and Guattari derive their influential concept of flow, which describes the antipsychoanalytic operations of desire, whether embodied in the secretion of bodily fluids or the global circulation of capital.

Deleuze and Guattari (1983, 96) call upon Bergson to authorize the claim that "the living being resembles the world" — a parallel that informs their famous description of capitalism as the body without organs. Prior to *Anti-Oedipus,* Deleuze also authored a study titled *Bergsonism* (1991, 46) which argues that the "heart of Bergson's project is to think differences in kind independently of all forms of negation." This relates directly to Deleuze and Guattari's later contention that flows operate by the logic of deterritorialization, resisting negation or containment by regulating psychological and/or geographical systems. According to *Anti-Oedipus,* the capitalist system provides the primary means of controlling or reterritorializing flows in the contemporary world, restricting their movement through state institutions or interstate agreements such as the GATT. "One sometimes has the impression," Deleuze and Guattari write, "that the flows of capital would willingly dispatch themselves to the moon if the capitalist State were not there to bring them back to earth" (258). Yet, as Berlitz (1974) reminds us, the Bermuda Triangle resists containment while maintaining a familiar presence on the earth's surface.

This anomalous space acts as an agency-without-subjectivity that repeatedly breaks the flows that broach it. Such a disruption of flows not only questions the sequential continuity of time but also signals a radical departure from capitalist modes of spatial organization. By resisting the forces of reterritorialization, the Bermuda Triangle exceeds what Deleuze and Guattari call the schizophrenic limit of capitalism, a limit that the capitalist system must constantly push back to ensure its regular survival. For Deleuze and Guattari (1983, 266), schizophrenia is "the *absolute limit* of every society, inasmuch as it sets in motion decoded and deterritorialized flows that it restores to desiring-production 'at the bounds' of all social production." In turn, capitalism generates a "displaced *interior limit*" that neutralizes or repels this "absolute exterior limit," directing flows so they no longer pass "between social production and the desiring-production that breaks away from social reproduction" (266). This has important implications for understanding the constant contraction and expansion of the Triangle's boundaries. To argue that the area's uncertain geography registers the failure of reterritorialization is to claim that capital does not exercise complete control over the flows that traverse the area. This suggests a very different state of affairs to the neoliberal fantasy of globalization, by which capital asserts its total domination over space and time. The Bermuda Triangle myth conjures a scenario in which capital forfeits control over the means of transnational mobility, causing flows to go astray, slow down, or simply disappear. It is as if some greater intelligence or agency had overpowered the axiomatic of capital, redeploying flows of transport and communication to heed some unannounced purpose (such as the protection of the earth from environmental catastrophe) or to altogether cut loose from the processes of capitalist accumulation. Not only does the Triangle produce a space that confounds emplacement, disavowing all talk of local knowledge, but it also outlines an alternative geography of globalization, one that refuses to abide capital's sovereign power.

In this regard, it is significant that the Bermuda Triangle is not the only anomalous area of its kind on the earth's surface. Researchers of paranormal phenomena have long recognized a similar mysterious zone off the southern coast of Japan, the so-called Dragon's Triangle. This second area of unexplained disappearances follows a line from western Japan, north of Tokyo, to a point in the Pacific at the approximate latitude of 145 degrees east. It turns southwest, past the Bonin Islands, then down to Guam and Yap and west toward Taiwan, before heading back to Japan in a northeasterly direction past Okinawa. Significantly, this second anomalous zone occupies the opposite side of the earth's crust to the Bermuda Triangle for both longitude and latitude. In *The Dragon's Triangle* (1989), the most complete account of the anomalous events in this area, Berlitz lists no less than fifty-two unexplained vanishings for the period 1949–89, including eight nuclear submarines with arms capabilities of up to 126 atomic warheads. To this Quasar adds a subsequent five losses, culminating with the massive twenty-three-thousand-ton *Honghae Sanyo*, which disappeared southeast of Japan in April 2001. While Japanese legend has it these vanishings are caused by the perturbations of a huge underwater dragon, Berlitz rehearses a host of speculations that resemble those used to explain the Bermuda Triangle mystery: volcanic activity, vanished civilizations, alien abductions, antigravity warps, space-time anomalies. He even suggests that KAL 007, the Korean passenger jet shot down when it drifted into Soviet airspace in September 1983, may have lost its course due to a temporary magnetic shift in the area.

There are a number of geophysical features shared by these two zones of enigmatic disappearances. Both are transected by the Agonic Line (along which compasses point to true north and magnetic north at the same time), and both encompass huge underwater trenches (the Mariana Trench in the Dragon's Triangle is the world's deepest). Berlitz also notes similarities in the reputed vanishings that have occurred in these areas. He suggests that the loss of three separate aircraft off Japan in March 1957 constitutes "a collective peacetime air tragedy comparable to one of the most famous Bermuda Triangle mysteries, the disappearance of Flight 19" (63). Furthermore, he finds the boundaries of the Dragon's Triangle to be no less flexible than those of its western Atlantic counterpart. Among the litany of disappearances, Berlitz lists the *Ming Song,* a Panamanian-registered vessel that vanished "north of Australia" in October 1975, and the *Glomar Java Sea,* a British oil-drilling craft that went missing near Hainan Island (off China's south coast) in October 1983. Clearly the boundaries of this anomalous zone, like those of the Bermuda Triangle, are subject to discrepant plural mappings.

Like the Bermuda Triangle, the Dragon's Triangle (or at least its extended version) is an important zone of refugee transit and detainment. Since the mid-1970s the seas to the south of China have claimed dozens of overloaded refugee boats, predominantly peopled by Vietnamese, Sino-Vietnamese, and Cambodian asylum seekers headed for Australia. While Australia accepted some 3,566 boat-arrivals between 1976 and 1981, when the Vietnamese government instituted an Orderly Departure Program, the situation changed dramatically after 1989, when successive waves of refugees began again to depart from the south China coast. Following the Bush-Clinton practice of forcibly detaining asylum seekers, Australia's government instituted a program of interception and detention in 1992, establishing on its territory Guantánamo-like prison camps, run under contract by the private firm Australasian Correctional Management, a subsidiary of the Miami-based Wackenhut Corporation. Housing thousands of asylum seekers, including children, in some cases for as long as three years, these camps became the focus of national controversy as detainees began to express their frustration with desperate acts of protest: riots, arson, hunger strikes, self-mutilation, attempted suicide by drinking shampoo, the sewing together of the lips, self-impalement on barbed-wire fences. Particularly after the election of the conservative Howard government in 1996, when the profile of the refugee shifted to those fleeing repressive regimes in the Middle East (Afghans, Iraqis, and Iranians), the politics surrounding these camps became extremely heated. With the mainstream public firmly on its side, the Australian government complained of judicial activism and subtly mobilized a xenophobic rhetoric reminiscent of the country's past racial exclusivism.

Australia's refugee situation came to a head in August 2001 when the Norwegian tanker *MV Tampa* rescued 433 asylum seekers (primarily Afghans and Iraqis) from the sinking Indonesian vessel *Aceng* and attempted to land them on Christmas Island. Ignoring the Norwegian captain's requests for medical help and in need of an election boost, Howard ordered that the tanker be stormed with elite SAS troops and left it adrift for six days while he negotiated his so-called Pacific solution. By this arrangement, the bulk of the *Tampa* refugees were detained on the impoverished Pacific island of Nauru — to the southwest of the central Dragon's Triangle — where they had no access to the legal rights available to detainees held on the Australian mainland. A former phosphate mine and money-laundering haven for the Russian Mafia, Nauru accepted some twenty million dollars from Australia to establish camps for 800 asylum seekers, increasing this to 1,200 some four months later with the offer of an additional ten million. By February 2002, the main Nauru camp, a litter-infested former sports ground surrounded by limestone pinnacles and disused mining shafts, housed some 1,159 asylum seekers, replete with security from the private firm Chubb Protection Services. Joined shortly by another Australian-funded detention center on New Guinea's Manus Island, these camps shadow the U.S. facility at Guantánamo's Camp X-Ray, suggesting further links between the Bermuda Triangle and its western Pacific counterpart. The primary difference is that while the Guantánamo camp houses detainees who allegedly fought for Al Qaeda or Afghanistan's Taliban regime — "the most dangerous, best trained vicious killers on the face of the earth" to cite U.S. Secretary of Defense Donald Rumsfeld (2002) — Australia's camps detain asylum seekers who seek only to find protection from these same "unlawful combatants."

Another important parallel between the Dragon's Triangle and the Bermuda Triangle is the status of the area with the U.S. military. While the Dragon's Triangle does not encompass U.S. territorial waters (apart from those surrounding the tiny island of Guam, which, like Puerto Rico, is an unincorporated U.S. territory), it has since the end of World War II been subject to intense surveillance and control by the U.S. armed forces. Crucial in this respect is the island of Taiwan, the sovereignty of which U.S. military power maintains in a virtually permanent state of exception, erecting a strategic trip wire between China and the western Pacific. As Solomon (2000) argues, this defensive posture no longer obeys the Cold War logic of containment. Rather, given China's status as the largest trading partner linking the interests of U.S. and Taiwanese capital, it abides a new imperial logic of sovereign police control aimed at keeping labor subject to the constraints of global production. Not only does the United States arm the Taiwanese military, which provides an important node in the Reagan-Bush fantasy of a missile-defense shield, but it also maintains bases on Guam and Okinawa, both of which border on the central Dragon's Triangle. Indeed the case of Okinawa, a Japanese territory that, like Vieques Island, is the site of U.S. military training exercises (including the firing of 1,520 depleted uranium shells by a Harrier AV-8B jet in late 1995), reveals an inconsistency in U.S. policy regarding such activities. While Okinawa has seen intense Vieques-style protests against the U.S. military presence (an effort redoubled with the rape of a Japanese woman by a U.S. marine in June 2001), the U.S. administration gives no indication of terminating military operations on the island. Recent troop realignment plans have indicated the possibility of downscaling U.S. military presence on Okinawa by moving some fifteen thousand marines to Australia, but the deterrent effect of maintaining a base close to Taiwan and the Korean peninsula means that a total cessation of military activities on the island is unlikely to occur.

Needless to say, the U.S. military's safeguarding of the interests of capital in the Dragon's Triangle has not always gone smoothly. Many of the incidents in the area involve U.S. military craft. For instance, all three of the disappearances in March 1957, the so-called nightmare month of aviation, involve the loss of U.S. military airplanes. The first of these occurred on 12 March, when a KB-50 tanker plane vanished in good weather with a crew of eight on a flight between Japan and Wake Island. The second involved a U.S. Navy JD-1 Invader, which disappeared on a routine flight from Japan to Okinawa on 17 March.

But the most spectacular of these vanishings was the last, which took place on 22 March when a U.S. Air Force C-97 military transport with sixty-seven personnel aboard disappeared southeast of Tokyo. Another incident involving the U.S. military occurred in December 1965, when an A-4E strike aircraft, equipped with a hydrogen bomb, rolled off the deck of the aircraft carrier *Ticonderoga*. The official report stated that the bomb and the plane, which have never been recovered, sank to the ocean depths some five hundred miles from Japan. But Berlitz (1989) claims that subsequently declassified documents indicate that the A-4E and its dangerous cargo tumbled into the sea near Okinawa. A more recent event involves a U.S. Navy EP-3 series spy plane, which was forced to make an emergency landing on Hainan Island after colliding with a Chinese F-8 fighter jet in the South China Sea, close by the 1983 disappearance site of the British vessel *Golmar Java Sea*. The collision, which took place on 1 April 2001, just days before the mysterious disappearance of the *Honghae Sanyo* in the central Dragon's Triangle, occurred under clouded circumstances about which U.S. and Chinese authorities have been unable to agree. Resulting in the death of the Chinese pilot and the eleven-day detention of twenty-four U.S. marines on Hainan Island, the event shifted the balance of U.S.-China relations, heightening tension at a time of sensitive arms sales to Taiwan and increasing U.S. interest in the penetration of Chinese markets.

Doubtless the prodigious economic activity in the western Pacific is one reason why the United States is keen to oversee capital's sovereign embrace of the area. As Berlitz (1989, 22) remarks: "That these disappearances continue right on the well-trafficked doorsteps of two of the developed world's leaders in electronics, computers, and high technology must be considered mysterious indeed." But if the technological, economic, and political preeminence of the United States and Japan has focused attention on the Bermuda and Dragon's Triangles, more ambitious scholars have sought out further abnormal zones in less-trafficked areas of the globe. Particularly active in this project have been the researchers at SITU, the Society for the Investigation of the Unexplained, an organization headed by Ivan Sanderson, crypto-zoologist and one-time science editor for *Argosy* magazine. Employing a host of innovative techniques, including the collection of data on television talk shows and the sticking of knitting needles through a child's globe, the SITU team was able to plot ten other aberrant zones on the earth's surface. Constellated at angles of seventy-two degrees around the thirtieth parallel of latitude north and

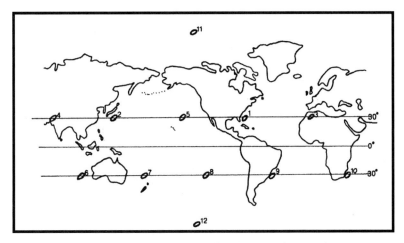

The twelve vile vortices. From Lawrence Kusche, *The Bermuda Triangle Mystery — Solved* (Amherst, N.Y.: Prometheus Books, 1986, 1995), 262. Reprinted by permission of the publisher.

south (and including the North and South Poles), these so-called vile vortices are all purported areas of strange disappearances. In "Worldwide Seas of Mystery" (1975), Sanderson asserts that these vortices are lozenge-shaped. But if we consider that in one mapping the Bermuda Triangle stretches from the Gulf coast of Mexico to the British Isles (over seventy-two degrees of longitude), there is reason to suspect that these lozenges might also expand to similar dimensions, in which case they would encompass the entire earth. What is the significance of this bizarre act of globalization, in which the whole world becomes a Bermuda Triangle?

Following my previous speculations, I suggest that the vile vortices scenario represents a fantasy of a globalization without limits. At stake is a process of wild globalization that functions neither as a means of cultural homogenization nor as a way of instituting differences to make the world a friendlier place for capital. Understood in this way, the Bermuda Triangle mystery questions two prevailing views of globalization. First, it problematizes the world-systems theory of Wallerstein (1991) and colleagues, which evolves from a mix of Marxist dependency theory and *Annales* school historiography. By this view, the globe is structured by a set of dynamic relations between all-powerful centers, relatively isolated peripheries, and mediating semiperipheries. Inequalities of wealth and power determine the intensity and direction of transnational flows, and the world moves slowly toward a higher form of order. The Bermuda Triangle legend suggests a far less stable scenario. Not only do the Triangle's space-time anomalies question the historical periodizations that lie behind this scheme, but, by constructing a situation that overpowers capital's control over global flows, the myth also undercuts the systemic claims of Wallerstein's approach. In a world of chaotic or disconnected flows, it becomes impossible to identify large-scale structural oppositions (between center and periphery, north and south, McWorld and Jihad world) with which to study the totalizing effects of the capitalist world-system. Boundaries between center and periphery are in constant flux, and flows of commodities, culture, people, and information are subject to unpredictable displacements, leading to a state of pronounced instability.

If the prospect of wild globalization plays havoc with such totalizing systemic models of the contemporary world, it also questions the alternative view by which the current global reorganization of space and time involves a mutual implication of global and local processes. Theorists who adhere to this paradigm argue that the world is becoming both more globalized (unified by flows moving across borders) and more localized (fragmented into enclaves of difference, coalition, and resistance). These thinkers, who work predominantly in cultural studies, contend that the operations of global capital must be studied in the context of their concrete local manifestations. At the same time, they offer symbolic tactics of cultural location and everyday life as modes of appropriation and resistance. But the Bermuda Triangle myth projects a world in which there is no way of localizing culture, where everyday practices and performances cannot be tied to the certainties of place. If cultural borders constantly shift and the idea of locality is swallowed in a whirlpool of disjointed flow, then local difference can no longer be identified as the privileged site of agency and resistance. What the vile vortices phenomenon suggests is a mode of globalization in which restraining measures of reterritorialization cannot control the processes of deterritorialization, and transcultural flows break free from the workings of capital. Clearly we do not live in such a world, but, at a time when it appears that capitalism is without systemic alternatives, such a scenario disrupts our sense of where the future lies.

Already in transnational cultural studies — I am thinking of the work of Appadurai (1996) — there exists a model of globalization that emphasizes not the conjunction of flows into unifying territorialities but their disjunction according to a multidimensional economy of -scapes. Appadurai's work is by his own admission exploratory, but it retains a model of socially produced space while stressing lags and disjunctures that question the totalizing propensities of the Marxist tradition. There is always the danger that this kind of gambit will become enmeshed in an overfamiliar and perhaps unresolvable struggle between Marxist and poststructuralist approaches. Such a theoretical tussle, however, assumes ready access to a set of structural principles that purport to describe the totality of the capitalist world-system. The ensuing debate rests on the susceptibility of these precepts to deconstruction, since deconstruction must seek out a seemingly coherent edifice upon which to perform its radical epistemological work. But what if such an edifice offers itself for neither structural nor deconstructive analysis, if the totality of world capitalism is already deconstructed insofar as its characteristic forms of command are by now entirely flexible, decentered, and deterritorialized? The problem then becomes how the experience of the here and now can be made to represent an absent and unrepresentable totality. As Jameson (1992, 9) argues, the difficulty of conceptualizing the totality of the capitalist system lends conspiracy theory a new lease on life, since as a narrative structure, it unites "the minimal basic components: a potentially infinite network, along with a plausible explanation of its invisibility."

In its various permutations, the Bermuda Triangle myth generates versions of such conspiracy theory. Commentators ascribe its mysterious agency to aliens, Atlanteans, or any number of shadowy actors whose influence is apparently as pervasive as it is invisible. Theories of this kind attribute the area's disruptive capacities to an agency that transcends global forces, claiming that an unknown or extraterrestrial intelligence protects the world from environmental degradation, nuclear destruction, or other catastrophic futures. As pundits gather evidence to substantiate the existence of such an invisible agency, the Triangle becomes a space in which anything can articulate to anything, regardless of social or historical circumstance. Following Jameson, I suggest that this kind of conspiracy theory must be read allegorically. At a time when capitalism's global reach cannot be conceived in separation from digital networks that bombard us with more information than we can possibly navigate or absorb, the figure of an extraterrestrial or supernatural agency supplies a means of representing the unrepresentable totality of the world-system.

After all, geographers like Cosgrove (1994) attribute the rising popular consciousness of globalization to the technical visualization of the world as one place in photographs taken from outer space. Similarly, Dean (1998) reminds us that extraterrestrial fantasies supply a means of imagining the immanence and fragility of life on earth, inspiring visions of global citizenship and interconnectedness if only by mobilizing an us-and-them rhetoric that implicitly reinforces existing economic and cultural divides. In any case, the positing of an agency or intelligence that exceeds capitalist rationality need not be understood as a claim for the transcendence of global processes. In its extraterrestrial or conspiratorial moments the Bermuda Triangle myth struggles to name destabilizing forces that are immanent to global capitalism itself. These unpredictable forces must be constantly controlled and reterritorialized if the system is to sustain itself. Thus capitalist globalization produces its own elaborate set of mythologies, including fanciful notions such as the self-regulating capability of markets, the protection of creative talents by intellectual property rights, or the obliteration of geography through information transfers.

Notwithstanding this, it is important to remember that the triumphant rhetoric of globalization does mark a substantial shift in the operations of capitalism. It would be foolish to deny that capital can now move with astonishing speed and take profitable advantage of new technologies of production, transport, and communication. But as Paul Smith (1997, 14) argues, celebratory narratives of capitalist globalization "are never without their contradictions; indeed, they often also exacerbate material contradictions at the same time as they project a transcendence of these very contradictions." In its disjoining of transnational flows, the Bermuda Triangle brings such contradictions to the fore, mapping out a space in which capitalism becomes dysfunctional and is no longer able to conceal its internal instabilities. As such, it is a realm where contemporary forms of global capitalist command are subverted and disabled — a space where the transcendental fantasy of capitalist sovereignty is repeatedly brought down to earth and the material contradictions of a triumphant globalism become all too hauntingly evident.

According to Hardt and Negri (2000, 345), the current world order sustains itself "through three global and absolute means: the bomb, money, and ether." The bomb designates the panoply of thermonuclear weapons, registering the possibility of destroying life as such and limiting the sovereignty of nation-states to make decisions regarding war and peace. Money supplies the primary means of controlling the global market, subordinating national economic regimes to powers of control that are concentrated in political and financial hubs — the so-called global cities. And finally, ether refers to the management of communication and information systems, the virtual production of the real by which capital submits society entirely and globally to its rule. The Bermuda Triangle and its various doubles (the Dragon's Triangle and vile vortices) disrupt and enfeeble these mechanisms of control at all three levels.

First, the Triangle undermines established forms of military power, mysteriously spiriting away vehicles and weapons, while also disabling the cybernetic technologies that support these transport and armament systems. This involves not only the subversion of sovereign police authority, such as the patrolling of territorial waters, but also the appropriation of the world thermonuclear arsenal. Berlitz (1989, 194) asks of the 126 nuclear warheads supposedly buried in the Dragon's Triangle: "Can there be a force beneath the sea stockpiling these nuclear weapons? And is it doing this as a form of protecting us from ourselves, or preparing for some counterstrike?" Whatever paranoia these questions may embody, they imply the wresting away of thermonuclear power from the existing agents of world domination, no matter how open or free these actors may prove to be. As Virilio (1988, 22) explains, the military "necessity of *controlling* constantly expanding territory, of scanning it in all directions (and, as of now, in three dimensions) while running up against as few obstacles as possible has constantly justified the increase in the penetration speed of means of transport and communication." The Bermuda Triangle subverts these ideologies of speed and control, scrambling and detaining flows of transport and communication to disorientate navigational and scanning technologies, not only on the marine surface but also in the global, 3-D-space of aeronautics, ballistics, and submarinology. In this domain, the smart bomb becomes dumb, and the fantasy of a clean just war, without civilian casualties, friendly fire, or collateral damage, is undermined. Thus the Triangle's victims, whether military personnel or otherwise, are always innocent bystanders, seized from their duties by unknown and invisible forces.

The Triangle also produces disturbances on the plane of monetary exchange, questioning the global capitalist vision of a worldwide marketplace wired up by a cybernetic grid that transcends space and time. At the literal level, the area disrupts financial flows, and has done so for centuries. The search for Bermuda Triangle wreckage has always been linked to the hunt for sunken treasure, such as the various coins, bullion, and jewelry lost with the sinking of eleven Spanish treasure galleons off the Florida Keys in July 1715. Weller (1999) documents the techniques of amateur treasure hunters off the Florida coast, describing sunken bounties that amply attest the area's ability to interrupt and detain monetary flows. In the current world formation, the Triangle also asserts its presence as a site of missing money due to its inclusion of offshore banking centers such as the Bahamas and the Grand Cayman Islands. Apart from serving as tax havens, these jurisdictions provide important nodes in the transnational networks of money laundering. Their proximity to the United States makes them key sites for the investment of illegally earned funds, which are then made to disappear in the undifferentiated flows of the world financial system. In addition to this disruption of financial flows, the Triangle also plays havoc with flows of transport, many of which carry valuable commodities, and communication vectors, which are essential to the smooth working of global finance.

In *Money/Space* (1997), Leyshon and Thrift argue that the world of money is constructed out of and through geography. Celebratory talk of capitalist globalization points to money's ability to transcend mundane boundaries, flickering around the world with a heady and boundless mobility. But for Leyshon and Thrift, the operations of global finance cannot be understood in separation from the spatial demarcations that structure monetary movements, whether due to jurisdictional differences in economic fundamentals, regulatory regimes, or geographically bound investment and tax incentive schemes. Foremost among the spatial frames of financial globalization are what Sassen (1991) calls the global cities, powerful urban hubs that concentrate the technological infrastructure required for financial networking alongside the necessary backup of service industries and unskilled labor supplies. These control hubs of the global economy reterritorialize financial power, putting lie to the narrative by which the worldwide reach of monetary networks detaches financial opportunity from geographical constraints. But the Bermuda Triangle works to scramble and undo the elaborate patterns of monetary flow generated by these financial centers, making them unreadable or wild. In this anomalous zone, which expands to encompass the entire globe, the deterritorializing powers of capital push beyond their internal limits, highlighting the inherent instability of the world economy. It is not simply a matter of capital encompassing the entire globe within its expanding flexible frontiers, registering the absence or impossibility of an outside. In the case of the Bermuda Triangle, these mechanisms of expansion and flexibility are amplified to the point that they override the spatial demarcations of world finance, relinquishing capital of its axiomatic control over transnational flows.

With regard to the ether or the global domain of communication, the situation is more complex. This is because the Bermuda Triangle is at once generated by information flows (insofar as it is a construction of the global media nexus) and disables them (insofar as it disrupts and scrambles the messages that cross its unstable borders). The area constantly reconstitutes itself, existing at the limit of communicational processes that dissolve the relationship between order and space. In this sense, the Triangle is both the representational problem and the representational solution for a world in which digital media technologies generate virtual topographies that threaten to eclipse actual geographical space. From the viewpoint of communication, the Bermuda Triangle has a self-reflexive quality, since its disruption of information flows might be taken to represent the complexities of the interactions between audiences, media producers, and popular texts. Alternatively, the anxieties and fantasies of the myth's diverse audiences might be said to give rise to stories about mysterious disappearances (through a process of projection or desiring-production). The interchangeability of these arguments registers the uncertain placement of communication networks in the current world order. At once standing as the symbol of global capitalism and suggesting the very possibility of its undoing, the communication nexus attests the impossibility of mapping out the world-system in a coherent or totalizing fashion. Any attempt to chart such a map leads either to postmodern anomie or to the anxieties that breed conspiracy theory. As Hardt and Negri (2000, 347) explain, "we cannot conceive this relationship [between order and space] except in *another space,* an elsewhere that cannot in principle be contained in the articulation of sovereign acts." The Bermuda Triangle is such an elsewhere, a domain in which the actualization of the virtual suffuses the production of geographical space. This nonsovereign realm at once confounds the logic of territoriality and confronts the deterritorialized networks of communication with a disruptive interactivity that disables the subordination of society to capital.

The ambivalent placement of the Bermuda Triangle within the networks of global capitalism does not offer an iron-cast guarantee of resistance or subversion. Popular narratives about the Bermuda Triangle leave open the possibility that capital might recolonize this domain, regaining control of the flows that traverse it, or, more accurately, seize upon its chaotic properties and turn them to the business of profit and accumulation. Most prominent among such fantasies is the scenario by which the Triangle furnishes capital with a cheap and renewable source of energy, allowing it to settle its scores with ecological movements and overcome the systemic crises marked by the exhaustion of fossil fuels. Such an ideological complexity also inhabits the myth's racial and sexual dimensions, suggesting that the Triangle's disruptive capacities might actually buffer the wealthy capitalist world from immigration flows or that the area might serve as an open space for the projection of male fantasies. But these permutations of the mystery countermand the dominant strain by which the Triangle's unstable borders upset the reterritorializing capacities of global capitalism. Primary to any reading of the Bermuda Triangle myth must be an attempt to understand the significance and effects of its renowned ability to interrupt and detain transnational flows. Whatever future this scenario implies, be it one of radical contingency or invisible conspiracy, it questions the triumphant narrative by which reality is reduced to the image of capital. As such, the myth points to forms of difference and immanence that elude the processes of global capitalist control. The Bermuda Triangle presents itself as a nonplace where the possible articulates the real and global space outshines the processes of circulation and accumulation that produce it in the first place.

Two

Transnational Transylvania, Europe's Monstrous Other

The ambiguous and contradictory nature of the modern *nation* is the same as that of vampires and other living dead: they are wrongly perceived as "leftovers from the past"; their place is constituted by the very break of modernity.
— Slavoj Žižek, *Tarrying with the Negative*

In August 2001, a dispute broke out between the Romanian government and the Hollywood production company Universal Studios regarding a Dracula theme park to be built five miles from the small medieval town of Sighişoara, Transylvania. Billed as the world's first terror park and financed by the German company Westernstadt Pullman City, the venue, to be known as Dracula Land, promises an estimated turnover of one million tourists per year. Plans include vampire rides, restaurants, hotels, cinemas, a golf course, and a Dracula Institute, complete with meeting rooms and library. A vital piece of infrastructure for Romania's struggling postsocialist economy, the project aims to capitalize on the reputation of Vlad the Impaler, the fifteenth-century ruler of Wallacia, who was born in Sighişoara and, according to McNally and Florescu (1972), provided the inspiration for Bram Stoker's *Dracula* (1983). Since the publication of Stoker's novel in 1897, the association of Transylvania with vampires (and Count Dracula in particular) has become a familiar motif of popular culture. But Universal Studios, the producer of seven Dracula films from 1930 to 1965, has strong ideas about the ownership of the materials and images associated with this most notorious of vampires. Demanding that the Romanian government pay extensive copyright fees for the use of the most iconic Dracula images in the park, the Hollywood giant raised the ire of money-needy Transylvanians. "Who do these Americans think they are?" complained one member of the Sighişoara tourist board. "Dracula is a part of our history and one of the few resources we can use to attract people from all over the world. There's more than enough money around in Hollywood as it is. Why do they need more?" (Coman 2001).

That the intellectual property surrounding a figure like Dracula should become a point of contention between one of the world's largest entertainment conglomerates and a peripheral postsocialist nation is not in itself surprising. Dracula was the object of one of the earliest and most renowned international copyright battles. In the 1920s, Bram Stoker's widow Florence took the German expressionist filmmaker F. W. Murnau to court for making an unauthorized version of *Dracula,* the classic *Nosferatu* (1922). Although Murnau had changed the character names and bankrupted his company in making the film, Florence Stoker pursued the case, and in July 1925 a German court ordered all copies of the film to be burned. A few years later, when Universal bought the rights to *Dracula* for its 1931 Tod Browning adaptation, a version that owes much to Murnau's cinematic technique, the remaining copies of *Nosferatu* in the United States and the United Kingdom were also seized and destroyed. Murnau's classic survives today due to a painstaking process of reconstruction, but in the meantime intellectual property laws have grown ever more complex and central to the international divisions of trade and labor. Today, state-sanctioned forms of intellectual property, such as patents, trademarks, and copyrights, are among the primary sites of struggle between the capitalist and the producing classes. Whether in the form of genetic information, Napster downloads, or ghoulish Lugosi images, knowledge and culture have been increasingly subject to privatization, supplying one of the primary motive forces for the latest wave of capitalist development.

The Dracula Land controversy unfolds in the context of interstate agreements such as TRIPs (Trade Related Intellectual Property), which was signed in 1995 and obliges nation-states to enforce intellectual property regimes at the cost of retaliatory sanctions under unfair trade provisions. As Toby Miller et al. (2001) explain, the global pursuit of copyright privileges by Universal and other Hollywood corporations occurs at a time when new delivery and screen duplication technologies facilitate the work of media piracy, flooding markets in many parts of the world with illegal CDs, videos, and DVDs. At the same time, Hollywood seeks to expand its markets in digital distribution arenas, often relying on these alternative, informal, and illegal distributional networks to establish a foothold in its most problematic — and increasingly most important — markets. Because copyright provisions derive from author's rights principles that attach to fixed works, they afford no protection to folklore and other forms of public culture, leaving institutions such as the Sighişoara tourist board, which appeal to traditional place-bound notions of cultural ownership, without recourse before the international legal system. Dracula stands as a perfect symbol of Romania's contested position in the contemporary capitalist order: at once a measure of the nation's attempts to plug into transnational flows of money, tourists, and commodities, and a register of the anxieties, frustrations, and insecurities generated by this same opening to transnational capitalism. Nowhere are these un-certainties more evident than in the virulent ethnic nationalisms that haunt contemporary Transylvania. To study the ongoing association of Transylvania with vampire culture is thus to confront the nexus of capitalist globalization and ethnic conflict in postsocialist Europe.

Only since 1918 has Transylvania been a Romanian province. Be-fore that, it was part of Hungary. Today the area has a majority Romanian population, but it also houses sizable Hungarian (Mag-yar), Szekely, German, and Roma minorities. (The Jewish population was mostly expelled during the Holocaust or traded with Israel in the 1970s.) The province is a site of intense ethnic contestation and holds immense symbolic significance as a borderland between the imag-ined geopolitical entities of eastern and western Europe. This is one reason why it has proved so popular a setting for vampire fiction. Stoker's *Dracula* is only the most famous text to associate Transyl-vania with vampires, depicting the region as a site of political and racial strife — "the whirlpool of European races" to recall the Count's own description (28). There is by now a highly developed literature on vampire culture, including approaches from psychoanalysis (Cop-jec 1991; Dolar 1991; Rickels 1999), literary studies (Arata 1990; Moretti 1983; Wicke 1992), communication studies (Donald 1992), queer theory (Case 1991), and cultural criticism (Gelder 1994). The present chapter draws on this literature to explore the mapping of Transylvania in vampire texts and its significance for the political, economic, and cultural conflicts that characterize contemporary Tran-sylvania and postsocialist Europe in general. Special attention is paid to the reorganization of geographical space and its relation to eth-nic nationalism, economic regionalism, and the wider processes of capitalist globalization. I argue that vampire texts produce Transyl-vania as a "monstrous geography" that is at once partially connected to and partially dislocated from the global/local topographies of contemporary capitalism. In this way, the chapter offers a radically defamiliarized reading of those icons of transformation (the resurgence of ethnic nationalism, the rise of market economies, and the renegotiation of gender roles) that present postsocialism as evidence of capitalism's global might.

According to the dominant narrative by which globalization involves the worldwide spread of market economics and liberal democracy, postsocialism is a stage in the transition of the former socialist nations to capitalist modes of political, economic, and social organization. Commentators like Fukuyama (1992), Drucker (1993), and Ohmae (1995) understand the decline of actually existing socialism to register a shift toward a new international order in which all systemic alternatives to capitalism have been eliminated. For these thinkers, the collapse of the former socialist bloc marks not only the end of the Cold War but also the possibility of imagining a truly global marketplace. Fukuyama in particular judges the post-1989 renegotiation of world power to announce "the end of history" — that is, the movement of all human societies toward liberal democracy under the guiding hand of the free market. But while the withering of state socialism has ushered in new forms of global power, it is uncertain that the present order is a harmonious concert orchestrated by the not-so-invisible hand of the market.

Paul Smith (1997) argues that contemporary capitalism sustains itself by means of an ideological formation that asserts the existence of a single world market as if it were a fait accompli rather than a continuous (and perhaps unrealizable) process of transformation. If, as the Frankfurt school theorists argued, modern capitalism sought to master the natural world, post–Cold War capitalism dreams of dominating even the metaphysical dimensions of space and time. Such a fantasy of a fully integrated global marketplace would be impossible without the tumultuous events that swept the former socialist bloc in 1989. The collapse of state socialism triggers not only a reorganization of world economic, political, and cultural relations but also a recasting of the ideology of the marketplace. I propose to critically interrogate this celebratory mythography of capitalist globalization by examining the popular fantasy that inhabits an important postsocialist site — the vampire mythography of Transylvania.

The Undead Question

Without doubt, the fall of the Berlin Wall was the most iconic event in the overthrowing of socialist regimes that swept eastern Europe in

1989. But the most spectacular and violent of these uprisings was the so-called Christmas Revolution in Romania. Culminating in the publicly broadcast execution of the socialist dictator Nicolae Ceauşescu and his wife, Elena, the exact unfolding of the Romanian revolution remains nebulous. It is generally agreed that Ceauşescu's fall resulted from the conjuncture of a popular insurrection (that began in Timişoara, Transylvania) and a coup of the Securitate (Ceauşescu's secret police) against itself. But there is no consensus on the relative importance of these events. Other areas of controversy are the role of the KGB, the involvement of Hungarian intelligence, and the identity of the terrorist forces that fought alongside the Securitate in the final days of the conflict (Ratesh 1991). Accounts of the revolution abound with conspiracy theories. Even the most dispassionate commentators resort to the language of plotting, intrigue, and mystery. Lévesque (1997, 199) remarks that "there was not one, but a multitude of plots, intrigues, and intended goals...and it is doubtful that the mystery will ever be fully unravelled." This discourse of mystification seems strangely appropriate to describe a revolution that was sparked by public unrest in Timişoara, the westernmost city of present-day Transylvania. One need not turn to vampire novels or films to legitimate Transylvania's reputation as a site of mystery and horror. The events surrounding the 1989 uprising in Timişoara are bizarre enough.

Although the exact relation of the Timişoara riots to the Bucharest coup remains a point of historical contention, the disturbances in Transylvania were clearly a catalyst to Ceauşescu's demise. The protests, which began on 16 December with the arrest of Lázló Tökes, a dissident ethnic Hungarian pastor, culminated when the Romanian army opened fire on the agitated crowds. Part of the importance of the Timişoara uprising was its close monitoring by foreign media, particularly Hungarian television, whose broadcast signals penetrated into Romania itself (Gross 1995). On 22 December, television audiences worldwide were treated to images of a mass grave in Timişoara, supposedly the burial place of some 4,630 protesters who had been slaughtered during the conflict. The timing of these reports was crucial to the ensuing revolutionary events, providing crucial evidence in Ceauşescu's trial. Several months later, doctors' reports revealed that some thirty of the corpses shown on television had been stolen from the city morgue and hospitals. Apparently, the mass grave had been constituted only after Hungarian and East German press agencies had announced its discovery.

The Timişoara massacre. Reprinted by permission of the Associated Press.

It is unclear who organized this simulation and to what ends. Certainly the reports of mass murder gave impetus to the revolution and rallied international support. They also heightened opposition to the Securitate, who took the blame for the carnage, clearing the reputation of the army and its leaders, who had by that time sided against Ceauşescu. Agamben (2000) characterizes this mock massacre as the Auschwitz of the age of the spectacle. Just as Adorno claims that after Auschwitz it was impossible to think and write as before, Agamben argues that it is impossible to look at a television screen in the same way after Timişoara. In these globally circulated images, which anticipated the media simulations of the Gulf War, truth became indistinguishable from falsehood, and the spectacle found legitimation in nothing but itself. Whatever the wider epistemological implications of this exhumation and display of corpses, which for Agamben is symptomatic of the course of world politics itself, the episode illustrates how the manipulation of the relations between the living and the dead is central to the birth of postsocialism.

In contemporary Transylvania, such mortuary practices are by no means confined to the extremities of mass uprising. In *What Was Socialism, and What Comes Next?* (1996), Katherine Verdery argues that the transition out of socialism involves ritual performances of liminality by which the living redefine their relations to each other through ties to the dead. She cites several examples in which post-socialist regimes signify a change in political order by moving dead bodies (or representations of dead bodies) around and reburying them. These include the dismantling of statues of Lenin and Stalin in the former Soviet Union and the reburial of the former socialist leaders Paderewski and Nagy in Poland and Hungary, respectively. A related incident involves the removal of a statue of Hungary's fifteenth-century king Mátyás from its central location in Cluj, Transylvania. In 1994 an international controversy resulted when the Romanian nationalist mayor, Gheorge Funar, announced plans to move the statue in order to excavate for ancestral bones in the Roman ruins thought to lie beneath it. Verdery extends her study of reburial and postsocialism in *The Political Lives of Dead Bodies* (1999). Here she presents case studies of reburial practices in the wars of Yugoslav succession and the 1997 reburial of Inochentie Micu, an eighteenth-century Greek Catholic bishop and Romanian nationalist hero whose body was transported from Rome for a second burial in the Transylvanian town of Blaj. In both instances, the reburial of the dead supplies a means of reordering worlds of meaning: endowing postsocialist politics with a sense of the sacred, assessing blame and seeking compensation, resignifying spatial and temporal boundaries, and seeking modes of national self-affirmation through connection with ancestors. Verdery concludes that the reshaping of social memory under postsocialism involves a strange form of investment by which political actors gain legitimacy by removing corpses from the grave and putting them back again.

The vampire mythology associated with Transylvania encompasses a similar negotiation of the relations between the living and the dead. Indeed, the famous description of the vampire as the living dead or the undead implies a reanimation of the corpse, a nightly rising from the vault before reburial at daybreak. In his classic study *The Vampire in Europe* (1929), Montague Summers links the vampire lore of Transylvania to peasant rituals that involve the exhumation of dead bodies. Summers explains that these rituals are a means of ascertaining if the deceased has become a vampire. If the body has not fully decomposed then it is supposedly a vampire, but if the bones are dry and white the soul has apparently passed to heaven. Mortuary practices of this type acquire a new significance in the light of Verdery's reflections on postsocialist reburial practices. Indeed she cites Gail Kligman's (1988) ethnographic study of Transylvanian peasant ritual to argue that these popular beliefs did not disappear during the socialist period. Verdery claims that while reburial rituals have not gone unchanged, they are reinvented in the postsocialist context. What is important is that these practices have a history that makes them available for numerous associations derived from presocialist times, forming a broader cultural system that shapes the possibilities for present action. Changes in political context give these ideas new relevance — for example, ideas about proper burial and harmonious kin relations prove politically powerful for people living through postsocialist transformations in which conflicts over property have exacerbated disputes within families. If, as Verdery suggests, reburial practices provide a privileged means of understanding the transition to postsocialism, the link between the sociospatial constitution of contemporary Transylvania and its popular reputation as the home of vampires is more than fortuitous.

According to Verdery, death and rebirth under postsocialism are conjoined not only through the treatment of corpses but also through two major systems of meaning — kinship and nationalism. Significantly, these meaning systems are also operative in vampire fiction. In Stoker's *Dracula,* Count Dracula delivers a long disquisition on Transylvanian history, linking his Szekely family heritage to a sense of national-racial pride. The Szekely are a minority group in Transylvania. Although their ethnic origins are obscure, many of them assumed a Magyar (or Hungarian) ethnic outlook, forming a tight cluster of Magyarized people in southeastern Transylvania, where they fulfilled the role of border guards, protecting Hungarian lands from the threat of Ottoman invasion. From the twelfth century, a count holding direct authority from the Hungarian king acted as their ruler. But despite their initial aristocratic status, by the mid–nineteenth century the condition of the Szekely was far from noble and egalitarian. The wealthy landholders had been assimilated into the Magyar aristocratic class, while the majority could barely be distinguished from peasants in their way of life. This is the background against which Stoker's Dracula makes his disquisition. Focusing on the patrimony of his own aristocratic house, Dracula attributes the present subjugation of his people to the preciousness of their blood: "The warlike days are over. Blood is too precious a thing in these days of dishonourable peace; and the glories of the great races are as a tale that is told" (Stoker 1983, 29–30). Although it unfolds in an altogether different historical context, postsocialist nationalism also insists on the importance of ancestors, blood, and past racial glories.

The rituals of reburial that mark the transition out of socialism are attempts to bury the socialist past and shape the postsocialist future.

They involve a complex system of representation that hinges upon notions of gender and substance: representations of the national soil as the body of ancestors, understandings of abortion as inimical to national rebirth, and concepts of ancestral patrimony as embodied in property ownership and national territory. If read through the symbolism of vampire culture these notions acquire a perverse quality, involving monstrous conceptions of the body politic, queer modalities of reproduction, and contested territorial boundaries. Above all the vampire's undead status questions the standard narrative by which postsocialism evinces the worldwide victory of capitalism. By suggesting that socialism's death is somehow incomplete or reversible, the trope of the living dead implies the postponement or deferral of socialism within postsocialism. This is why the popular geography of Transylvania provides a platform on which to interrogate triumphal narratives that take postsocialism as evidence of capitalism's total domination of space and time.

In *Conflict and Chaos in Eastern Europe* (1995), historian Dennis Hupchick describes the ethnonational dispute surrounding Transylvania as "the undead question." He begins his investigation of the historical conflict over the province by recalling its mythical aura: "It seems to conjure up images of dark, forlorn castles perched precipitously on craggy, forested mountain cliffs that are perpetually swathed in lowering mist and rain" (50). Like other analysts of the Romanian-Hungarian situation, he feels obliged to remind his readers that Transylvania "is a real region in Central-Eastern Europe, today about the size of Kentucky, and one of three component provinces of Romania" (50). But despite Hupchick's efforts to distance Transylvania from its popular cultural reputation, the symbology of vampirism returns to haunt his account of the area's racial history. By describing the question of Transylvania's ethnic makeup as undead, he gives lie to the myth that the area's ethnonationalist tensions were somehow put to rest under socialism. According to the dominant "ancient hatreds" theory, favored by Western politicians and journalists, the appearance of nationalist movements and sentiments in the wake of socialism attests the return of an archaic order of ethnic or tribal conflict that had been suppressed by socialist internationalism. There are a number of difficulties with this argument, not least the implication that ethnonationalist tension springs from premodern enmities that attest the inability or refusal of the conflicting parties to adhere to modern principles of rationality and governance. In fact the national identities at stake in the Transylvanian dispute are thoroughly modern,

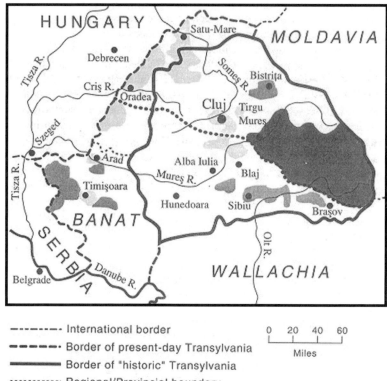

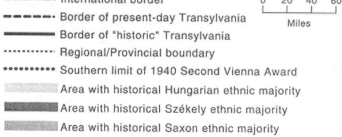

The Transylvanian question: the historical fluctuation of Transylvania's borders. From Dennis P. Hupchick, *Conflict and Chaos in Eastern Europe* (New York: Palgrave Macmillan, 1995). Copyright Dennis P. Hupchick. Reprinted with permission of Palgrave.

stemming from eighteenth- and nineteenth-century struggles in which the Romanian peasants sought to gain religious and economic rights equal to their aristocratic Hungarian counterparts.

Although the Hungarian presence in Transylvania dates from the eleventh century, when the Magyar king István conquered the area, a modern national consciousness began to take hold only in the eighteenth century. Until 1699, when the area was placed under direct

Hapsburg control, Transylvania was a semi-independent entity, governed by a royally appointed *vajda* (or *voivode* in Romanian) and a diet composed of representatives from the three privileged ethnic groups: Magyars, Szekely, and Saxons. Unlike the Magyar groups in the Pannonian and Slovakian regions of the Hapsburg empire, the Transylvanian Magyars retained the administrative use of their language, refused to accept Hapsburg rule after the Turkish defeat of 1526, and played an important role in western European affairs for the following 160 years. Even after the Hapsburgs gained direct control over Transylvania, the great anti-Hapsburg rebellion of 1703–11 and the political concessions later won from Emperor Charles IV and Empress Maria Theresa placed the Transylvanian Magyars at the forefront of Hungarian national development. In an important sense, Transylvania was the historical breeding ground of Hungarian nationalism. Its Magyar-led anti-Hapsburg struggles preceded the popular nationalism that emerged among the Pannonian Magyars in the early nineteenth century. Even after the revolution of 1848 and the 1867 *Ausgleich* separating Austria from Hungary, Transylvanian aristocrats continued to exert a high degree of power since Hungary adopted what Anderson (1991) calls an official nationalism — a provisional but ultimately doomed attempt to marshal the popular energies released by the nationalist movement to the retention of dynastic privilege.

Significantly enough, Romanian nationalism also finds its historical roots in Transylvania. While the extent of Romanian presence in the region prior to the eleventh century is a matter of historical contention, there can be no doubt that Romanians made up the bulk of the peasant class during the centuries of Magyar dominance. Even during the period 1526–1699, when the semi-independent Transylvania was a center of religious tolerance, extending rights to Lutherans, Calvinists, and Roman Catholics alike, the Orthodox Romanians received no official recognition. When the Hapsburgs gained control of the principality in 1699, they sought to strengthen their position against the Magyar nobles by converting the Romanians to Catholicism, specifically through the instrument of Uniatism — a Christian denomination that combined Orthodox ritual with Catholic doctrine to form the so-called Greek Catholic Church. While this program was largely successful, it ultimately served the ends of Hapsburg centralism less than it enabled the emergence of a specifically Romanian national consciousness.

The crucial figure in the rise of Romanian nationalism is Inochentie Micu, the same eighteenth-century Greek Catholic bishop who was reburied in Blaj in 1997. Micu used the institutions of Greek Catholicism to formulate a program of political and social action that aimed at emancipating the Romanian peasants and raising them up to nationhood. As a student in a Jesuit seminary in modern-day Slovakia, he had been instructed in the techniques of philology, and these would prove crucial to his development of an ethnopolitical doctrine that asserted the historical precedence of the Romanians in Transylvania. According to Micu's theory, which drew on linguistic and archaeological evidence (including inscriptions on monuments in Rome), the Romanians were direct descendants of the Daks, the supposed indigenous inhabitants of Transylvania who were Romanized after the Roman emperor Trajan conquered the area in the second century C.E. The intellectual and cultural traditions forged by Micu provided the foundation on which modern Romanian nationalists would build, first in Transylvania and, from there, in the two Romanian principalities of Wallachia and Moldavia.

Until 1914, when the outbreak of World War I altered the geopolitical balance of power in the region, the nationalism of Transylvanian Romanians remained largely distinct from that of their counterparts in the Romanian principalities. While the Transylvanian Romanians struggled to gain parity with other nationalities within the Hapsburg empire, those in the principalities, under heavy French influence, were concerned mainly with blotting out their Ottoman past and building a Greater Romania that would encompass Transylvania. Prior to 1914, those in Transylvania had little interest in the Greater Romania ideal, not least because the highly aristocratic form of nationalism that existed in the principalities conflicted with their efforts to gain a more egalitarian position under the Hapsburgs. Toward the end of the nineteenth century, however, the Romanian monarch began to agitate among the Transylvanians for union with his kingdom. This was also the period in which Stoker set his *Dracula* in Transylvania. In choosing the province as the location for his vampire tale, Stoker drew on several British travel narratives, including Charles Boner's *Transylvania: Its Products and Its People* (1865), Andrew F. Crosse's *Round about the Carpathians* (1878), Emily Gerard's "Transylvanian Superstitions" (1885), and Major E. C. Johnson's *On the Track of the Crescent* (1885). As Arata (1990) notes, these works resemble British colonial travel narratives in their rhetorical strategies, evidencing a growing interest in the region on the part of the western European powers. Indeed, the influence of Britain and France would prove crucial for Transylvania during World War I and its aftermath.

Siding with the Allied powers, Romania took advantage of a weakened Austria-Hungary to launch an invasion of the province, first unsuccessfully in 1916 and then successfully in 1918. The subsequent award of Transylvania (as well as the adjacent regions of Maramureş, Crisana, and the Banat) to Romania with the Trianon Treaty of 1920 brought the question of the area's ethnonational affiliations to the forefront of European international affairs.

Hungary, which had been stripped of almost two-thirds of its former historic territories by the Trianon Treaty, considered the ruling a national humiliation — a sentiment that would eventually drive the nation toward an alliance with Nazi Germany. Through the institutions of the League of Nations and the international press, Magyar nationalists argued that they had been robbed of territories that were an integral part of their ancestral homelands. According to their version of history, when the Hungarian king István moved into Transylvania in the eleventh century the sole inhabitants were a few Magyars who had settled there from about 800 C.E. The Romanians, they asserted, had arrived in Transylvania only in the thirteenth century, when they drifted across the Carpathians from their homelands in the Balkan south. In addition the area had been a stronghold of Magyar culture during the Ottoman period and had served as a safe haven for Hungarian agitators and nationalists during the 1848 revolution.

Initially the Romanians responded to these claims by arguing that they enjoyed a demographic majority in Transylvania. Eventually, however, they were obliged to make a viable historical case to counter that of the Hungarians. To do this, they drew on the theory of Daco-Roman origins first expounded by Inochentie Micu and his followers. According to Micu, there existed an indigenous Transylvanian population prior to the Roman invasion of the second century C.E. — the so-called Daks. When the Romans abandoned the province after 160 years, they left behind a pastoral Dak population that had become Latin-speaking (hence the Latin structure of the modern Romanian language). These Daco-Romans weathered the numerous storms of invasion that swept the province from the fifth to the ninth centuries, living primarily in inaccessible mountain areas, and finally emerging as the modern Romanians under the Magyars. Thus the Romanians, and not the Magyars, were the first people of Transylvania. The Hungarians were modern latecomers who had usurped the region from its rightful inhabitants by force.

Whatever the merits of these rival historical narratives, neither was successful in establishing an international consensus regarding the province's past. Like the vampire stories that had begun to circulate about Transylvania in popular films and books, each of these narratives drew upon murky historical claims that were ultimately unsusceptible to empirical verification. During the interwar period, Romanian control of Transylvania found its basis in political factors alone: namely, the status quo of the Trianon Treaty and the refusal of England, France, and their allies to budge before Magyar petitions. Not surprisingly the Hungarians were driven into an alliance with Hitler, the most prominent European critic of the treaty system. By a twist of fate, Romania also found itself allied with Nazi Germany as World War II approached. Although Romania had every reason to support the Versailles arrangements, it had drifted toward the Nazis due to deep internal political and economic unrest caused by rabid anti-Semitism and deep class conflicts expressed through native fascist, Christian rightist, and peasant movements. From the German perspective, both Hungary and Romania were necessary allies to ensure their domination of eastern Europe. An alliance with Hungary afforded a degree of stability in the region, while Romania was a valuable source of petroleum. The problem was that these allies were at loggerheads over Transylvania. Indeed in 1940 the Hungarians were actively preparing to invade the province. To stave off conflict, Hitler pursued a territorial solution, issuing a decree that granted the northern two-fifths of Transylvania to Hungary. But neither the Magyars nor the Romanians were content with this settlement, viewing it as a temporary arrangement that would be resolved when the war was over. Unfortunately for the Hungarians, the German defeat meant that the award was nullified. In 1944, the Romanians had defected to the anti-German allies, and, when the war was over, they received all of Transylvania as a reward.

By the judgment of many commentators, the rise of socialism in eastern Europe served to suppress Romanian-Hungarian ethnonationalist conflict under a Soviet-imposed hegemony. This is a crucial assumption for the ancient-hatreds theory that explains the resurgence of nationalist sentiment under postsocialism as a return to tribalism. As outlined above, however, the national identities at stake in the Transylvanian dispute date to the break of modernity, having their origins in eighteenth- and nineteenth-century struggles against monarchical states. There is no basis in the claim that postsocialist ethnonational allegiances stem from premodern affiliations that are antithetical to modern conventions of secularism, cosmopolitanism, and tolerance. Equally problematic is the commonplace that socialist party rule served to override nationalist sentiment and identification. On the contrary, centralized party rule created political subjectivities that were especially susceptible to the symbols inherent in nationalist appeals.

While the jurisdictional conflict between Romania and Hungary declined in the early years of the socialist period, the Romanian government took active steps to dampen ethnic tension in Transylvania, establishing a Hungarian Autonomous Zone in the province's east in 1952. This Autonomous Zone, which would endure for only eight years, was safely tucked away from the Hungarian border and did not enjoy any significant form of self-government. Under the rule of Gheorghiu-Dej, who came to power in 1952, the Romanian state pursued a policy of assimilation (or homogenization, as it was officially dubbed) with respect to its minorities, a strategy that would continue when Ceauşescu emerged as party secretary in 1965. Deletant (1995) outlines three main elements to this policy: first, the migration of Romanians into Transylvania and the movement away from the province of Hungarians and Germans (the latter by emigration); second, the decrease of minority language schools through the application of quotas; and, third, the promotion of Romanian as the majority language necessary for social mobility. Despite these efforts, ethnic identifications continued to play an important role in the daily lives of Transylvanians.

Verdery (1996) argues that one reason for the continued importance of ethnonational identifications under socialism was the pivotal role played by personal connections in a system of centralized economic command. Because the Romanian economy functioned as a system of organized shortage, placing social actors in competition for scarce resources, any device that increased one's chance of obtaining the goods one needed had a functional role to play. The tightening of ethnic boundaries offered an effective means of expelling competitors from networks of supply, often through the creation of ethnic occupational specializations. In this way, the proliferation of ethnonational identities was integrally tied to the organization of socialism, and, as the mechanisms of centralized rule grew stronger, so the incentives to forge exclusive bonds with members of one's own ethnicity strengthened.

This dynamic was particularly evident in the final decade of Ceauşescu's rule, when a failing economy pushed the leadership to clamp down on a growing Hungarian nationalism in Transylvania. In 1983 the editors of a clandestine Hungarian-language journal *Ellenpotok*

(Counterpoints) were arrested, beaten, and expelled to Hungary. Similarly in 1986, the editor of another underground publication, *Erdelyi Magyar Hirugynokseg* (The Hungarian press of Transylvania), was forced to leave the country. Meanwhile Ceauşescu began a massive program of village redevelopment that aimed to reduce the number of villages in Romania by more than half, shifting the inhabitants into new agroindustrial towns. Although the program was not specifically targeted at Hungarian villages, it had a disproportionate effect upon Hungarians in Transylvania, where many small rural communities were marked for phasing out. In 1988 the issue drew the attention of an emerging opposition group in Hungary, the Hungarian Democratic Forum, which organized a massive rally opposing systematization in Budapest and a series of smaller demonstrations at Romanian embassies in European capitals and the United States. Much to Ceauşescu's dismay, the Transylvanian question had reemerged as an internal Hungarian problem as much as it remained an unresolved issue within Romania itself.

The Transylvanian dispute also surfaced as a difficulty in the bilateral relations between the two nations. In December 1986, the Hungarian Academy published a three-volume history of Transylvania that directly questioned the official Romanian argument according to which the Daks inhabited the province prior to the eleventh century. So outraged were the Romanian authorities that in April 1987 they placed a full-page advertisement in *The Times* of London, charging the Hungarian Academy and government (the Hungarian minister of education had edited the volume) with falsifying history with irredentist intent. Clearly, on the eve of the Christmas Revolution, the nationalist emotions surrounding Transylvania were running high, transformed and escalated by forty years of socialist rule rather than suddenly looming up from the ancient past. The metaphor of the undead or reanimated corpse provides an appropriate means of describing the status of the Hungarian-Romanian controversy at the birth of postsocialism, since it succinctly registers the way in which such ethnonationalist tension was neither dead nor buried during the socialist era. As the December 1989 events in Timişoara attest, the figure of the living corpse supplies more than a rhetorical device for describing a situation that might otherwise be outlined in more straightforward terms. Under postsocialism, the disinterment, display, and reburial of dead bodies emerge as obsessive means of dramatizing the end of centralized party rule, reshaping public memory, and building a sense of national legitimacy. In this context, the popular reputation of Transylvania as the home of vampires converges on its status as a site of ethnonational conflict and postsocialist transition.

Dracula Lives

Not accidentally does the post–World War I escalation of the dispute in Transylvania accompany the rapid dissemination of the Dracula myth in the popular media. A standard reference work on vampire culture, Gordon J. Melton's *The Vampire Book: The Encyclopaedia of the Undead* (1994), cites two early silent film versions of Stoker's novel, both subsequently lost: a Russian *Dracula* made in 1920 and a 1921 film titled *Drakula* made by the Hungarian filmmaker Károly Lajthay. While it is impossible to speculate on the content of these works, both made within twelve months of the signing of the Trianon Treaty, it is known that the Hungarian film was suppressed by the Horthy regime, which had risen to power after Romania's defeat of Béla Kun's communist forces. Doubtless, the material of Stoker's novel provided fertile ground for allegorizing the political struggles that wracked Hungary and its former Transylvanian territories. The following year saw the release of Murnau's *Nosferatu*, which characterizes Transylvania as "the land of phantoms." In Murnau's silent classic, Dracula doubles for Count Orlock, a Transylvanian aristocrat who travels to real estate he has purchased in the city of Bremen, where he finds a constant source of victims. Two years later a theatrical version of *Dracula* premiered in Derby, England, eventually to be staged both in London and New York City in 1927, with the U.S. version featuring the Hungarian Transylvanian actor Béla Lugosi. In 1931, Lugosi appeared in Universal's *Dracula,* which set the archetype of Transylvania for decades to come, with its journey into a land of dark shadows, superstitious peasants, and craggy mountains, and with a castle, enshrouded in fog, perched on a steep precipice. From here, the Dracula story began to reproduce itself in a multiplicity of media, genres, and cultural contexts, giving rise to a seemingly endless web of remakes, parodies, and sequels.

A Spanish version of *Dracula* appeared in 1931, also made by Universal and released simultaneously with the Lugosi classic. As if to celebrate the vampire's reproductive powers, Universal released *Dracula's Daughter* in 1936, followed in 1943 by *Son of Dracula.* In 1953, *Drakula Istanbul'da,* a Turkish version of *Dracula,* was produced, and the first comic book adaptation of *Dracula* appeared in a publication called *Eerie.* The first television version of *Dracula,* which starred

Béla Lugosi in *Dracula*, 1931. Reprinted by permission of MPTV and the Australian Picture Library.

John Carradine, was broadcast as part of NBC's Matinee Theater in 1956, the same year that *Kyuketsuki Ga,* the first Japanese vampire movie, appeared. In 1958, the British company Hammer Films initiated a new wave of interest in vampires with its first Dracula movie, *Horror of Dracula,* starring Christopher Lee. Although the film made no explicit mention of Transylvania, the area would feature prominently in subsequent Hammer releases, such as *The Brides of Dracula* (1960) in which a voice-over intones: "Transylvania — land of dark forests, dread mountains and black, unfathomed lakes. Still the home of magic and devilry." The 1960s saw the production of the first Korean *Dracula, Ahkea Kkots* (1961), the appearance of Roman Polanski's controversial *The Fearless Vampire Killers* (1967), and the release of the first explicitly gay vampire movie, *Dracula and the Boys* (1969). During the 1970s, a host of classic adaptations of *Dracula* appeared, including the BBC *Count Dracula* (1978), the Universal remake of *Dracula* (1979), and Werner Herzog's remake of Murnau's classic, *Nosferatu, the Vampyre* (1979). The same decade saw a rush of parodies and generic crossovers, most prominently Jim Sharman's *The Rocky Horror Picture Show* (1975) and Stan Dragoti's *Love at First Bite* (1979) but also the Blaxploitation *Blacula* (1972), *Dragula* (1973), as well as the sign-languaged *Deafula* (1974).

In the 1970s, there also appeared a rush of popular vampire novels, with the publication of bestsellers such as Stephen King's *'Salem's Lot* (1975), Anne Rice's *Interview with the Vampire* (1976), and Chelsea Quinn Yarbro's *Hotel Transylvania* (1978). While not all of these works were set in Transylvania, the association of the province with vampires was by this time well established. In the 1980s, amid the release of vampire films such as *The Hunger* (1983) and *The Lost Boys* (1987) with no putative link to Transylvania, there also appeared works such as the comedy *Transylvania 6-5000* (1985) and *Daughter of Darkness* (1989), which maintained the connection with the region. Not until the 1990s, however, with the fall of the Ceauşescu regime, did Transylvania reemerge as the preferred site for films such as Ted Nicolaou's *Subspecies* (1991) series and Francis Ford Coppola's *Bram Stoker's Dracula* (1992), both shot on location in Romania. With the turn of the twenty-first century, the vampire's reproductive capacities again became caught in a millennial cycle of expectation and letdown, spurring works like *Dracula 2000* (2000) and *Shadow of the Vampire* (2000), a skillful reconstruction of the making of Murnau's *Nosferatu*. Given the tendency of vampire culture to graft itself onto the latest cultural technology, it is no surprise to learn that Dracula has by now a formidable presence on the Internet, with Web sites devoted to fanship, history, scholarship, and tourism.

While there exist over one hundred *Dracula* movies and well over six hundred commercially produced vampire films, the above account gives only the barest sketch of the myth's migration from medium to medium: novel, stage, film, comic book, television, and Internet. To parse apart the processes of transmission responsible for this diffusion would be a massive task, already partially completed by David Skal in *Hollywood Gothic: The Tangled Web of Dracula from Novel to Stage to Screen* (1990). There can be no doubt that Dracula's capacity to migrate from technology to technology is part of the myth's attraction. Stoker's *Dracula* is a consummate piece of techno-fiction, running the gamut of late-nineteenth-century technologies of consumption: the gramophone, stenography, the typewriter, the Kodak camera, the newspaper, the telegraph (Wicke 1992). As Halberstam (1995) argues, this propensity to animate the processes of technical reproduction is inseparable from a production of monstrosity, by which the vampire emerges as the embodiment of an infinitely interpretable otherness, variously understood to represent the Jew, the homosexual, the hysterical woman, or the colonial subject. The vampire's polymorphous perversity, its apparently unlimited ability to adapt, mutate, and occupy these various subject positions, allows it to proliferate, reproducing itself in a series of copies, each slightly different from the other. Stoker's figure of hypermasculine seduction slowly metamorphoses into a photosensitive claustrophobe (Murnau), an outlandish serial killer (Polanski), a high camp icon (Sharman), and a postfeminist symbol of sexual potency (Rice). This repetition confers a sense of immortality upon the vampire, endowing it with a seemingly unstoppable cultural longevity. Vampire stories never quite drop out of circulation, but constantly return, entangling their audiences in a complex web of desires, fears, and paranoia. What interests me is the way in which this process of othering, which is always technological, insinuates itself in the mapping of Transylvania. For while the vampire's resistance to representation makes it notoriously difficult to pin down — throwing no shadow in the light, leaving no footprints on the ground, casting no reflection in the mirror — the reputation of Transylvania as the home of vampires continues to haunt the popular imagination.

The association of Transylvania with vampires has not diminished even if many contemporary vampires have drifted away from this geographic base. In Anne Rice's *Interview with the Vampire* (1976, 207) the central vampire, Louis, and his child companion, Claudia, who both hail from New Orleans, travel to Transylvania in search of kin, only to encounter "a mindless, animated corpse." "We had met the European vampire, the creature of the Old World," declares Louis, "He was dead" (207). But for every work that deprives Transylvania of its vampiric host, another can be found that maintains the connection. Besides, the name Transylvania readily detaches itself from its material ground, becoming a transferable sign that carries its meanings to other parts of the earth's surface, Rice's New Orleans among them. Gelder (1994) points out that this process had begun even before the publication of Stoker's *Dracula*. He cites an 1830 map of Tasmania, the large island south of mainland Australia, which designates the uncolonized (and uncharted) part of the territory as Transylvania. In this case, the otherness evoked by the term Transylvania is strangely literalized, since behind the dense forests that separated the mapped from the unmapped sections of Tasmania lived the island's indigenous people, whom the colonists had violently pushed away and would eventually completely exterminate. This tendency for Transylvania to serve as a mobile sign that bestows its sense of otherness upon distant geographic locations continues today, when the connection with vampires is more or less intractable.

Take the example of the Kentucky-based Transylvania University, which, as Elizabeth Miller (1997) recounts, threatened to take the Hallmark Corporation to court for its production of a T-shirt with the words "Transylvania University. We Go for the Throat! E Pluribus Bitum" inscribed across the front. Although the university has no ostensible connection with Romania, the association with vampires is endemic and apparently impossible to reverse. Transylvania's capacity to usurp the names of distant places is evident also in texts like Rudy de Luca's film comedy, *Transylvania 6-5000*, or the 1996 teen novel *Transylvania 90210*, ghost-written for actress and former Las Vegas showgirl Cassandra Peterson, a.k.a. Elvira, Mistress of the Night. As their titles suggest, these works fold North American popular culture into an extravagantly inauthentic Transylvanian ambiance, as if this supposedly remote place had always belonged in Hollywood, or at least in Beverly Hills.

Whatever the cosmopolitan or diasporic tendencies of vampire culture, the link with Transylvania persists in the era of postsocialism and globalization, particularly among audiences in the wealthy capitalist world. In *American Vampires* (1990), the folklorist Norine Dresser reports a survey in which over five hundred U.S. students were asked where vampires come from. Over half of them answered Transylvania. By contrast, Elizabeth Miller (1997) notes a tendency among contemporary Romanians to deny the existence of vampires in their folk beliefs. Partly this is due to a semantic difficulty, since the word "vampire" in modern Romanian refers to a supernatural creature that originates in Western culture and can be extended to describe murderers or assassins. Ethnographic studies, such as Harry Senn's *Were-Wolf and Vampire in Romania* (1982, 41), indicate that vampires do exist in the Romanian tradition, although these creatures are distinct from the vampires of the West, which derive from "the literary and philosophical contexts of romanticism and decadent Marquis-de-Sadism." Such a tendency to classify vampires according to an East-West cultural typology reflects the geopolitical imaginary of vampire tales themselves, where the identification of Transylvania as an Eastern site serves to mark its supposed eeriness and otherness.

At the beginning of Stoker's *Dracula,* as Jonathan Harker moves closer to Transylvania, he remarks in his diary: "The impression I had was that we were leaving the West and entering the East" (2). Similarly, in Murnau's *Nosferatu,* the crossing of Harker (or Hütter as he is known) into Transylvania receives a spectacular technological rendering, as a photographic negative reverses light and dark — a technique that implies the binary opposition of Dracula's lair and the German city from which Harker travels. This technological construction of Transylvania's otherness continues as the vampire genre evolves, burying itself in an ever more elaborate array of special effects. As recent a film as Coppola's *Bram Stoker's Dracula* perpetuates the Orientalist identification of Transylvania, directly quoting the sentence from Jonathan Harker's diary above and deploying extravagant makeup and costuming to suggest Dracula's connection with the East. Here, the Orientalist conceit derives from the identification of Dracula with Vlad Țepeş (also known as Vlad the Impaler or the historical Dracula), the fifteenth-century Wallachian *voivode* born in Sighişoara and renowned for his bloodthirsty slaughter of the Turks. Glover (1996) explains that Vlad had passed his youth in Istanbul and that Coppola's identification of Dracula with this historical personage makes him into a figure like Joseph Conrad's Kurtz, who submits to the sensual Orient even as he struggles against it.

It is no surprise to learn that this Orientalist construction of Transylvania also features in Cold War era commentaries on Stoker's *Dracula* that evoke the rhetoric of the iron curtain and the evil empire. Wasson (1966, 27) describes Transylvania as a "threat to the progress of Western Civilization," while Ronay (1972, 169) labels it the home of "the potent spiritual poison of the Communist East." Similar epithets attach themselves to Nicolae Ceauşescu, particularly in the final years of his rule when the question of Hungarian nationalism acquired a new urgency. Fueled by rumors that Ceauşescu (who suffered from prostate cancer) regularly received blood transfusions from children, Hungarian nationalists began to deploy the trope of vampirism to demonize the Romanian leader. Kurti (1989) reports that during Ceauşescu's 1978 visit to Washington, D.C., protesters from Hungarian communities in the United States and Canada carried placards proclaiming "Dracula Lives." Although Stoker's novel and the films following from it were banned in Romania during the socialist era, Ceauşescu made a deliberate attempt in the 1970s to rehabilitate the reputation of Vlad Ţepeş. Statues were erected, streets renamed, a postage stamp issued, and a feature film produced. During this same period, the U.S.-based scholars Raymond McNally and Radu Florescu published two influential studies, *In Search of Dracula* (1972) and *Dracula: A Biography of Vlad the Impaler* (1973). These volumes argued that Stoker had based his vampire on the historical Dracula, sourcing his material through a Hungarian professor named Arminius Vambery. Placed in the context of Ceauşescu's admiration for Vlad Ţepeş, McNally and Florescu's argument further implicated the Romanian leader in an association with Dracula, a connection that Hungarian commentators and their Western sympathizers did not fail to exploit following the Christmas Revolution of 1989.

The early 1990s saw a run of biographies that traced Ceauşescu's downfall, drawing on a readily available vampire iconography. Significantly, Ceauşescu and his wife, Elena, had been executed in Tirgoviste, the fifteenth-century seat of Vlad the Impaler — a coincidence that further legitimated the identification of the former leader as a vampire. In *Kiss the Hand You Cannot Bite: The Rise and Fall of the Ceauşescus* (1991, 190), Edward Behr describes Ceauşescu as the communist Dracula, noting the rumors that he "regularly received blood transfusions from sacrificed Romanian children." John Sweeney's *The Life and Evil Times of Nicolae Ceauşescu* (1991) offers a more sensational account that blends the nationalistic myth of Vlad Ţepeş, vampires, and the life story of Ceauşescu. The book, which begins, "This is a horror story... about a monster" (23), depicts Romanian political culture as a combination of submission and authoritarianism explained by the country's historical incorporation into the Ottoman empire. Here the portrayal of Ceauşescu as a vampire directly joins an Orientalist construction of Romanian culture, implicitly affirming the geopolitical myth by which Transylvania maintains a separate Western heritage. Sweeney's biography thus intersects Hungarian accounts of Transylvanian history — as represented, for instance, by Gyula Zathureczky's *Transylvania: Citadel of the West* (1967) — illustrating the complex intermingling of nationalist historical narrative with vampire mythology.

The parallel between Ceauşescu and Dracula is also apparent in what Gelder (1994) calls post-Ceauşescu vampire narratives. A case in point is Douglas Borton's short story "Voivode" (1992), which, like Sweeney's biography, combines elements of Stoker's novel, McNally and Florescu's biography of Vlad the Impaler, and Ceauşescu's life story. In this text, Ceauşescu is the twentieth-century incarnation of Vlad Ţepeş who has survived as a vampire. A similar post-Ceauşescu allegory is found in Ted Nicolaou's 1991 film *Subspecies,* which, with its primarily Hungarian crew and actors, traces the fortunes of three young female researchers who travel to Transylvania from the United States to conduct an ethnographic study of vampire beliefs. They become embroiled in a battle between two vampire brothers, the good Stephan and the evil Radu, who has killed his father. The bloodsucking antics of Radu are clearly intended to represent the political excesses of Ceauşescu. He even has an army of tiny offspring — the subspecies — who fulfill the role of the Securitate. Another important post-Ceauşescu vampire narrative is Dan Simmons's 1992 novel *Children of the Night,* which skillfully combines postrevolution Romanian history, the Vlad Ţepeş myth, and AIDS allegory. The story finds its background in Ceauşescu's pronatalist population policies, which created a flood of abandoned children who were housed in state orphanages. Due to the practice of giving these malnourished children microtransfusions of blood in the belief that it would boost their immune system, an AIDS epidemic broke out among them. *Children of the Night* posits a vampire strain with a weakness in their immune systems that can only be offset by drinking human blood, as an inherited retrovirus allows them to rebuild tissue to the point of cannibalizing themselves. This confers powers of longevity upon them, allowing an eternalized Vlad Ţepeş figure to emerge as the central character. Posing as the head of one of the world's largest corporations, this protagonist becomes engaged in a struggle for an orphan boy who promises to continue the Dracula line but is protected by an American hematologist who believes that his condition promises a cure for AIDS. In the course of events, it becomes evident that the vampire clan has orchestrated Ceauşescu's demise and is responsible for the turbulent condition of postsocialist Romania, the results of a conspiracy that extends back to the fifteenth century.

What is interesting about Simmons's *Children of the Night* is that it identifies vampires not with the former Romanian regime but with the forces of transnational capital that dislocate the socialist system of centralized command. In this novel, Dracula is a venture capitalist who must reinvest in Romania to ensure his own perpetuation. While the metaphorical equation of vampirism and capital is at least as old as Marx and plays a crucial role in Stoker's *Dracula,* where the vampire is a real estate magnate, it acquires a new significance in the postsocialist context. In Simmons's novel, the trope of vampirism represents not the political excesses of Ceauşescu or his menace to the Hungarian national minority but the very market reforms that drive ethnic Romanians toward a new sense of nationalism. As Verdery (1996) explains, the fall of the Ceauşescu regime forced many Romanians to revise their sense of identity or self, which under socialism had been constructed in tacit opposition to party rule. While there was a necessity to affirm one's commitment to the regime in public, there was an equal and opposite tendency to disavow its legitimacy in private, leading to a divided identity structure that separated "us" from the socialist "them." With the demise of Ceauşescu, this organization of selfhood fell into crisis, and new enemies had to be found in the ethnic minorities that inhabit the Romanian state: primarily Hungarians but also Jews and Roma (who exist only in small numbers). After the revolution, when politicians began to reorganize popular sentiment, the rhetoric and symbols with the greatest electoral appeal proved to be nationalist ones.

In Romania, as in other former Soviet bloc countries, there emerged a new entrepreneurial class — usually former communist apparatchiks — who saw nationalist politics as a means of protecting emerging national markets for their own interests, rather than opening them to outside predators. As a result, nationalist political rhetoric became tightly entwined with a symbolism that depicted ethnic minorities as agents of a threatening and encroaching transnational capitalism. This was most evident in the 1992 elections, when the Party for Social Democracy (PDSR), led by Ion Iliescu, an estranged member of Ceauşescu's inner circle, was returned to power. During the campaign, national populist organizations such as the Romanian Hearth (Vatra Romaneasca), its associated political Party of Romanian National Unity (PUNR), and the Greater Romania Party (PRM) inflamed public emotion with xenophobic anti-Hungarian rhetoric, linking the Transylvanian minority with the transnational Soros Foundation (the nongovernmental organization headed by expatriate Hungarian financier George Soros) and recalling Hitler's 1940 partition of the province. In 1990, Hungarian prime minister Joszef Antall had declared himself the prime minister of all Hungarians, including those living as minorities in border states. Picking up on this rhetoric, Romanian nationalists capitalized on longstanding fears of Hungarian separatism.

This anti-Hungarian rhetoric developed in tandem with the time-honored discourse of opposition to Europe, deployed since the nineteenth century to ward off penetration by foreign capital and the dislocating introduction of Western political forms. For Romanian nationalist groups, the Hungarian presence in Transylvania involved not only a defilement of sacred Romanian soil but also the renewed possibility of the nation's territorial dismemberment. In this context, the imagery and rhetoric of vampirism provided an irresistible means of representing the ethnic other. Verdery (1996) reports that a book written in 1991 to warn Romanians of Hungarian autonomist intentions featured on its cover a map of Romania being threatened from the north by a huge set of teeth, about to take a bite out of the country's rounded shape. Here, as in Simmons's novel, the familiar conceit of the vampire's Eastern origin is turned head on heels, so the threat of vampiric encroachment comes to represent the design of the Hungarian minority (with the supposed backing of transnational capital) upon the Romanian heartland.

While the tension between Romanians and Hungarians in post-1989 Transylvania has never produced the heightened violence of the wars in the former Yugoslavia, there have been important moments when the apparently peaceful coexistence of these groups has been tested. In March 1990, a violent conflict erupted between Romanians and Hungarians in Tîrgu-Mureş, the capital of the Szekely section of Transylvania, leaving eight dead and hundreds injured. Three symbolic events triggered this clash: a pharmacist's announcement that he would replace a Romanian sign with a Hungarian one, mass celebrations of the Hungarian national day on 15 March, and a campaign to push Romanian students out of a school. On 19 March, a group of Romanians attacked the local headquarters of the Hungarian Alliance (DAHR). The following day retaliations took place, resulting in multiple Romanian deaths and injuries. A television crew filmed a man who savagely kicked a fallen old peasant, and the image was circulated around the world as a Romanian beating a Hungarian. Two days later, when the people involved were identified, it proved the other way round. The victim, who suffered serious trauma, was depicted by Romanian state television as a victim of the Hungarian nationalists, while DAHR lawyers set about the process of freeing the aggressor from prison. Subsequent research reveals that the majority of each national group blames the Tîrgu-Mureş incident on the other party: either directly on the rioters or indirectly on the administration identified with the other's culture (Mungiu-Pippidi 1999). This ongoing suspicion epitomizes the relations between Romanians and Hungarians in postsocialist Transylvania, explaining why the vampire provides a ready symbol for representing the rival nationality, whether understood as Eastern or Western in origin, capitalist or socialist, transnationally mobile or rooted in ancestral soil.

In 1997, another near conflict between Romanians and Hungarians occurred in the city of Odorheiu Secuiesc, again in the Szekely region of Transylvania. The city council gave permission to a Swiss charity to build an orphanage. When it was discovered that the institution would house orphans from all over Romania and not just children from the immediate area, a Hungarian mob seized the building, expelling the Greek Catholic nuns who had been installed there. Had the town boasted a larger Romanian population, a violent confrontation would likely have ensued. In *Subjective Transylvania* (1999), Mungiu-Pippidi contends that the Odorheiu incident shows that events similar to Tîrgu-Mureş could occur again in Transylvania. Although the DAHR has been a power sharer in the Romanian government since 1996, when a center-right coalition was elected under the leadership of Victor Ciorbea, there remain persistent difficulties that stem from the Hungarian demand to be treated not as a minority but as a nation — a constitutive unit of the state *in corpore*.

The DAHR is the largest ethnic party in Europe, representing 1.7 million Hungarians and occupying 7 percent of the seats in the Romanian parliament. Far from quelling nationalist political sentiment, however, the presence of this party in the government has provoked a daily struggle: of the government with the media and a rebellious parliament, of the DAHR leaders with discontent wings of their own party, and of the Romanian coalition leaders with their members and constituents. In the late 1990s, Romanian politics was extremely turbulent, with Ciorbea's resignation in March 1998 and the dismissal of his successor, Radu Vasile, in December 1999. Although this turmoil was largely a result of faltering economic conditions, it also affected the position of the DAHR, as successively weakened administrations had less political leeway for working with the Hungarians. With the election of a minority social democrat (PDSR) government led by Adrian Nastase in November 2000, and Iliescu's reinstallation as president the following month, the DAHR remained in government only due to the new coalition's need to fend off the Greater Romania Party

(PRM), which had received 20 percent of the vote. The strength of the Romanian nationalist vote suggests that the Nastase government will also experience instability. As recently as February 2001, the PRM launched a vote of no confidence against the government and organized demonstrations in Cluj to protest laws, brokered by the DAHR, allowing the use of minority languages in local public administrations.

A future challenge for Transylvania involves the fact that Hungary is due to enter the European Union in 2004, leaving Romania on the backlist of candidate nations. If Hungary joins the Schengen agreements, it will need to introduce a visa for Romanian citizens, a situation that will undoubtedly lead to heightened demands for double citizenship among Romanian Hungarians. The question of EU integration is particularly complex in relation to Transylvania, not only because the stronger performance of Hungary in the accession process affirms the self-identification of ethnic Hungarians as Westerners but also because Transylvania itself is imagined as a borderland that delineates the eastern fringe of Europe. During the 1996 election campaign, the PDSR published a map from Samuel Huntington's *The Clash of Civilizations* (1996) showing a line separating Transylvania, considered as belonging to central Europe, from the rest of Romania, supposedly belonging to the Orthodox East. Accompanying the map was a note suggesting that if the center right won the election, the NATO powers would divide Romania along this line. Huntington's model finds its origins in a geopolitical tradition that proposes that "Europe ends where Western Christianity ends and Islam and Orthodoxy begin" (158). Such a civilizational paradigm, he contends, finds confirmation in the model of EU enlargement proposed by figures such as former French prime minister Alain Juppé. By this scheme, an implicit map of concentric circles divides an inner core of member states from a group of central European countries (including Hungary) likely to achieve accession and an eastern European periphery (including Romania) beyond the pale of integration. While Hungary's 1998 admittance to NATO and passage to the second stage of EU accession partnership in June 2000 corroborate this geopolitical vision, the uncertain territorial status of Transylvania problematizes any attempt to draw a neat dividing line between Europe and its supposed periphery. In so doing, it destabilizes the geopolitical opposition East/West, allowing Europe to be understood not as a unified territory but, as Critchley (2000) writes, a "series of europeanisations, of processes involving multiple geographies, many interconnected histories, stories, and multifarious presents."

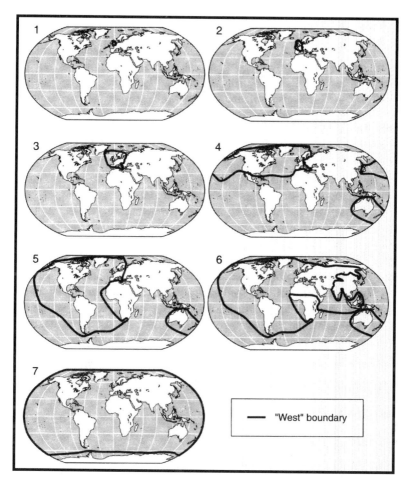

Seven versions of the West. From Martin W. Lewis and Kären E. Wigen, *The Myth of Continents: A Critique of Metageography* (Berkeley: University of California Press, 1997), 50; copyright 1997 the Regents of the University of California. Reprinted with permission.

In *The Myth of Continents* (1997), Martin Lewis and Kären Wigen trace the shifting fortunes of the longitudinal divide between East and West, arguing that this metageographical binarism has no stable spatial coordinates. They point to no less than seven mappings of the East-West divide, the first with the West encompassing only the British Isles and the last with the West covering the entire globe with the exception of Antarctica. Each of these cartographies serves different ideological purposes, positing large-scale civilizational essences and superimposing them over surprisingly elastic spatial expanses. At stake in the split between Western Christianity and Orthodoxy that Huntington correlates with the probable limits of the European Union (Lewis and Wigen's third version of the West) is an attempt to remap and reinforce patterns of economic and military power that were thrown open to negotiation with the end of the Cold War. By suggesting that "the identification of Europe with Western Christendom provides a clear criterion for the admission of new members to Western organizations" (160), Huntington explains the current machinations of political and economic globalization by reference to a civilizational fault line that he dates back to the medieval era. What this perspective ignores is the numerous crosscutting groupings and deep internal subdivisions that fracture these supposed civilizational units. The geographical specificity of conflict is reduced to reified identities and attributes, transforming their ambiguities and indeterminacies into graspable certainties and solid truths.

In the case of Transylvania, these indeterminacies are evident not only in the historical shifting of boundaries but also in everyday confusions as to who belongs to which ethnic group. The same ambiguities are apparent in vampire texts, which, in mapping Transylvania alternately as an Eastern or Western site, open it to a territorial uncertainty that parallels the vampire's own unstable identity. Ultimately, this geographical unsettlement not only destabilizes the East/West divide but also empties these binary terms of any positive cultural content. It is not simply a matter of Transylvania sitting between eastern and western Europe but of this ethnic "whirlpool" (as Stoker would have it) undoing the myth of a bounded Europe altogether. In this respect, the lesson of the vampire is the same as that extrapolated by Balibar (1998, 226) from the vacillation of borders and overlapping of cultures that constitutes contemporary Europe: "...that Europe is everywhere outside of itself, and that in this sense there is no more Europe — or that there will be less and less of it."

Monstrous Geography

As the Nazis discovered in 1940, the prospects for overcoming ethnic conflict in Transylvania are not served by a simple geographical division that attempts to separate the rival groups into two distinct territories. With the exception of the Szekely area, there exists poor segregation of ethnic communities in Transylvania — Romanians and Hungarians mingle within the same counties, cities, villages, and even apartment blocks. In an article titled "Dead Certainty: Ethnic Violence in the Era of Globalization" (1998), Appadurai argues that this kind of social intimacy generates uncertainty about otherness. Under conditions of ethnic mixing, questions arise as to the identity of intimates — are they one of "us" or one of "them," are they attempting to infiltrate my family or gain access to my entitlements, or am I accepting an imposter as my confidante, lover, or friend? In Transylvania, such an indeterminacy of identity has been exacerbated by a long history of assimilation that encouraged subjects to disguise themselves as members of the other ethnic group to gain access to education or economic opportunity, depending who exercised the greater power at the time. Livezeanu (1995) reports that as early as 1922, attempts to reform the Transylvanian school system were complicated by difficulties of ethnic identification. Romanians complained that Hungarian assimilation policies had denationalized ethnic Romanians, creating a class of hidden Romanians — people who declared themselves Hungarian but who had Romanian names or backgrounds. Similarly, during the Ceauşescu era, when Romanian became the language of social mobility and the application of quotas resulted in a decrease in minority language schools, census reports reflect a fall-off in Hungarian population growth (Árápad 1999).

According to Appadurai, the indeterminacy of identity that results from this kind of assimilation and cultural mixing can produce confusion that leads to ethnic violence. Particularly in the postsocialist context, where uncertainty is exacerbated by the opening of national boundaries to global capitalist flows, the ethnic body becomes a theater for establishing the parameters of otherness — taking the body apart, so to speak, to discover the enemy within. Such violence is an effort to expose, penetrate, and occupy the material form of the other, an attempt to stabilize identity by eliminating the flux introduced by mixture and indeterminacy. Like the vampire that must be staked through the heart to expel its monstrosity, the ethnic body must be pulled to pieces to rid it of the possibility of further change or slippage.

Much work on vampire culture understands the monster as a means of sociologizing the other, defining the boundaries of community as a defense against the violence that is the root of the sociosymbolic bond. But there is an alternative approach that claims that the vampire fulfills the *need* for an other, designating an excess that defines the very terms and limits of identity. Donald (1992, 119–20) draws on Todorov's notion of the fantastic to argue that vampire films exhibit "the instability of culture," using "terror and desire" to "highlight the fragility of any identity that is wrought from abjection." Likewise, Cohen (1996, 7) invokes the Derridean concept of *différance* to argue that the monster is a "third-term supplement," an "incorporation of the Outside, the Beyond — of all those loci that are rhetorically placed as distant and distinct but originate Within." In a similar manner, Copjec (1991) and Dolar (1991) deploy the techniques of Lacanian psychoanalysis, rejecting the attempt to correlate the vampire with a stable allegorical other (the proletariat, sexuality, other cultures, alternative ways of living, heterogeneity, and so forth). This they understand as an attempt to assign a specific content to the uncanny, a category that in Freud's account is constitutively unstable, being located at the point where the most intimate interiority becomes exterior, producing horror and anxiety. For Copjec and Dolar, the vampire is always a double of the victim — its distorted bodily form indicating the possession of an excess object, which is the dangerous source of its radical enjoyment or *jouissance*. The attempt to kill the vampire (the wooden stake through the heart and so on) is an effort to rid the monster of this excess, to deprive it of its perverse enjoyment, and, in so doing, to stake out a stable place for the self. To illustrate this dynamic, Žižek (1991) revisits the scene from Stoker's *Dracula* where Arthur stakes Lucy, his ex-fiancée who has been violated by Dracula and become a vampire herself:

> The Thing in the coffin writhed; and a hideous, blood curdling screech came from the opened red lips. The body shook and quivered and twisted in wild contortions; the sharp white teeth champed together till the lips were cut, and the mouth was smeared with a crimson foam. (Stoker 1983, 216)

Žižek is fascinated by Stoker's use of the word "Thing," which describes Lucy's body at the moment of orgasm, treating her enjoyment as a substance or object. The passage depicts Lucy's climax as a desperate resistance of the Thing, of pleasure fighting not to be released from the body. For Žižek, this Thing is the very locus of enjoyment, an imaginary surplus that refuses to be incorporated into the symbolic network of language and identity. Thus, the attempt to drive it out of the body is always unsuccessful — the vampire cannot help but return (even if in another bodily form) since it is a fantasy formation that inhabits the gap carved out by the other within the self. Like the perpetrator of ethnic violence described by Appadurai, the vampire slayer never gains any real or sustainable knowledge but only perpetuates the uncertainty and frustration that he or she sought to eliminate. In this way, vampire narratives offer a way of understanding ethnic conflict as an attempt to deprive the other of its enjoyment.

In *Tarrying with the Negative* (1993), Žižek contends that the nation not only is a product constructed by specific discursive practices (such as the rival Hungarian and Romanian narratives of Transylvanian history) but also consists of an underlying substance — a "Nation-Thing" that, like Lucy's ecstasy, is the remainder of some real, nondiscursive kernel of enjoyment. By this analysis, ethnic tensions always involve the clash between different modes of enjoyment. The other's excess of enjoyment is bothersome, and often regarded as a threat, because it also signifies the theft of one's own enjoyment, even if only as a symbolic menace:

> We always impute to the "other" an excessive enjoyment: he wants to steal our enjoyment (by ruining our way of life) and/or he has access to some secret, perverse enjoyment. In short, what really bothers us about the "other" is the peculiar way he organizes his enjoyment, precisely the surplus, the "excess" that pertains to this way: the smell of "their" food, "their" noisy songs and dances, "their" strange manners, "their" attitude to work. To the racist, the "other" is either a workaholic stealing our jobs or an idler living on our labor, and it is quite amusing to notice the haste with which one passes from reproaching the other with a refusal to work to reproaching him for the theft of work. The basic paradox is that our Thing is conceived as something inaccessible to the other and at the same time threatened by him. (Žižek 1993, 203)

Mungiu-Pippidi's (1999) ethnographic study of interethnic cohabitation in Transylvania shows that Žižek's understanding of ethnic hatred as grounded in the fear of the other's enjoyment is consistent with Romanian-Hungarian relations as experienced in everyday life. Hungarians feel that Romanians deny them their enjoyment, since they are uncivilized, speak too loud, need less to feel happy, and make too many children. Conversely, Romanians feel robbed by Hungarians, who supposedly work too hard, follow too strictly the commands of the church, and have a stronger national identity. In both cases, these fantasies are rooted in hatred of one's own enjoyment. Hungarians, for instance, see themselves as repressing their enjoyment by means of obsessional activity, and it is this same enjoyment that returns in the figure of the loud, easy-going Romanian. One of Mungiu-Pippidi's informants, a Hungarian peasant from Mureş County, explains as follows:

> The German and us learned from the Romanians to sit in front of the gate to speak with passers-by. And we still don't do this enough. The Hungarian once returned home shuts the gate and starts working without further delay.

Here, the self-reproach is obvious. The Hungarian peasant reprimands himself for working too much, and finds the Romanian to offer an example of a more measured lifestyle. Behind this recognition of the other's equanimity, however, lie all the stereotypes of Romanian noisiness, apathy, and laziness. Consider the testimony of the coach of a Hungarian handball team:

> The evening before the match with the Romanian team I send my boys jogging and then put them to bed early stressing the importance of the next day match. The Romanian team occupies the porch of the hotel, smokes a little, drinks a lot of beer, dances in the near-by disco, goes to bed at two in the morning and the next day we are better than they but they win.

In this case, the Hungarians are denied the enjoyment of victory by the Romanian team. The coach deals with his disappointment by complaining of the Romanians' behavior on the night before the match, a stance that only heightens his anger, since the Romanians win despite their undisciplined partying. Clearly the Romanian excess is perceived as a threat because it comes to signify the Hungarians' own loss of enjoyment — both the pleasure they deny themselves by resting before the game and their frustration with the defeat.

In the case of the Romanian perception of Hungarians, this same dynamic works in reverse. Mungiu-Pippidi quotes workers in Cluj and peasants from Livezi-Harghita who lament the Hungarians' stronger national awareness:

> Wherever one of them is born he is a Hungarian, and he will be a Hungarian in 200 years still.

> Romanians have less personality, they're more conformist, and they don't stand like Hungarians.

The perception that Hungarians enjoy a greater sense of national identity is linked to the self-denigrating claim that Romanians are

conformist and lacking in character — a condition apparently manifest in the way they hold their bodies. For Greek Catholics, many
of whom became Orthodox during the communist period when their
religion was outlawed, the supposed strength of Hungarian national
identity reveals their own sense of shame and humiliation. Romanians
in Hungary were assimilated. Look at the Romanians who go to the
United States, they become American, while the Hungarians are still
Hungarian. It's the same with the millions who were Greek Catholic
when communists forbade it and who became Orthodox without any
problem.

For Žižek, this fantasy structure, by which hatred of the other stems
from hatred of one's own enjoyment, is set in motion not merely by
the proximate living conditions of different ethnic communities but by
the inner antagonism inherent within these communities themselves.
What is at stake is the possession of a national Thing, which com-
pensates for this constitutive split in the community by pointing to an
imaginary surplus that refuses symbolization and makes the nation
appear to itself as a homogeneous entity. In attempting to rob the
other of its national Thing, however, the community deprives itself
of its own enjoyment, and thus the cycle of resentment and violence
continues.

Not accidentally does Žižek compare this national Thing to the
vampire, which in Stoker's account is a human body inhabited by a
Thing. It is not a matter of the vampire allegorizing the ethnic other
in some direct way, although this may be the case in certain vampire
stories. Rather the vampire's excess of enjoyment (its uncanny ability
to occupy the place of all sorts of allegorical others) corresponds to the
shared enjoyment that links members of a community to the nation
qua Thing. Žižek argues that this national Thing occupies the locus of
the Thing-in-itself in Kantian philosophy, opening up "the space for
the 'undead' and similar incarnations of some monstrous radical Evil"
(221). "It was already the 'pre-critical' Kant," he writes, "who used
the dreams of a ghost-seer to explain the metaphysical dream; today,
one should refer to the dream of the 'undead' monsters to explain
nationalism" (221). In this way, the vampire becomes something more
than a symbol that attaches itself to the perceived excesses of the
ethnic other. Rather, its very indeterminacy or blurring of the line
between inside and outside specifies the feeling of dread that befalls
the subject whenever it too closely approaches the other in the self.

In the case of Transylvania, this indeterminacy manifests itself as
an uncertainty over territory. This is evident not only in the rapid

fluctuation of borders (the boundary between Romania and Hungary shifted four times during the twentieth century) but also in the disputes over land that have plagued the process of property restitution in the postsocialist era. Verdery (1996) offers a case study of the difficulties surrounding land restitution in the Transylvanian village of Aurel Vlaicu, located in Hunedoara County. Although property restitution has been a complex process throughout Romania, it has proved particularly troublesome in Transylvania, due to the region's inclusion in the former Hapsburg empire. During the 1860s, the Austrians introduced property registration into Transylvania, and consequently records of prior ownership are more complete in this region than in other areas of Romania, where land records were instituted in a later and more provisional form. This means that Transylvanians have had much greater chances of reestablishing ownership of property and resisting usurpation by local authorities, making the struggles over land particularly intense.

In 1991, the Romanian parliament passed a law liquidating collective farms and returning their lands to the households that had handed them over during the period of collectivization, 1959–62. This process was complicated by the fact that collectivization had erased the grid of property from the earth's surface, removing the boundaries that immobilized land and engendering a landscape with elastic qualities. When the property restitution process began in 1991, a series of geographic and demographic shifts made the business of restoring land to its previous owners difficult if not impossible. In the case of Aurel Vlaicu, a river had been diverted, reducing the overall size of the village's territory and producing a situation where there were more claims than land to be distributed. To some extent, this was alleviated by the fact that communist bureaucrats had hidden land by manipulating figures to make it seem as if the collective farms were producing a greater yield. Nonetheless, a shortfall remained, leaving topographers and officials to engage in creative cartographic practices that often benefited their own family members or ethnic cohorts. Verdery explains that the map of a fixed landscape became destabilized: "Parcels and whole fields seemed to stretch and shrink; a rigid surface was becoming pliable. . . . It was as if the earth heaved and sank, expanding and diminishing the area contained within a set of two-dimensional coordinates" (139). Here, the indeterminacy that presides over the vampire's otherness emerges as a principle of cartographic projection itself. In postsocialist Transylvania there remains no possibility of mapping the land in a scalar, transparent, and consistent fashion. The vampire lends its uncertainty to even the most official processes of demarcation and plotting, making the area a truly monstrous geography.

Cohen (1996, 7) affirms that "the geography of the monster is an imperiling expanse, and therefore always a contested cultural space." In contemporary Transylvania, the monster's presence is apparent in the heightened ethnic contestation between Romanians and Hungarians. But the uncertainty and ambivalence that animate these rival nationalisms cannot be understood in separation from the dislocating effects of global capitalism. Indeed, the decline of socialism in the former Soviet bloc was precipitated not only by internal political instabilities but also by an encounter with a changing world system. As communist party leaders attempted to solve their structural problems without major reform, they were driven to monetary import and debt servicing from the capitalist world. This brought socialism into contact with a global capitalist economy that was itself undergoing transformation in response to the systemic crisis that had set in during the early 1970s, shifting to become more flexible through accelerated technological innovation, decreased turnover times, financial deregulation, and geographical decentralization. The centrally controlled socialist economies were unable to compete with this emerging system of flexible accumulation, leading to aggravated divisions within communist parties, an increased receptivity to capital, and the eventual fall of socialist regimes.

It is a mistake, however, to understand this collision between socialist and capitalist systems as a straightforward victory for capitalism. The opening of socialist economies to transnational capital generated a new order of social uncertainty, particularly as the redrawing of borders led to the creation of new nationalisms and diasporas in the former eastern bloc. Paradoxically, the same processes that engendered cross-border influence also produced political groups and symbols that aimed at reinforcing borders against, or channeling, that influence. Capitalism was still perceived as an other, carrying with it all the uncertainties associated with the vampire. In this context, the vampire's continued haunting of the former socialist bloc is registered by the trans- in Transylvania. As Rickels (1999, 55) writes: "Transylvania is a place entirely of the 'trans,' of moving across, a place of transference, of switch-over, of long-distance communications or transmissions." Under postsocialism, the vampire appears in the complex transference between capitalism and socialism, serving at once as a figure of flow and as a sign of the obstructionism practiced by those whom circulation threatens to drain.

Circulate, Circulate

In *The Order of Things* (1973), Michel Foucault attempts to rescue the eighteenth-century analysis of wealth from its traditional role as an imperfect anticipation of political economy by arguing that circulation provided its fundamental category, its conceptual and discursive unity. Circulation, rather than the category of production formulated by nineteenth-century theorists, determined the emphases of the dominant schools of economic thought in the eighteenth century, Mercantilism and Physiocracy. As early as 1651, Thomas Hobbes had picked up on the metaphor of circulation to describe the passage of money through the social body as "the sanguification of the commonwealth." Similarly in 1698, Charles Davenant deployed the same trope to argue that trade and money are "like blood and serum, which though different juices, yet run through the same veins mingled together" (350). In the late-eighteenth and early-nineteenth centuries, the metaphor of circulation, which finds its origins in William Harvey's 1628 discoveries concerning blood flow, was largely displaced as the central principle of political economy as a result of the work of Adam Smith and David Ricardo. Nonetheless, it continues to inform Marx's analysis of the reproduction of capital in *Capital,* vol. 2 (1885), which specifies the formula for circulation as M–C...P...C′–M′, where M is money capital, C is the commodity, P is production, and the primes indicate an increase by surplus value.

Anyone who doubts that Marx's account of circulation continues to draw on the metaphor of blood flow need only remember the famous passage from *Capital,* vol. 1 (1867), that likens capital to the vampire: "Capital is dead labour which, vampire-like, lives only by sucking living labour, and lives the more, the more labour it sucks" (342). Not surprisingly, the sentence has become a favorite with critics who understand vampire texts as allegorical representations of the capitalist system. Moretti (1983), for instance, interprets Stoker's *Dracula* as an elaborate gloss on the workings of late-nineteenth-century monopoly capital, in which the monster silences dissent by generating fear. But what becomes of the vampire in the current era of globalization, when flow and circulation once again emerge as buzzwords for a transnational capitalism that seeks to satisfy its seemingly endless thirst for profit by deregulating financial systems, continually opening new markets, and colonizing sites for the cheaper production of commodities?

One compelling feature of the analysis of the new order of global capitalism offered by Hardt and Negri (2000) is their understanding of the fall of the socialist bloc as at once a symptom of and a strike against an emergent world empire. For Hardt and Negri, contemporary capitalism engenders "a *decentered* and *deterritorialized* apparatus of rule that progressively incorporates the entire global realm within its open, expanding frontiers" (xii). Rather than relying on a transcendent center of power (or a master signifier that brings about the closure of the ideological field), the latest stage of capitalism operates on the plane of immanence, managing hybrid identities, flexible hierarchies, and plural exchanges through modulating networks of command. At the same time, it generates new forms of resistance and subjectivity, producing a multitude (or a new barbarian horde) that provides both the force that sustains global capitalism and the impetus that calls for and makes necessary its destruction. The chief example Hardt and Negri offer of the power of this multitude is the crumbling of the socialist bloc in 1989. The disciplinary apparatus of state socialism, they contend, was unable to react to the demands and desires of globally emerging subjectivities and this drove the system into crisis. In particular, mass migration and the desertion of productive cadres (particularly in technically skilled areas such as software design) struck at socialism's bureaucratic heart, demonstrating how the mobility of the labor force can express open political conflict and contribute to the destruction of all-powerful regimes. But while the creative movement of these subjectivities pushes capitalism toward an abstract and empty unity, to which it appears as an alternative, this new imperial sovereignty also stands over the multitude and subjects it to its rule. Hardt and Negri explain by recalling Marx's metaphor for capital: "The multitude is the real productive force of our social world, whereas Empire is a mere apparatus of capture that lives off the vitality of the multitude — as Marx would say, a vampire regime of accumulated dead labor that survives only by sucking off the blood of the living" (62). Here, the vampire reappears as a symbol of global capital, its ability to metamorphize recast as a principle of flexibility that allows the regime of accumulation to continue indefinitely.

Žižek (1993) offers a similar vision of the fall of state socialism. He remembers a picture from the time of Ceaușescu's overthrow that showed the rebels waving the national flag with the red star, the communist symbol, cut out, so that instead of the symbol standing for the organizing principle of national life, there was nothing but a hole in its center. For Žižek, the image provides an index of the open character of the historical situation, at least as experienced by the masses that poured into the streets. At the time of the revolution, the crowd was driven by enthusiasm over this hole, which was not yet hegemonized by any ideological project. Only after did ideological forces (whether nationalist or liberal democratic) enter the stage and attempt to kidnap a process that originally was not their own. To suggest that in the postsocialist era the vampire has filled this hole is not to claim that a symbol of capitalism has replaced a symbol of communism in a straightforward relation of substitution. In reading the complex inter-actions between postsocialism, capitalism, and globalization through the figure of the vampire, what comes to the fore is the undead character of socialism — its continued haunting of postsocialist society whether in terms of nationalism, political and economic organization, or the practices of everyday life. This gives lie to the myth of capitalism's total engulfment of the world, pointing to the continued existence of spaces where the logic of global capital becomes dysfunctional and the internal instability of the world system is revealed.

As much as Romania struggles to become a player in the global economy (to enter the European Union, for instance), it continues to bear the brunt of exclusion. Far from embodying a transition to lib-eral democracy and a market economy, the Romanian state has ceded many of its formerly central instruments of rule, including coercion, to lower level actors, effecting what Verdery (1996) calls a transition from socialism to feudalism. In this postsocialist formation, marked by various forms of Mafia and ethnonationalism, liberal democracy encounters its uncanny reverse, usually qualified (and at the same time disqualified) as fundamentalism, the end of cosmopolitanism, the re-turn of tribalism, and so forth. But these forms of fundamentalist identification are an inherent reaction to capital's universalism, and will not subside as long as the universal dimension of the social forma-tion remains defined in terms of capital. Postsocialism thus provides the mirror in which global capitalism and liberal democracy recognize their own ugly reflection or, perhaps more accurately, the mirror in which global capitalism and liberal democracy, like the vampire, fail to recognize themselves.

Needless to say, this postsocialist formation is not in any straight-forward sense anticapitalist. Its nationalist identifications are a direct reaction to a clamoring for inclusion in the circuits of global capital and the experiences of uncertainty that this sets off. Not accidentally does the opening of Transylvania to transnational flows occur under the stewardship of the vampire. This is particularly obvious in rela-tion to tourism and Dracula-related travel. While the socialist regime attempted to capitalize on the Western interest in Dracula during the

1970s, the resulting tourism was largely directed to sites associated with Vlad Ţepeş, and was closely associated with Ceauşescu's attempt to rehabilitate the reputation of this fifteenth-century national hero. In the 1980s, there was a decline in tourist visits to Romania due to an internal austerity program coupled with deterioration in services and facilities. But a revitalized Dracula tour industry emerged after 1989. In postsocialist Romania, vampire tourism is a highly organized business and an important source of revenue for the struggling national economy.

Contemporary Dracula tours combine visits to the Transylvanian sites mentioned in Stoker's novel with visits to locations associated with the historical Dracula: Sighişoara, the birthplace of Vlad Ţepeş; Peonari, the site of a partially restored fortress built by Vlad in the mountains between Wallachia and Transylvania; and Bran Castle in southern Transylvania, a site with no connection to Vlad Ţepeş or Stoker's novel but promoted by Romanian authorities as Dracula's castle due to its appearance and accessibility. Whatever their connection to historical figures, these places are possessed by a marked inauthenticity, as if the Hollywood Dracula had returned to haunt his putative birth site and to oversee the region's opening to global networks of circulation.

Elizabeth Miller (1997) reports that tourists can follow Jonathan Harker's route up the Borgo Pass, stopping in Bistriţa to eat robber steak at the Golden Krone Hotel, and then continuing to Castle Dracula Hotel, an unconvincing reproduction of a vampire's castle built in the early 1980s. While many Romanian intellectuals complain that such tourist activity (particularly that associated with Vlad Ţepeş) leads their fellow nationals to accept an imported and corrupted version of national history, the Dracula industry enjoys the official endorsement of the Romanian state. In 1991, a historical-cultural organization by the name of the Transylvanian Society of Dracula was formed in partnership with the Romanian Ministry of Tourism. Led by Nicolae Padaruru, a former tour operator, the society not only organizes Dracula tours but has also successfully staged two World Dracula Congresses (1995 and 2000) and expanded its membership to include chapters in Canada, the United States, Japan, Spain, Germany, Italy, and Sweden. At the 1995 congress, Dan Matei Agaton, the minister for tourism now responsible for the Sighişoara Dracula Land project, announced the launch of a major offensive on the part of Romanian tourism, allowing himself to be made a Knight of the Dracula Order in a midnight ceremony featuring a black cloak.

Bran Castle, Transylvania. Photograph by Simon Marsden. Reprinted by permission of Simon Marsden/The Marsden Archive.

This playful marketing activity attests the lengths to which post-socialist officials will go to attract direct foreign investment, but it also angers nationalists who claim that such a welcoming of transnational capital promotes mythologies that eclipse the historical record and endanger the healthy reproduction of the national body.

Such concerns about the reproduction of the national body have ramifications not simply on the economic level but also in the realm of biopolitics. In Marx's account, the workings of economic circulation are intimately connected to the processes of reproduction. These involve not only the perpetuation of ideologies that support the continuity of social systems but also the constitution of a labor force through practices of biological reproduction that are highly politicized, often at the expense of women. Reproduction is fundamentally associated with identity: both that of the nation, over which it exercises authority, and that of the family, which perpetuates itself most frequently through patrilineal descent. But as Western feminists have argued, the vampire's reproductive activity (the direct exchange of blood), technological perpetuation, and nonnormative kinship relations (vampires create families of choice) signal an alternative to the dominant gender regime of compulsory heterosexuality (Case 1991; Halberstam 1995, Haraway 1997).

Even in Stoker's novel, where the vampire assumes the role of a masculine seducer who preys exclusively on women, there is already an attempt to outline a biopolitics that strays from white patriarchal norms. Not only does Dracula tend his female prey, offering those who inhabit his castle a small child to feed upon, but his reproductive capacities also prove dangerously threatening to the traditional Victorian males who hunt him down. As Haraway (1997, 214) explains, the vampire "drinks and infuses blood in a paradigmatic act of infecting whatever poses as pure." Particularly in the contemporary technological environment, in which digital communication provides the bases — or at least the conditions of possibility — for many of our relations, the traditional criterion of blood to determine who is related to whom no longer applies. For the vampire, the joining of race and sex in an unsullied patrilineal bloodline is a radically temporary and contingent effect, sedimented by repetition into a pattern that appears natural. Vampiric desire opens new vectors of kinship, generating possibilities for connection through affinities, affections, tastes, distastes, labors, pleasures, technical wirings, attractions, repulsions, and chemical reactions. Not surprisingly does the vampire become a figure for queer sexualities, whether in the relatively tame

homoeroticism of Anne Rice's gothic blockbusters or the more outlandish lesbian allegories of writers like Pat Califia (1988) and Jewelle
Gomez (1991). Contrary to the infertility that banishes queer sexuality
from the realm of the natural, the vampiric moment of transubstanti-
ation disrupts the normative gender codes that organize subjectivities
into regular Oedipal units. Accordingly the vampire also threatens
paternalist state ideologies, particularly those that aim to secure their
perpetuation by control of women's bodies.

As is well documented, the Romanian state, beginning in 1966,
sought to supply the labor force necessary for its self-reproduction by
means of a pronatalist political demography that outlawed abortion
and contraception. Ceaușescu famously declared: "The fetus is the
socialist property of the whole society." As Kligman (1998) explains,
this control of reproduction — both biological and social — became
the basis of state power. The result was the emergence of illegal abortion as the most common form of birth control, a high maternal
death rate, the overcrowding of orphanages, an infant AIDS epidemic, and, after 1989, the international trafficking in babies through
adoption. Although the first post-Ceaușescu government revoked all
prohibitions against abortion and contraception, the effects of this
pronatalist biopolitics were enduring. Socialism not only exercised
control over women's sexual and domestic activities but also required
their participation in the labor force, these both conceived as a necessary contribution to the public good. With the shift to postsocialism,
there occurred a retraditionalization of gender roles, which encouraged women to abandon the workforce. As in other postsocialist
societies, the transition fostered a renewed public emphasis on family
life and religion, forcing women back into the domestic sphere despite the rising cost of living. Indeed, many Romanian women are still
compelled to reproduce not at the behest of the state but at the command of the international market, which offers sizable rewards for
the provision of children for adoption. Despite the greater availability of contraception, abortion remains the primary method of birth
control in Romania (Baban 2000). Clearly there is little attention to
sexual inequality in this context. With the exception of a small, urban-
ized feminist movement, the only political force that addresses issues
of gender is the nationalist right, which instructs women to discover
their natural mission and revives the pronatalist rhetoric by which
abortion occasions the nation's death.

Antiabortion rhetoric in the West centers on the claim that the fetus
is a human being who is murdered. As Salecl (1994) explains, in the

postsocialist context pronatalists reinterpret this ideology to present abortion as a threat to the nation. The key to their argument is the idea that the life of a human being has special meaning because he or she belongs to a national community. By allowing abortion, the society not only kills a human being but also erodes the national substance, leading eventually to the extinction of the nation. In other words, the fetus becomes the bearer of what Žižek calls the national Thing, embodying the enjoyment that binds the nation together. This makes the pronatalist fetus not so much the correlate of the person but the correlate of the vampire, which, according to Žižek, carries the excessive enjoyment that must be present for the nation to achieve its ontological consistency. The act of abortion thus becomes an attempt to expel this Thing from the national body, to render the nation inanimate, a mere lifeless corpse (like the Transylvanian revenant in Rice's *Interview with the Vampire*) at the mercy of transnational forces.

Such a parallel between the unborn child and the undead vampire finds strong precedents in popular culture. Rodman Flender's 1991 film *The Unborn* traces the fortunes of a heterosexual couple who check into an in-vitro fertilization clinic after experiencing several miscarriages. The fertility treatment works, but when the mother and other patients break out in oozing rashes it becomes clear that the fetus she carries is a vampire. The movie proceeds with a series of gratuitously horrifying effects (exploding bellies, ersatz embryos, mutant babies) before a back-alley abortionist puts an end to the pregnancy in its third trimester. This text, produced only two years after the crumbling of the socialist bloc, makes explicit the parallel between the unborn child and the undead vampire that remains implicit in pronatalist discourse. If, with Salecl, one understands the pronatalist stance against abortion as an attempt to prevent the theft of national enjoyment, the fetus, like the vampire, appears as the bearer of an excess pleasure that is the very stuff of national belonging. As long as nationalist politicians view abortion as an attempt to diminish the national substance, the figure of the vampire will continue to haunt postsocialist nationalism.

Needless to say, the rhetoric of vampirism is not an explicit element of pronatalist discourses. Pronatalist nationalists are likely to express displeasure at the figure of the vampire and its characteristic practices of sexual profligacy. Not only does the vampire represent the imposition of a Western mythology upon their homeland, but also, in troubling the boundaries between life/death, natural/unnatural, and male/female, it unleashes a desire that unsettles the heterosexist notion of being that informs pronatalist politics. For contemporary queer theorists, the vampire is nothing less than an icon of deviant sexuality, a cipher that enables the thinking of the subject beyond the logic of identity and difference that underlies the Freudian distinction between hetero- and homosexuality. Whatever the predilections of antiabortion campaigners, there is reason to link this queer theoretical understanding of subjectivity with the work of contemporary globalization theorists, particularly those who point to the decline of the nation-state sovereignty at the hands of global capital.

The complexity of the relations between queer theory and global capitalism are highlighted by the controversy surrounding Dennis Altman's 1996 article "On Global Queering," criticized by Halperin (1996) and others for its implication that queer theorists have abandoned the political struggles of an earlier generation of gay and lesbian activists. Altman contends that the transnational spread of queer studies is doing for sexual cultures what "McDonalds has done for food and what Disney has done for entertainment." As Morton (1996) points out, Altman understands queer as an aesthetic category that does little to highlight the structural inequalities of the current world system. He thus posits an unresolvable standoff between desire-based notions of changing sexuality and need-based theories of political economy. What is lacking in Altman's argument is an appreciation of the way in which the contemporary globalization of capital impacts upon the constitution of subjectivity, particularly with respect to nation-state belonging. One effect of the processes of globalization is to blur national boundaries, that is, to make less clear what should be situated inside and outside the nation-state. This entails not only the reconceptualization of geographical space (and a correlate remapping of economic inequality) but also the reorganization of subjectivity, especially in relation to notions of political participation and citizenship.

The problematization of subjectivity, citizenship, and identity under globalization parallels the queer theoretical questioning of stable sexual allegiances since both suggest that identity and difference are no longer adequate concepts for recognizing the constitution and interaction of subjects. Although the category of queer has doubtless entered the canons of marketing demography, it is not a matter, as Altman suggests, of queer theory acting as an agent of global inequality — its export from the United States homogenizing nonnormative sexualities on a worldwide scale. Rather global capitalism itself functions according to a queer dynamic, decentering and dislocating the dominant modern paradigm of nation-state sovereignty and its concomitant model of political subjectivity. One register of the affinity between global capitalism and queer notions of subjectivity is the fact that the vampire stands for both. This is why postsocialist nationalists so often perceive the vampire as a threat — on the one hand, it undermines heteronormative modes of reproduction, which fuel the pronatalist agenda, while on the other, it motivates transnational flows of capital, which override the integrity of national borders. As the popular cultural home of vampires, Transylvania is the repository of all these anxieties, being at once the site of vampire tourism, a contested terrain of national identity, and a symbolic domain of queer sexuality (transsexual Transylvania, as *The Rocky Horror Picture Show* would have it).

By virtue of its monstrosity, the geography of Transylvania carries multiple and irreconcilable meanings. These must be considered in interrelation to unravel the complexity of the site's relation to global capitalism — a difficult task since each has different relations to transnational patterns of economic, cultural, and technological flow. One constant of vampirism, however, is that its medium of exchange is blood, whether extracted voluntarily or involuntarily from the victim. While Harvey's 1628 discovery of the circulation of blood through the human body supplies the basis for the economic metaphor of circulation, blood is one of the few objects in the contemporary world that resists integration into the system of market capital. This is because, for the most part, blood exchange is governed by protocols of donation rather than sale. For Titmuss (1970, 212), who compares the British system of blood donation to the U.S. system (at that time) of blood purchase, the donation of blood points to the existence of a domain of transactions that stands outside of economic quantification and carries "no explicit right, expectation or moral enforcement of a return gift." While the U.S. blood banking system has largely shifted to a mix of voluntary and insurance-credit schemes (Drake, Finkelstein, and Sapolsky 1982), Titmuss's assertion of an outside to capitalist rationality contradicts the prevailing anthropological argument by which the gift carries an expectation of return (Mauss 1967). As Frow (1997, 102) explains, "the gift and the commodity seem to partake of each other: the gift to be structured ... according to forms of calculation and interest that in some sense resemble those of a market economy, and commodities in turn to be constantly endowed with noncommodity meanings as they move within the moral economy of everyday life." Nonetheless, the question of blood exchange, and the related issues of AIDS, body organ trade, and the ownership of genetic information, run capitalism up against a limit, where the unlimited exchange of goods threatens biodiversity and potentially endangers the life of the world body politic. In particular, the intellectual property relations surrounding biological materials delineate a zone of intense commercial and ethical contestation, linking the vampire's perverse bodily performances to the interpretive and proprietary struggles surrounding its cultural representation — most recently exemplified by the copyright battle over the use of vampire images in Transylvania's proposed Dracula Land.

If Ceauşescu's pronatalist demography appears unacceptably repressive to contemporary liberal-democratic sensibilities, it is important to recognize that global capitalism is no less driven by a biopolitical paradigm of power. Whether in the business of symbolic analysis and problem solving, the immaterial nexuses of language and communication, or the production and manipulation of bodily affects, transnational capital spreads across the earth's surface, imposing its power not merely by the external disciplining of subjects but by incorporating them into its very functioning. In this context, where power functions as a control that saturates the consciousnesses and bodies of the population, the vampire stands as a register not of fear but of hope — the index of an alternative biopolitics that promises an open-ended set of affections, affinities, and possibilities.

Granted the vampire's biopolitics are highly ambivalent, often hedged by unspoken sexual and racial anxieties, but the fact that this monster trades in bodily materials means that it inevitably encounters a boundary that restricts its enjoyment — its feeding frenzy is always curbed by the ecstasy that accompanies its satiation. In some cases, this limitation is quite clear. In Abel Ferarra's 1995 movie *The Addiction,* the principal vampire, played by Christopher Walken, is also a Zen Buddhist who meditates to curb his desire, instructing his brethren to partake of human blood only once a year. Clearly we do not live at a time when some heroic agent promises to stake capitalism through the heart or when a new dawn threatens to shrivel the free market beneath its rays. But the image of the vampire implies something more than an uncontrolled reign of commodity transactions. It stands variously as an icon of nationalism, a figure of queer sexuality, a symbol of oppressed and impoverished peoples — the credits could roll on. What matters is the excess generated by this apparently limitless interpretability and the unbearable enjoyment that accompanies it. The vampire does not exist outside of capitalist rationality, but its compulsion to keep its pleasure alive at any price registers capitalism's danger to itself, the point at which the system begins to verge on unsustainability and can no longer hide its internal instabilities. For this reason, the vampire's demesne, Transylvania, becomes a site that troubles the myth of capitalism's total domination of space and time, suggesting a mode of political and social practice that, while by no means utopian, refuses to recognize the fall of socialism as the moment of capital's global triumph.

Perhaps it is time to reconsider the well-worn Marxist metaphor by which the vampire is dead capital that sucks the blood of living labor. Perhaps the real living dead are we common mortals, condemned to vegetate among seemingly indisputable realities, passing a life in which the death of capitalism figures only as a delusion. In its incessant return, its filling of the gap that separates the backward view that perceives the current state of affairs as insurmountable from the forward view that perceives the situation as open, the vampire appears as a fantasy formation that refuses complete integration into the capitalist imaginary. It remains a figure that registers the possibilities for working through capitalism, of moving beyond the current regimes of control and exploitation by pushing them to a limit where alternatives begin to appear within the capitalist system itself.

Three

Unmapping the Golden Triangle; or, The World on Drugs

> Circulation sweats money from every pore.
> —Karl Marx, *Capital*, Vol. 1

Since first named by U.S. journalists in the early 1970s, the high-land area of Southeast Asia known as the Golden Triangle has been renowned for the cultivation of opium and its refinement into heroin. This chapter studies the workings of the global drug economy to understand another mode of production that occurs in the Golden Triangle, the production of space. That one of the world's primary zones for heroin production should occupy as regular a space as an equilateral triangle is indeed wondrous. The shape immediately conjures up images of godhead, Oedipal desire, or the female pubic area. Clearly the borders of the Golden Triangle are arbitrarily imposed, providing a catchy if geographically imprecise identity for an important narcotics production zone. I argue that a substance as nomadic and addictive as opium cannot be contained by these geographical limits.

The Golden Triangle poses as a hidden interior to the global drug economy, an outlaw zone inaccessible to the mapping systems of national governments and law enforcement agencies. But its secrets are constantly emptied out, jettisoned around the world, plainly visible in the arms and eyes of addicts. With the acceleration of economic globalization and the opening of international markets to increasingly deregulated trade systems, the business of heroin trafficking has been greatly eased. The governments of advanced capitalist states have launched a war against drugs, but the narcotics industry thrives on the global economic agendas promoted by these same powerful institutions. To study the geographical parameters of drug trafficking and addiction is to confront the limits of global capital, the very difficulty of its relation to other regimes of political, moral, and legal

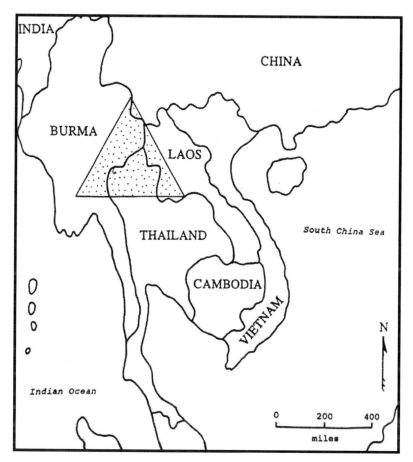

Location of the Golden Triangle. Reprinted by permission of the International Boundaries Research Unit (IBRU).

authority. This involves developing an account of geoeconomic and geopolitical change that treats the drug business and global capitalism not as separate phenomena occurring in discrete locations, but rather as interrelated processes that intersect in the organization and reproduction of contemporary modes of capitalist accumulation.

As usually mapped the Golden Triangle covers parts of northern Thailand, the Burmese highlands, western Laos, and a segment of China's Yunnan Province. The area comprises three different types of overlapping space: the indigenous space of the Triangle's hill tribes (among them the Hmong, the Lisu, the Kachin, the Karen, the Lahu), the modern space of nation-states (with borders policed by military and government personnel of varying degrees of corruption), and the global space of transnational flows (where the Triangle is defined by the inexorable flows of addiction that emanate from it). The unstable intersection of these spaces makes the area particularly suitable for the production and export of opium and heroin. As Lintner (1991, 4) explains, "as long as the political, economic and social situation in these remote and neglected border areas remains unsettled, there is little likelihood of the flow of opium from the Golden Triangle showing any sign of slowing down." But the modes of instability characteristic of the Golden Triangle cannot be confined to its borders. Economic resources invested in the drug industry must be subtracted from the legitimate economy of participant nations, reducing their output and rate of growth. Moreover, the laundering of drug money distorts the world allocation of resources, generating instabilities in the international financial system. The Golden Triangle is a surface representation of an underground economy of huge proportions, a vast network of smuggling, dealing, taxing, and laundering that eludes the regulatory mechanisms of both markets and states.

One difficulty with studying the workings of capitalist globalization via the underground narcotics trade is that drugs are too readily appropriable. Not only do they exist at the intersection of several powerful sociocultural discourses (medicine, law, and economics, not to mention sex and rock'n'roll), but they also partake of an indeterminacy that poststructuralist thinkers associate with the temporal flux of language. Derrida (1993, 16) claims that it is possible to "extend the concept and experience of drugs far beyond its legal, medical definition, and in a space at once idiosyncratic and public, arrange all sorts of practices, pleasures and pains that no one could rigorously show to be unrelated and without analogy to drug addiction." This argument finds confirmation in a multitude of discourses that use drugs as a metaphor to describe other forms of activity or consumption: religion as the opiate of the masses, television as the plug-in drug, addiction to sex, exercise, or work. It is all too easy and all too dangerous to level these terms of association (religion = television = sex = exercise = work), creating chains of equivalence that grow weaker as they inevitably expand. Yet to limit or enclose this slippage is to ignore the addictive capacity of drugs, their propensity to sneak across borders (material, discursive, and epistemological). De Certeau (1984) explains that the Greek *metaphor* refers literally to a carrying over, an act of movement or transport between identifiable places on the earth's surface. The present chapter studies the transnational circulation of drugs to argue that such movement is more than simply rhetorical. Matching Derrida's emphasis on the temporality of language with Lefebvre's interest in spatial politics, my investigation of the global drug trade moves beyond both Marxist approaches, which stress the analysis of commodities, production, social relations, and organized resistance, and cultural approaches, which emphasize issues of representation, consumption, individual subjectivity, and discourse.

The logic of the inquiry is synthetic and analogical, shifting between several critical discourses to investigate the complexity and evasiveness of the relations between drugs and global capital. I explore the role of the Golden Triangle as a site for the acting out of fantasies regarding travel and tourism, before switching to consider the way in which the area interrupts the geopolitical agendas of antidrug international agencies. The chapter then turns to examine the economic significance of heroin trafficking and money laundering. Drawing on psychoanalytic and anthropological theories of money and its relation to cleanliness, I compare the global economy's dependence upon capital with the addicted condition of the drug user's body. This central metaphor underlies a final discussion of globalization and consumption, a crucial hinge in debates about the complicated nexus of economics and culture. By making these rhetorical connections, the study reveals a deeper, mutually constitutive link between contemporary conceptions of the body as the theater of power and the spatiotemporal formations of global capitalism. I ask how notions of human corporeality and selfhood relate to the system of money valuations and capital accumulation, arguing for the impossibility of understanding economic globalization outside of notions of addiction. The inquiry thus supersedes its interest in the rhetoric of flow. It suggests that drugs collapse the distinction between need and desire, exposing the mutual implication of homogenizing and heterogenizing theories of globalization: political economic theories of structural dependency and poststructuralist theories that stress the hybridizing effects of consumer resistance and fantasy.

Wonderland of Opium

The modern history of opium cannot be understood in separation from other illicit economic activities, including the slave trade, prostitution, and the clandestine market for arms. Among the world's underground economies, however, the drug industry is the largest, restricted since the early twentieth century by nothing but its illegality. Before that, opium was a legitimate commodity. The historical entanglement of opium trading with European imperialism is central to geopolitical relations in the Indian Ocean and western Pacific from the late eighteenth century on. In 1773, the British East India Company took control of the export of Bengali opium to China, an essential link in the triangular trade between Britain, India, and China. Despite China's outlawing of the drug in the 1790s, British commerce transformed the narcotic from a luxury item to a bulk commodity of the same proportions as commercial stimulants like coffee, tea, and tobacco. Indeed the British fought two Opium Wars with China (1839–42 and 1856–58) to protect the free passage of the drug into the country (Beeching 1975; Inglis 1976). By the end of the nineteenth century, opium had become a global commodity with markets not only in China but also in Southeast Asia, Europe, and the Americas. For Europeans and North Americans, it was the chemical production of the opium's derivatives (morphine and heroin) that facilitated the drug's popularity. In 1898, the Bayer Company of Eberfeld, Germany, coined the trade name heroin and began to market the product, alongside aspirin, through saturation campaigns in newspapers and magazines (Berridge and Edwards 1987). In the form of morphine and laudanum, opiates proved popular with middle-class women, and legal trade continued until the signing of five League of Nations treaties (in the period 1923–31) that outlawed the nonmedicinal use of narcotics (Chaterjee 1981). After this organized crime took over, refining opium into heroin and shifting the profile of the user to the working-class male. From the 1930s to the 1960s, European markets were supplied with Turkish opium refined by Corsican syndicates in Marseilles (Bequai 1979). Meanwhile, Southeast Asian governments maintained tight monopolies on local production and consumption, at least until 1949 when the expulsion of the Kuomintang (KMT) from China into Burma began an illicit opium trade to fund anticommunist military activity.

Not until the 1970s did the Golden Triangle acquire its name as the world's principal zone for opium and heroin production, supposedly due to the direct exchange of the drug for gold in the Burma-Thailand-Laos border region. The rise of the area for opium cultivation is directly linked to the war in Vietnam. During the early phases of the war, French military and intelligence officers dealt in opium to pay and arm local groups to fight the Viet Minh. As the fighting progressed, the CIA began to transport opium for Hmong/Laotian tribes who in turn offered resistance to the North Vietnamese. With this CIA involvement, heroin addiction spread among U.S. forces in Vietnam and through them to the metropolitan centers of the capitalist world (McCoy 1972). This global expansion of the Southeast Asian drug trade prompted new modes of transnational distribution, remittance, and accumulation that, in many ways, parallel the rise of post-Fordist capitalism. For all the triumphant rhetoric surrounding contemporary capitalism's imagined victory over space and time, the fantasy of unlimited global mobility also dominated the aspirations of early 1970s drug-trafficking organizations. Consider the trademark of the notorious Double U-O Globe heroin, the favored brand with U.S. troops during the later stages of the Vietnam War. The label features two lions leaning over a tilted globe. Across the top are Chinese characters reading "Double Lion Earth brand," below which are two statements, also in Chinese — "Beware of Counterfeits" and "Pure 100 Percent." Outside the circle are further characters that read "Travel Safely by Sea," the Chinese equivalent to bon voyage, implying not only that the drug might reach its destination safely but also that the addict might have a "good trip" with it.

As a testament to the transnational mobility of drugs, the trademark foresees the present era when the global heroin trade has experienced an unprecedented boom. In the 1980s, with the rise of the Latin American cartels, cocaine became the most popular narcotic in Western markets, alongside a host of chemically synthesized drugs: crack, ecstasy, ice, special-K, crystal-meth. During this same period, heroin production took hold in central Asia, particularly in Afghanistan, where CIA sponsorship of the Islamic Mujahideen's war against the Soviet Union provided the political protection and logistic linkages to join the country's fledging opium industry to markets in Europe and America. The parallels between the central Asian heroin trade and that of the Golden Triangle are striking, in terms of both their origins in CIA-sponsored military activities and the involvement of rival ethnic groups, often engaged in internecine struggles (Chouvy 2001). Like the Golden Triangle, the central Asian opium-growing operation spills across national borders, covering Afghanistan, northern Pakistan, and parts of Iran. Indeed, the similarities between the two regions are sufficiently strong to license the naming of the central Asian after the Southeast Asian zone, not the Golden Triangle but the Golden Crescent. This act of naming, which takes place in the 1980s, not only suggests that the Golden Triangle reproduces itself in another part of the world but also points to the historical entanglement

提防假冒

純淨100%.

DOUBLE UOGLOBE BRAND

一帆風順

Trademark for Double U-O Globe heroin brand. Photograph by Alfred McCoy. From Alfred McCoy, *The Politics of Heroin: CIA Complicity in the Global Drug Trade* (New York: Lawrence Hill Books, 1991). Reprinted with permission.

of the two regions. It is impossible to study the production of space in the Golden Triangle without considering the mutual implication and linked destiny of these areas. Particularly in the past decade, when world opium production has soared, the unstable relations between the Golden Triangle and the Golden Crescent have led to the street availability of heroin at low cost and unprecedented purity.

By the end of the Soviet-Afghan war in 1989, the Golden Triangle and the Golden Crescent vied for supremacy in the global heroin market, the former supplying North America, East Asia, and Australia, and the latter supplying Russia and Europe. In Afghanistan, rival Mujahideen groups battled for control over the industry. Fighting was particularly intense for the fertile Helmand Valley area, controlled by Mullah Nasim Akhundzada. Under the leadership of Gulbuddin Hekmatyar, the Hezb-i-Islami militia group attempted unsuccessfully to seize the valley. But two years later, they assassinated Nasim (by then, deputy defense minister of Afghanistan), and fighting broke out again between the two factions, with the Helmand Valley group led by Nasim's older brother. This infighting between the Mujahideen over heroin-producing regions gave rise to a pronounced instability, paving the way for the rise of the Taliban regime in the mid-1990s.

Meanwhile in the Golden Triangle, opium production was thriving in Burma, where a military junta known as the State Law and Order Restoration Council (SLORC) had seized power in September 1988. Particularly in the northern Shan State area, controlled by opium warlord Khun Sa and his Mong Tai Army, the cultivation of the drug outstripped all other areas in the world. In 1990, a U.S. court indicted Khun Sa on charges of importing thirty-five hundred pounds of heroin into New York City. But despite this indictment (and corroborative efforts by the Thai army to eradicate opium crops), production continued to skyrocket, reaching a peak of 1,914 tonnes in 1996 according to the United Nations Office for Drug Control and Crime Prevention (UNDCP 2001). In January of the same year, Khun Sa made his so-called surrender to the SLORC, by that time known as the State Peace and Development Council (SPDC). This event, which caused a massive jump in Golden Triangle heroin prices, resulted from a deal between Burma's military government and the United Wa State Army (UWSA), another northern militia group. Basically the agreement involved the UWSA displacing Khun Sa, who had become a diplomatic liability, in return for government authorization to conduct and develop the heroin trade. This led not only to the establishment of a number of sophisticated heroin refineries in the Shan and Kokang state areas but also to a diversification of the area's drug production to include methamphetamines, known in Thailand as ya-ba or mad pills. Since 1996, the UWSA-sponsored manufacture of methamphetamines has exponentially increased, predominantly in laboratories along the Thai-Burma border, resulting in the production of between 200 and 300 million pills per annum (Chouvy 1999). There can be no doubt that this product diversification, which supplements the area's already prodigious opium cultivation, was partly a reaction to the expansion of the Golden Crescent opium industry, which in 1996 began to produce massive yields, sending prices down on a global scale.

In October 1996, the Islamic fundamentalist group known as the Taliban seized Afghanistan's capital, Kabul, partly at the instigation of the ISI, the Pakistani intelligence agency that had been a key player in Afghan affairs since the Soviet war. While the Taliban regime promised to bring a semblance of stability to the region, introducing strict laws regulating religious practice and the role of women, they remained locked in conflict with a loose coalition of ethnic opposition groups confined to the country's north, the so-called Northern Alliance. Both parties in the ongoing civil war drew on opium as a source of funds, although the Taliban, who controlled 90 percent of the nation's territory, including the prime poppy growing areas in the Helmand Valley and south of Jalalabad, had access to far more crops. Under their rule, Afghanistan's opium production increased rapidly, outstripping the Golden Triangle in 1999 with a massive crop of 4,600 tonnes, approximately 75 percent of the opium produced in the world that year (UNDCP 2001).

In the late 1990s, Afghanistan also developed the ability to manufacture the more pure and expensive white version of heroin known as China White, the trademark product of the Golden Triangle since the late 1960s. Much of this heroin was trafficked into China through its northwest Xinjiang province or smuggled into Thailand where it was repackaged and passed off as more favored Southeast Asian brands in the North American and Australian markets (Lintner 2001). All this changed in July 2000, when the Taliban leader Mullah Mohammed Omar declared opium cultivation a religious crime and began serious efforts to suppress the industry. By May 2001, the Afghan regime's antidrug effort had been so successful that they were rewarded 43 million dollars by the U.S. government as part of an aid program for nations engaged in crop eradication programs. But the Taliban had acted shrewdly, stockpiling an estimated 2,900 tonnes of the drug, and forcing market prices up by almost 170 percent. The situation changed again in September 2001, when it became clear that an international coalition led by the United States would launch an uncompromising military attack on Afghanistan for harboring members of the Al Qaeda network suspected of planning and executing that month's attacks on New York City and Washington, D.C. At this point, the Taliban began to release its stockpile and, according to Western intelligence sources, lifted the ban on opium production (Lintner 2001). Throughout the ban, however, poppy cultivation continued in Northern Alliance controlled areas, making them the largest beneficiaries of the region's opium trade by the time the United States recruited them as allies in its so-called war against terror (Agence France Presse 2001).

The future of opium production in the Golden Crescent remains uncertain. Hamid Karzai, Afghanistan's elegantly dressed interim leader in the wake of the U.S.-led coalition's tumbling of the Taliban, has reaffirmed the ban on poppy production. But this will be difficult to enforce given the support for the opium trade within the Afghan Transitional Authority — specifically from Northern Alliance factions that control export routes to Tajikistan, Uzbekistan, and Turkmenistan (Synovitz 2002). While the U.S. government uses the occasion of the Superbowl to inform consumers that to buy illegal drugs is to help terrorism, history indicates that the presence of the U.S. military will do nothing to abate the heroin industry. As Colonel Salomatsho Khushvakhtov of the Tajik Drug Control Agency puts it: "I'm pretty sure, when Americans come to Afghanistan to stay, some of them will become drug dealers" (quoted in Orth 2002). In any case, the war in Afghanistan has had a tremendous impact upon the global drug economy, leading to the Golden Triangle's reemergence as the world's largest heroin producing area. As the UNDCP reports, the Burmese poppy crop of 2001 outstripped Afghan production by almost 600 percent (UNDCP 2002). Constituting the bulk of Golden Triangle production, Burma's opium output has declined since 1996, stabilizing at about two-thirds of the levels produced in the early 1990s. But a February 2002 editorial in the *Bangkok Post* reports increasing heroin production in Burma, warning that the recent focus of drug enforcement agencies on methamphetamines may pave the way for another explosion of poppy crops ("Burma Must Show It Deserves Drug Aid" 2002). History suggests that traffickers turn to other cultivation areas when an established source dries up, and there is nothing to suggest that Burma's SPDC would oppose an expansion in opium production. The government-sponsored UWSA remains a key player in the global heroin trade, controlling production in the Shan and Kokang state areas and maintaining strong links with China's triad crime syndicates. Clearly the Southeast Asian heroin trade remains linked to the events in the Golden Crescent. But whatever the future holds, the Golden Triangle has been the world's principal source of opium since the late 1960s, and the fictional, journalistic, and cinematic production surrounding this area has shaped popular attitudes toward heroin production, trafficking, and addiction.

In an interview with David Barsamian (1990), Alfred McCoy, the author of *The Politics of Heroin in Southeast Asia* (1972) and *The Politics of Heroin: CIA Complicity in the Global Drug Trade* (1991), expresses uncertainty as to the origin of the term "Golden Triangle." McCoy attributes the invention of this "imaginary geographical construct" to "some unknown journalist wag or geographer" (5). Renard (1996) attributes the first official use of the phrase to Marshall Green, U.S. assistant secretary of state for East Asian and Pacific affairs, at a 12 July 1971 press conference. An earlier article in *Ramparts* magazine identifies the area as the Fertile Triangle (Browning and Garrett 1971, 33), but the expression "Golden Triangle" is clearly in circulation by mid-1971. Significantly, this act of naming corresponds with the Nixon administration's declaration of a war on drugs, a massive antinarcotics effort that brought official U.S. recognition of Southeast Asia's centrality to the heroin trade. With this increased scrutiny, the Golden Triangle became subject to heavy surveillance by institutions such as the U.S. Bureau of Narcotics, which opened an office in Vientiane, Laos, in November of the same year. By this time, the Golden Triangle had acquired a reputation as a problem zone in which military and/or diplomatic intervention was unlikely to stop the flow of drugs. A February 1972 special task force report to the U.S. cabinet states: "The most basic problem, and the one that unfortunately appears least likely of any solution, is the corruption, collusion and indifference at some places in some governments, particularly Thailand and South Vietnam, that precludes more effective suppression of traffic by the governments on whose territory it takes place" (U.S. Department of State 1972, 1). As McCoy (1991) argues, this rhetoric ignores the ongoing involvement of the CIA in the heroin trade. The Golden Triangle stands as a cartographic register of hidden conflicts within the U.S. government that fueled the global expansion of the heroin industry in the early 1970s.

Despite this official interest in the area, the Golden Triangle is immediately repossessed by popular cultural fantasy. Journalistic reportage paints it as a hidden ecotopia, inhospitable and inaccessible to the U.S. military and thus a site of symbolic resistance to the increasingly unpopular Vietnam War. Typical of this work is a feature article in the *Far Eastern Economic Review* titled "Wonderland of Opium" (1971). The magazine's cover pictures a hill tribe woman brightly clad in traditional dress nursing a ripe opium poppy between her hands. This type of representation sharply contrasts with Vietnam War photography that highlights violence and suffering, such as Ron Haeberle's famous images of the My Lai massacre published in *Life* magazine in December 1969. The headline accompanying the cover shot of the indigenous opium cultivator draws on Lewis Carroll's *Alice's Adventures in Wonderland* to depict the Golden Triangle as a strange alternative world. An article from the following year in *Natural History* magazine continues this exoticization of the area. Written by the anthropologist Alain Y. Dessaint and featuring large color photographs of Lisu tribespeople harvesting and smoking opium, the piece is simply called "The Poppies Are Beautiful This Year" (1972). Dessaint, whose research involved eighteen months of fieldwork in Evil Peaks (a Lisu village in northern Thailand), focuses on the processes of opium cultivation and harvesting, the role of the drug in religious life, and the potential for interethnic conflict. Suggesting that the Lisu's "dependence on opium production carries foreboding and uncertain prospects for their future" (34), he writes in the ethnographic present, subtracting his own presence from the situation, and at times aestheticizing the relation of the tribespeople to their crop. Thus he describes the mature opium fields with lyrical rapture: "Entire mountainsides are covered with white and purple poppies swaying in the wind, and the Lisu comment enthusiastically on the beauty of the fields, the promise of a good harvest" (36).

Lutz and Collins (1993) argue that similar representations of indigenous people in *National Geographic* magazine work to domesticate cultural differences, promoting themes of natural man and denying the historical dynamism of traditional societies. This is also true of popular reportage of the Golden Triangle. But it is important to remember that such journalistic fantasy also taps into the political desires of the anti–Vietnam War movement. Many early reports on the Golden Triangle heroin trade are critical of the U.S. military presence in Vietnam, exposing and criticizing the CIA involvement with opium trafficking. For instance, an article by T. D. Allman (1971, 37) in the "Wonderland of Opium" edition of the *Far Eastern Economic Review* notes, "several U.S. clandestine agencies and a number of allied Asian military leaders have been involved in the traffic for years." Clearly the journalistic discourses that first map the Golden Triangle fuel and are fueled by the growing U.S. domestic opposition to the Vietnam War.

On the heels of this reportage, similar representations of the Golden Triangle emerge in popular literature and film. Franklin M. Proud's spy thriller *The Golden Triangle* (1976) traces the fortunes of Joe Stanford, a rugged individualist and undercover CIA operative posted to Chiang Mai in Thailand's north. Stanford pursues his mission of supplying arms to Burma's Shan State rebels with unexpected efficiency, raising the suspicion of the KGB, which detects his cover and comes after him. But he also crosses his superiors in the CIA by learning too much about their complicity in the heroin trade, specifically through contact with another CIA agent stationed in Laos, who owes his first allegiance to the Corsican opium syndicate, Union Corse. During an overland mission, Stanford is shot by Meo tribesmen and rescued by the Lahu, a rival indigenous group. Safe in a Lahu village, he is nursed to health by Na Hti, daughter of a Lutheran missionary and a Lahu woman. This "sylph-like creature of exquisite beauty" (148) becomes his lover and companion in the ensuing manhunt. Episodes of vigorous pursuit are contrasted with idyllic scenes of the couple's lovemaking as the fugitives disguise themselves, first as a Buddhist monk and his boy guide and then as American hippies, escaping through Bangkok to Singapore. After Na Hti is shot dead by Stanford's CIA superior, the agent makes his way to Virginia, only to discover that his original cover was devised to distract attention from another operative who was preparing the resumption of U.S.-China diplomatic relations. Proud's *The Golden Triangle* is notable for its depiction of the opium-growing area as, on the one hand, a site of political chaos and ethnic animosity, the arena of clandestine deals and violent masculine struggles, and, on the other hand, a feminized zone of undiscovered exotic beauty. In this context, the allure of opium is articulated to white male fantasies about the sexual availability of young indigenous women — fantasies inseparable from the development of the Thai prostitution industry from the 1960s onward. Significantly, when Stanford checks into a Bangkok hotel with Na Hti, still disguised as a boy, the clerk pays her little attention since she "could be a transvestite *katoy,* a masculine *puying,* or an effeminate *puchai*" (222). In this way, the novel registers the abduction of hill tribe women into the prostitution racket — a business strongly linked to the organized crime networks involved in the production and smuggling of narcotics (Phongpaichit, Piriyarangsan, and Treerat 1998).

Paul Bonnecarrère's *Triangle d'Or* (1976) is another spy thriller, translated into English as *The Golden Triangle* (1977). Unlike Proud's novel, little of the action takes place in the Burma-Thailand-Laos border area. The story begins in Paris where François Sérignan, a wealthy industrialist and decorated commander from the French Indochina War, is drawn into the crusade against drugs by his daughter's death.

Joining forces with the French police and the U.S. Drug Enforcement Agency (DEA), Sérignan vows to destroy the organization responsible for the distribution of the impure "Brown Sugar" heroin that killed his daughter. His first stop is Hanoi, where some former Vietnamese associates provide him with intelligence and a safe passage into Thailand via Laos. Sérignan plans to foil the Brown Sugar trafficking organization by convincing its kingpin, Axel von Kersting, that he is the head of a rival cartel that threatens to take over the world market by distributing the purer China White, manufactured in Laotian refineries. All goes well until von Kersting discovers the existence of Flossie, daughter to Sérignan and a Vietnamese woman whom the agent had planned to marry before being wounded in the Indochina campaign. Sérignan has been unaware of Flossie's existence but the placing of a death threat on this newly found daughter assures his cooperation with von Kersting's outfit. Promising to transfer the China White traffic to the Brown Sugar syndicate, Sérignan begins a game of global intrigue in which he appears to operate in von Kersting's interests while actually undermining them. The action switches quickly from Bangkok to Paris, Reunion, Sumatra, Los Angeles, Marseilles, Washington, Venezuela, and the Bahamas. Meanwhile, Warren Drake, a charismatic DEA operative, conceals Flossie on a yacht, and the CIA devises a host of technological gadgets to catch von Kersting's operatives in the act of smuggling. Sérignan's associates repeatedly vouch for his integrity, but, in the end, it remains unclear whether von Kersting's downfall represents a major drug bust or merely the victory of one syndicate over another. A more formally complex text than Proud's *The Golden Triangle,* Bonnecarrère's novel remains ambiguous about the complicity of the CIA and other Western intelligence agencies in the heroin trade. Both books display a fascination with a young Eurasian woman, who, in her supposed innocence, provides a foil to the nefarious operations of heroin traffickers. The chief difference is that Bonnecarrère's work focuses on the global machinations of the drug industry, while Proud's novel confines the bulk of its action to the Golden Triangle.

The Southeast Asian heroin trade also provides a stock theme for Hong Kong action cinema, perhaps because that city's organized crime triads have been particularly active in trafficking activities (Booth 1996). Among the Hong Kong action films set in the area are Rome Bunnag's *The Golden Triangle* (1980), Sumat Saichur's *Raiders of the Golden Triangle* (1985), Bruce Le's *Black Spot* (1991), and Chin Siu-Ho's *Challenge to Devil Area* (1991). But the most notorious Hong

Kong movie to treat the Southeast Asian heroin trade is John Woo's *Heroes Shed No Tears* (1986), famous for the suppression of the director's original cut, which the producer considered far too violent. Combining plot elements from Coppola's *Apocalypse Now* (1978) and the Japanese *manga* series *Lone Wolf and Club, Heroes Shed No Tears* traces the conflict between a group of Chinese mercenaries (hired by the Thai government) and one of the Triangle's major drug barons. After witnessing a group of soldiers torturing and executing a group of French journalists on the Thailand-Vietnam border, the mercenaries shoot the drug lord through the eye, and there begins a long, manic, and intensely violent pursuit through the jungle. As the chase goes on, things become increasingly weird and alien. The fugitives encounter a variety of otherworldly characters, including a pot-smoking American soldier based on the Dennis Hopper character in *Apocalypse Now*. At one point, a mercenary is trapped in a burning field and must bury himself to survive — an episode adapted from *Lone Wolf and Cub*. The violence culminates with a grueling scene in which the drug kingpin takes revenge on the mercenary leader by sewing his eyelids open. This is shown from the victim's point of view. The audience sees only the dangling, bloody thread dropping in and out of the screen, as the sound track switches between sadistic giggles and desperate screams. Described on the video cover as "a visual tone poem in blood," *Heroes Shed No Tears* is one the most surreal and nihilistic depictions of drug-related violence in the Golden Triangle. The film is especially notable for its representation of hill tribe people as headhunters. This identification not only counterpoints the more prevalent image of the area's indigenous people as idyllic peace-loving creatures but also contradicts the available ethnographic evidence. Only Burma's Wa, who once offered human skulls as sacrifices, might qualify for such a classification, but to depict them as such is to ignore the massive transformations that have beset hill tribe communities with the arrival of the opium trade in the Golden Triangle.

Another register of Chinese interest in the Triangle is *Golden Triangle: Wilderness and Frontier* (1987), a book by the Taiwanese human rights activist Bo Yang, who was imprisoned for nine years after publishing an adaptation of an American comic that proved insulting to the Chiang Kai-Shek regime. Originally published as a series of articles in the *China Times,* the book focuses on the remnants of the KMT army, expelled into highland Southeast Asia in 1949. Like Woo, Yang offers a desperate and relentless view of the Triangle. He

begins by claiming that foreign reports on "the mysterious and enigmatic Golden Triangle" have succeeded "in penetrating only half the
layers of the mystery." There are more "astounding substrata . . . to be
discovered," he explains, "strata that perhaps only the Chinese could
comprehend" (2). Describing the drug business as a case of filial rec-
ompense by which the narcotics used to poison the Chinese in the past
are returned to their rightful owners in the West, he draws explicit parallels between the nineteenth-century opium wars and the struggles
between national armies and rebel forces in the Triangle. According
to Yang, the Golden Triangle is a "gargantuan monster . . . kept and
raised by the civilized western world" (64). The clear victims of this
monster are the descendants of the KMT or Lone Army forces, who
are subjected to a kind of ethnocide, occupying squalid refugee villages in northern Thailand. Yang goes to great lengths to emphasize
that these communities are not involved in the opium trade, but, in
so doing, he strategically ignores the long engagement of the KMT
in the drug business, often with the direct support of the CIA (Belanger 1989). His primary purpose is to reprimand the Taiwanese
government for refusing to support the occupants of these refugee villages, and thus he downplays KMT military complicity, contrasting
the condition of their descendants with the apparent well-being of the
hill tribes that cultivate the poppy. For him, the Golden Triangle is a
site of intrigue and danger in which the offspring of the KMT slowly
abandon their cultural identity and disappear "into the empty outer
space of Thailand" (177).

Yang's vision of the Triangle sharply contrasts the accounts of
North American anthropologists, who strongly concur that the area's
hill tribe communities are the principal victims of the opium trade.
Ethnographic studies such as Paul and Elaine Lewis's *People of the
Golden Triangle* (1984) and Edward Anderson's *Plants and People
of the Golden Triangle: Ethnobotany of the Hill Tribes of Northern
Thailand* (1993) document how opium cultivation imbalances local
ecosystems, leading to deforestation and devastating indigenous cultures and lifestyles. Anderson (1993, 18) writes: "it is crucial that the
wisdom and experience of these tribal people, who for generations
have lived in a close, balanced relationship with the ambient environment, be recorded. Otherwise, this knowledge will be lost forever."
For him, the knowledge of these people is "a treasure of immense
value to Thailand and to the rest of the world" (18). As Clifford
(1997) explains, this type of salvage ethnography places the anthropologist in the role of cosmopolitan traveler and the native in the

position of place-bound local. Anderson makes no attempt to consider how hill tribe cultures articulate to, change with, and even produce forms of modernity. Rather the Triangle's indigenous cultures are assigned to an atavistic past that struggles to survive in the modern world, even as it suggests modes of enchantment that promise to rescue contemporary society from its rationalized scramble for profit — in this case represented by the voracious profiteering of the opium industry. These carefully researched ethnographies, which construct the Triangle as their geographical object, supply compelling accounts of the transformations to which indigenous communities are subjected by the opium industry. But they fail to register the modernity displayed by these same communities as they negotiate the economic transactions of the drug business and the related movements of technology, information, military personnel, and tourists. As such, they promote a romanticized view of the Triangle as a hidden paradise, which might be reclaimed only if modern societies were to abandon their instrumental domination of the world and accept the indigenous gift of harmonious living in the natural environment.

This type of ecological fantasy has also dominated the promotion of the Golden Triangle as a tourist destination. Starting from the late 1970s, travel companies began to exploit the area's notoriety as an opium cultivation zone, using the name Golden Triangle as a marketing label to promote a variety of tourist activities. These range from packaged mass tourism in Chiang Mai to the ethnotouristic hill tribe treks organized by firms like the Australian adventure company Intrepid. Today the tourist industry in the Thai sections of the Triangle is highly developed. The U.K.-based firm Wild and Exotic Thailand, which bills itself as "an environmentally and culturally focused organization," offers a typical five-day tour, marketed under the name "Mystery of the Golden Triangle." Tourists are flown into the northern city of Chiang Rai and accommodated in a Western-style hotel. On the second day, they travel to the border town of Mae Sai, where they can cross into Burma and purchase Russian and Chinese goods in the markets on the other side. Following this, they are transported to the tri-border area, where signs declaring that they have arrived at the center of the Golden Triangle provide a popular photo opportunity. Day three takes them to the highland temple of Doi Mae Salong and the King's Mother's Royal Palace and Gardens at Doi Tung. The remaining days are devoted to hill tribe visits, including Karen, Akha, and Lahu villages — the first of which offers elephant trekking. Travelers not disposed to such organized tours can join hill tribe treks in Chiang Mai or Chiang Rai, some of them involving transport by motorbike. Many treks court the dangers of the opium industry, following its allure and sampling its products. Tour guides sometimes peddle the drug, seeking either to supplement their incomes or to support their own habits. European, North American, and Australian youth on Bangkok's Khaosan Road boast of sharing pipes with the Akha or white water rafting on amphetamines, before flying home in Golden Triangle T-shirts, some of them featuring the Belgian comic strip character Tintin. But whether Western tourism involves drug use or not, it is clear that opium cultivation creates an aura of exoticism that attaches itself to the Triangle. One symptom of this is the tendency of the term "Golden Triangle" to detach itself from its geographical base and to circulate through global networks as an indicator of Southeast Asian exoticism and authenticity. The name reappears in distant and unexpected places, such as Chicago's West Hubbard Street, where a curiosity store called The Golden Triangle advertises itself on the Internet as a supplier of antique furniture, sculpture, and other artifacts from Burma, Thailand, and Laos.

In recent years, the Thai sections of the Triangle have become so overcoded with Orientalist tourist fantasies (inseparable from the constructions of the sex industry) that the opium cultivation is actually in decline. With its sophisticated market infrastructure, Thailand has become the main line of distribution for Golden Triangle opium, approximately 80 percent of which is grown in the highlands of Burma (U.S. Department of State 2001). The thinly disguised complicity of Burma's military government means that opium cultivation, heroin refining, and the associated production of methamphetamines continue under its rule, particularly in the Kokang and Shan State regions. Following the 1996 surrender of Khun Sa, who now functions as a legitimate businessman in Rangoon, the Burmese government has assumed a direct role in the opium business and large amounts of drug money have entered the country's above-ground economy. According to an article in the *Guardian* (Levy and Scott-Clark 1997), Khun Sa's former hideout has been converted into a tourist theme park known as Khun Sa World. Visitors trucked in from Thailand can drink at the Khun Sa karaoke bar and take a tour of the leader's mansion, ironically nicknamed the White House. Meanwhile, Thailand's Doi Tung hosts the Golden Triangle Park — a massive piece of tourist infrastructure, featuring the Hall of Opium, a multimedia exhibition that focuses on the history of opium and the impacts of illegal drugs. An initiative of the Thai monarchy, the project incorporates amusement park elements such as a 130-meter entrance tunnel designed to evoke "the contradictory moods associated with opium: mystery, danger, fear, sleep, dreams, ease of pain, and suppressed suffering" (Golden Triangle Park 2001). In the early twenty-first century, the Golden Triangle maintains a delicate balance between such tourist initiatives and the global drug economy. While most tourist activity avoids direct engagement with the insurgent forces that control the heroin trade, the promotion of the Triangle as a tourist destination rests heavily on the area's reputation as an opium-growing region. Nonetheless, governments suggest that tourism reveals the area's transparency, legitimating the claim that there is nothing to hide. With the opening of these tourist theme parks, the construction of the Triangle as a wonderland is strangely literalized. Western fantasy turns back upon itself, providing the most effective guise for the opium production that continues in the Golden Triangle.

Mapping the Unmappable

The continued prominence of the Golden Triangle as an opium production zone stems from the growing disjunctures between the three types of space that constitute it: indigenous space, modern space, and global space. These overlapping topographies interact in complex and unpredictable ways, but it is possible to discern a general trend by which the indigenous and global formations collude to diminish the control that modern states exert over the area. It is largely due to the inability and/or refusal of nation-states to police drug production activities in the Golden Triangle that the area maintains its status as an opium cultivation zone. As is so often the case in the drug industry, this waning of state power reflects an informal alliance between indigenous cultural practices and postmodern economic activities that key into global capitalist agendas. A closer consideration of the spatial regimes constituting the Golden Triangle reveals the extent to which this contestation of modern space calls into doubt the cartographic techniques responsible for the area's initial identification and mapping.

The highland areas of Burma, Thailand, and Laos are inhabited by indigenous hill tribes who cultivate the opium poppy under the direction of powerful leaders known as warlords. The production process generally begins in late winter, when the high mountain slopes used for opium growing are cleared and burned. As the rains begin in May,

Opium harvesting. Publicity still from the documentary *Dealing with the Demon.*
Copyright Hilton Cordell Productions, 1995.

maize is planted in the future poppy fields. In September and October, this maize is harvested and the poppy seeds are sown. As the
flowers grow, the maize stems are gently weeded. Often other plants
are cultivated amid the crop: peaches, pears, beans, sorghum, peas,
lemon grass, coriander, or marijuana. At the end of December the
poppies begin to flower. When the petals fall, there is a short period
of time in which to extract the valuable latex from the capsule. The
hill tribe cultivators use a curved knife to score the bulb's surface,
leaving it overnight to secrete the thick white fluid. The following day
the laborers return with scrapers to remove the latex, which turns
a yellow-brown color overnight. For each poppy the process is repeated three or four times, and slowly the sticky resin is compiled and
wrapped in thick paper. While some of this raw opium is kept aside
for local consumption, most is sold to drug syndicates, who transport
the substance to chemical refineries along jungle trading routes, often
under heavy guard. It is important to emphasize that opium cultivation is not a traditional activity among the area's indigenous groups.
Many of the hill tribes that inhabited the Golden Triangle prior to
World War II (the Karen, the Lawa, the Khamu, the H'tin) began to
grow the crop only half a century ago. Those tribes that drifted south
into the area after World War II (the Hmong, the Mien, the Lahu,
the Lisu, the Akha) learned to cultivate the poppy in China's Yunnan

Province, where the drug was grown from the mid–nineteenth century to offset dependence upon British imports (Anderson 1993). In any case, the participation of hill tribes in opium cultivation attests the complex articulation of indigenous cultures to the global drug economy — an articulation that impairs the ability of nation-states to exercise sovereign control over the area.

Indigenous groups in the Golden Triangle offer no straightforward allegiance to any nation-state and are often, like the Shan and Kachin rebels in Burma, in direct conflict with national governments (M. Smith 1991; Lintner 1993). Edmund Leach's article "The Frontiers of Burma" (1960) is a classic study of the geographical quandaries produced by the area's multiform ethnic population. Placing the word "Burma" in quotation marks, Leach studies what he describes as an imprecisely defined frontier region lying between India and China and having modern political Burma as its center. Although he conducted fieldwork with the Shan communities of Burma's north, there is the clear implication that he is also writing about parts of Thailand and Laos. Leach explains that the notions of frontiers and nation-states are the products of modern European colonial expansion in the area. He draws on the thirteenth-century account of Angkhor by Chou Ta-Kuan to make a distinction between hill people, with Chinese notions of kinship, leadership, religion, and marriage, and valley people, with an Indian understanding of these matters. In this way, he characterizes "Burma" as a frontier region under continuous influence from both China and India, describing precolonial frontiers as undefined ecological boundaries that map out zones of mutual interest. Tongchai Winichakul develops a similar argument in *Siam Mapped: A History of the Geo-Body of a Nation* (1994). Studying the premodern mapping of Siam as an unbound kingdom, Winichakul explains that the hill tribes of the Golden Triangle understand the idea of a border not as a metaphysical line dividing sovereign states but as an overlapping frontier open for trade and cultural negotiation. He thus argues for a conception of indigenous space that is nonscalar and makes no reference to the earth's larger surface, such as latitude and longitude lines. This indigenous space was largely displaced by the hegemony of modern space instituted by French and British colonial authorities (in Vietnam and Burma) in the nineteenth century, but it remains as a residual force, undermining the sovereign territoriality of nation-states. The Golden Triangle thus comprises a complex nexus of overlapping indigenous spaces, fostering networks of transport and communication that facilitate the movement of drugs across national

The Golden Triangle as global space: heroin trafficking routes. Reprinted by permission of United Nations Publications.

boundaries, despite policing measures that aim to seal these frontiers against illegal flows.

At the same time, the Golden Triangle produces emergent forms of global space, which question the impermeability of its borders as barriers that contain the opium trade. As a global space, the Triangle is defined less by territoriality than by the inexorable flow of opium and heroin from its plantations and refineries. The area positions itself in a borderless world, pumping narcotics across national and regional boundaries and into the veins of addicts. Even staunch antidrug campaigners admit to the futility of closing nation-state borders against the drug trade. For instance, Paul Stares in his *Global Habit: The Drug Problem in a Borderless World* (1996, 67) writes that cross-border drug mobility is "very difficult, if not impossible, to monitor effectively." The triumphant rhetoric of the borderless world as developed by conservative commentators such as Ohmae (1990) has received harsh criticism for its failure to account for the way in which global capitalism hastens the development of new borders marked by stark inequalities and digital divides (Miyoshi 1993). Given the massive profits generated by the heroin industry, the hill tribes of the Golden Triangle are undoubtedly positioned on the losing side of these barriers, even as the processes of globalization alter their everyday lives, constructing them in some cases as objects of the tourist gaze. But this does not change the fact that the modern space of the Golden Triangle is under threat from both global and indigenous formations, the emergent and residual forms of space working against the bound territoriality of the nation-state.

Just as indigenous space destabilizes boundaries within the Triangle, so the global space of heroin trafficking works to transgress national frontiers around the world. If this is the case, there is also a need to explore the status of the Triangle's own borders. Clearly these are arbitrarily imposed, representing an effort to localize a source for transnational drug flows, an attempt to assign a place of origin to an illicit economy of worldwide proportions. Ultimately such limits cannot stand. The drug trade is a bad infinity of global complicities, with no clear beginning and no foreseeable end. Without transnational trafficking systems and widespread consumer demand, the Golden Triangle would not exist. Once boundaries are drawn around this area, they are compromised by the very phenomena they purport to contain. In a sense, the Triangle unmaps itself, since as soon as it is recognized as a discrete geographical entity it becomes susceptible to dislocating forces that undermine its territorial integrity. Put simply, the Golden Triangle interrupts the techniques of observation responsible for charting it in the first place.

With the post–Cold War escalation of the war against drugs, the Golden Triangle has become a site of intense geopolitical surveillance. The past decade has seen the establishment of several geopolitical observatories, which have remapped the world in an attempt to locate sources for and track the passage of transnational drug flows. These include the Paris-based Observatoire Géopolitique des Drogues (OGD), publishers of the confidential newsletter *The Geopolitical Drug Dispatch,* and the International Drug Watch, a U.S. information network and advocacy organization. As their names suggest, these agencies seek to expose or make visible "the hidden stakes of narcotics production and trafficking" (OGD 1996, xi). Such a fantasy of objective, panoramic observation corresponds to what Ó Tuathail (1996, 53) calls the geopolitical gaze, a panoptic vision that "depluralizes the surface of the earth by organizing it into essential zones...identities...and perspectives." But while organizations such as the OGD have considerable technological resources at their disposal, they are unable to fully map the activities of drug producers and traffickers. One example of this is the difficulty involved in satellite imaging of the Golden Triangle. Not only are there problems with cloud coverage, but also opium cultivators plant their crops on sharp mountain ridges. Positioned in this way, the poppy fields are protected from satellite surveillance, obscured by shadows or placed at an angle that flusters the data-gathering process, due to the satellite's inability to alter its orbit to take accurate images of the crops. In this way, the Triangle remains unmappable to even the most powerful geographic information systems. As a geopolitical entity it resists clear or transparent cartographic representation, producing disturbances in the scopic regimes that make possible the strategic maps of the contemporary world order.

At the level of trafficking, the mapping of drug flows is no less vexed. The Golden Triangle displaces the borders of contemporary geopower, making it difficult, if not impossible, to trace the passage of opium from its plantations. As soon as interdiction is successful at one point, the drugs begin to flow across another border. Crackdowns on the Thai-Burmese frontier have led to the opening of new smuggling paths through India, China, and Vietnam (UNDCP 2001). But regardless of the means or direction of travel, almost all heroin trafficking is financed by organized crime (U.S., Italian, Russian, Chinese). The drug is usually destined for markets in wealthy metropolitan centers, but it leaves a trail of addiction along the way, especially among the hill tribe cultivators (with male addiction rates of up to 80 percent) and its diverse courier communities (Nigerian students; Senegalese immigrant workers; clans from Kosovo, Chechnya, or Morocco; Croat, Serb, or Bosnian fighters; Russian businessmen). As depicted in Alastair Reid's British miniseries *Traffik* (1989) and its Oscar-winning U.S. remake, Stephen Soderbergh's *Traffic* (2000), heroin trafficking is a complex game of international intrigue in which nobody gets off clean. Both based around a scenario that recalls Bonnecarrère's *Triangle d'Or* (a powerful antidrugs campaigner discovers his daughter's heroin use), these films knit together a convoluted plot that links impoverished opium cultivators and smugglers with corrupt officials and politicians in a number of international locations. While the British version is far more extensive, moving from the poppy fields of Pakistan across the corrupt rich of Hamburg to the power elite and needle-infested drug haunts of London, the Hollywood version confines itself to the drug trade connecting Mexico and the United States. But both films depict drug traffickers and profiteers, who are at once closely bound and, for the most part, distanced from each other, particularly along ethnic and racial lines.

Certainly the association of heroin smuggling with diasporic ethnic communities (for example, the Vietnamese in Sydney's Cabramatta) has led to the demonization of minority groups, reinforcing local racial prejudices. But as Reid's and Soderbergh's films suggest, the businesses of heroin trafficking cannot be confined to any particular diasporic network, consisting rather of hidden complicities that traverse racial barriers and extend all the way up the political food chain. The OGD (1996, 6–8) reports the rise of newer, more flexible heroin-trafficking strategies that question the long-tentacles model of diasporic conspiracy. Known as short networking, these techniques involve mobile raiders who stay in a target location for only a few weeks, or even a few days, striking up short-lived relationships and selling directly to local purchasers. Such practices have made the work of interdiction even more difficult, forcing down street prices and leading to the international availability of heroin of unprecedented purity. Nonetheless, the practice of cutting the drug continues. Successive dealers increase their profits by diluting the heroin with substances such as caffeine and talc. By the time it reaches the street, the drug is usually only about 5 percent pure.

Dirty Laundry

In January 1980, Frank Nugan, Australian lawyer and playboy heir to a modest food-processing fortune, was found dead in a late-model Mercedes on the western outskirts of Sydney. In his pocket police discovered a business card from William Colby, the former director of the CIA. From there began a long and incomplete paper chase, tracing Nugan's association with Michael Hand, a former Green Beret and CIA trainer of hill tribe militia in Vietnam and Laos. Together these men had founded the Nugan Hand Bank, a CIA money-laundering front based in Australia's largest city. McCoy (1991) traces the history of this rogue financial institution, which was established in 1973 through a basic accounting fraud and, by the time of its collapse in 1980, encompassed a global web of illicit financial dealing spanning six continents. Loosely organized around a set of underworld criminals and U.S. intelligence agents who gathered at the Bourbon and Beefsteak Restaurant in Sydney's Kings Cross vice district, the Nugan Hand Bank's activities included arms dealing in South Africa, corporate fraud in Saudi Arabia, off-shore banking in the Cayman Islands, and the covert backing of a constitutional coup that ousted Australia's Whitlam Labor government in 1975. By far its most extensive business involved the channeling of money between Australian financial institutions and money-laundering outfits in Hong Kong. A large heroin market had developed in Australia in the late 1960s, when American troops began to arrive in Sydney on recreational leave from Vietnam.

By the mid 1970s, addiction rates had skyrocketed and criminal syndicates were arranging regular shipments from the Golden Triangle. Conveniently the Nugan Hand Bank also established a branch in Chiang Mai, lodged in the same building as the DEA. Records show that the bank was removing millions of dollars from Thailand. More voluminous were the transactions of the Hong Kong office, which offered Sydney depositors a facility for illegal transfers out of Australia and Hong Kong clients a higher interest rate for funds deposited in Sydney. While it is certain that the outfit provided an avenue out of Australia for funds earned from the sale of Golden Triangle heroin, the exact details of its operations remain obscure. Despite numerous government reports and massive investigative journalism, the vast majority of Nugan Hand's activities are shrouded in secrecy. What is the money launderer's secret and what does it tell us about the global machinations of the drug economy?

As most financial exchanges in the heroin industry involve small cash transactions, criminal syndicates need some way of consolidating and concealing the source of their funds. There are many reasons why an individual or organization may wish to hide wealth: the concealment of money earned from clandestine arms dealing or illegal prostitution, tax evasion, the bankrolling of paramilitary or terrorist organizations, the funding of intelligence and counterintelligence activities, the defrauding of share holders by corporate directors, the draining of wealth from national economies by postcolonial comprador classes. But the drug industry is the primary contributor to the world's black economy. Money laundering is a complex business, and methods vary according to the source of funds, the purposes for which the money is required, and the time available. The basic idea is to keep the money moving, creating a web of transactions, often involving a multitude of parties, with various legal statuses in as many different jurisdictions as possible. Experts such as Barry Rider and Michael Ashe (1996) identify three stages in the process.

The first and most dangerous stage, which involves getting the money into the financial system, is known as *placement*. Small deposits are made in a wide range of banks, preferably in a number of international locations so as to avoid suspicion and cash-transaction-reporting legislation. Sometimes money is prewashed by passing it through fronts such as art dealerships, travel agencies, fabric shops, or jewelry stores. In many countries, launderers place their money by means of alternative banking methods — for example, *Hawala/Hundi* banking throughout the Indian diaspora and Islamic world (transactions involving promissory notes, secret words and gestures, or encrypted e-mail messages) or *Fei Ch'ien* (Flying Money) banking in China (transactions involving cash certificates, secret symbols, or coded objects such as colored sugar cubes). Similar methods involve passing money through casinos, particularly those that make funds available in multiple jurisdictions, or by using illegally earned funds to make legitimate business purchases for parties who pay reimbursement in another jurisdiction to avoid taxes or tariffs.

Within hours of the money entering the networks of the financial system, it becomes available anywhere in the world. From here begins the second stage of *layering,* by which white-collar criminals shift the funds from bank to bank and jurisdiction to jurisdiction, stopping in each only briefly and sometimes consolidating on the way. This is a tricky operation, often involving shell companies that trade in imaginary services and commodities. Sometimes the money passes through legitimate commodity or bullion markets, especially in financial centers such as Hong Kong or Switzerland, which combine strict confidentiality requirements with loose regulatory frameworks. With the increased deregulation of world financial markets and the formation of trading blocs such as the European Union and NAFTA, these operations have become ever more prevalent and technical. Today most layering occurs via electronic fund transfers (EFTs) that involve no physical movement of cash. Funds are moved quickly or in parallel through Internet e-cash systems or private banking networks with names like CHIPS, CHAPS, and SWIFT. As Sassen (2000) notes, the privileging of the Internet in studies of digital networking has obscured a focus on private computer networks, although they have arguably had a greater impact upon national sovereignty and regulatory regimes, especially in the domain of global finance. Certainly, these private networks are the primary domain for the layering of laundered funds. The money is shuffled from one virtual space to another, and as it becomes increasingly unlocatable, so it becomes clean. Eventually, the funds are ready for *integration,* the third stage of money laundering involving reinvestment in the legitimate world via property markets, stocks and bonds, or other financial mechanisms.

So vast is the amount of laundered drug money in the world that it forms a huge alternative economy, the world's third largest after money and oil. Estimates point to a total annual volume in the range of U.S. $500 billion to 1 trillion (Petras 2001). No national economy or financial institution is untouched. Capital movements induced by

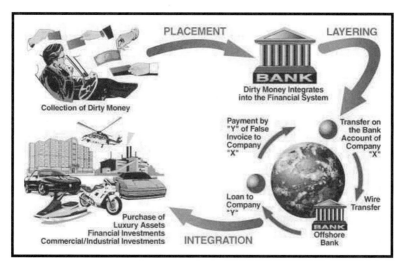

A typical money-laundering scheme. Reprinted by permission of United Nations Publications.

money laundering are promoted not by differences in economic fundamentals but by differences in controls and regulations that make the activity safer in some countries than others. Launderers will move money to jurisdictions where the risk of detection is smaller even if this means accepting a lower rate of return. Consequently, there are large amounts of money circulating through the international financial system in apparent defiance of the laws of economics. Money laundering is clearly a source of anxiety for the sovereign authorities of global finance. As Tanzi (1996, 7) notes in an IMF working paper, the practice has important macroeconomic effects that "bring some inherent instability to the world economy." Not only is the world's capital invested less optimally than might otherwise be the case, but financial movements originating from money laundering can influence variables at the national level, such as exchange and interest rates. This can confuse policy makers, and, due to the integration of financial markets, difficulties arising in one center can quickly spread to others, turning national problems into global-systemic ones. Just as trade liberalization aids the business of drug trafficking, so financial globalization eases the work of money laundering. The two practices feed off each other, producing a pronounced disequilibrium within the global capitalist system.

If the reported estimates of the proceeds of money laundering are correct, the value of the assets controlled by criminal organizations must be very large. While not all clandestine economic activity is drug related, there is an obvious link between the illegality of drugs and the need to launder money earned from their sale. The prevention of money laundering is no easy business, not least because it involves capitalism in a struggle against its own fantasies of deregulation, decoding, and abstraction-to-the-max. Given the largely state-based nature of the agencies that seek to control the practice, the work of prevention is extremely difficult. Even institutions like the Financial Action Task Force of the OECD, which coordinates antilaundering efforts across twenty-eight state jurisdictions, cannot penalize countries that encourage the investment of illegal capital. The problem is that the global marketplace recognizes no difference between funds obtained from criminal activities and legitimate assets. The distinction between clean and dirty money applies only within legal, political, and moral regimes. It has no essential impact upon the economic value of the funds in question or their ability to generate a surplus. As Georg Simmel explains in *The Philosophy of Money* (1978, 130), money is "the pure form of exchangeability." The rise of the money economy has a multitude of social, psychological, and philosophical implications, but as the general equivalent of value under capitalism, money is "the autonomous manifestation of the exchange relation" (119). It is due to the autonomy of its economic function that money retains its exchange value regardless of its legal, political, or moral status in different jurisdictions.

Most published studies of money laundering employ the legalistic discourse of regulatory institutions. This obscures a discussion of capitalism's relation to laundered money and its significance for theories of value. There is a wide gap between works that develop strategies for money-laundering prevention and discourses that theorize the connection of money to cleanliness. It is worth exploring this later link in detail since it sheds light on capitalism's uneasy relationship with legal, political, and moral regimes of value.

The most coherent body of theory concerning money's relation to cleanliness is psychoanalysis. In essays such as "Character and Anal Eroticism" (1908) and "On Transformation of Instinct as Exemplified in Anal Eroticism" (1917), Freud argues that money is intrinsically dirty. Drawing on a range of case histories plus examples from literature, anthropology, and mythology, he claims that the traditional association between money and excrement reveals a deeper psychological connection between sublimation and anality. For Freud, the rational, calculating attitude induced by money requires a sublimation of libidinal instincts or repudiation of the body. This implies an unconscious link between the interest in money and the infantile fascination with excrement, since the act of defecation is a physical reminder of the body's degeneration. As Norman O. Brown (1959, 294) explains: "In the true life of the body (which is also the life of the id) value can be detached from the body only by attaching value to the nonbodily excreta of the body, which are at the same time the dead matter produced by the body, and which incorporate the body's daily dying." According to psychoanalytic orthodoxy, money is dead matter that has been made alive by inheriting the magic power that infantile narcissism attributes to excrement. There can be no such thing as clean money. If money were not excrement, it would have no value. This means that money derived from legitimate sources is just as dirty as money earned from illegal economic activities. Only if considered in some aspect other than the economic — for example, the political or the legal — does the distinction between clean and dirty money begin to make sense.

Clearly the launderer does not attempt to cleanse money of its value. To launder money is to hide money, to conceal it in the abstract flow of capital as a means of avoiding state-imposed illegalities. But in the era of computer networking, isn't all finance capital washed in this sense? Speculation withdraws funds from commodity production to search for the new kinds of profits available through financial transactions themselves. This abbreviates Marx's famous formula for circulation $M-C\ldots P\ldots C'-M'$, bracketing out the moment of production and the commodity to become $M-M'$, money begets money. As Jameson (1997) argues, money, under the latest stage of capitalism, is doubly abstracted, not only because it stores up and congeals abstract labor power but also because it takes flight from an older form of productive content:

> Capital itself becomes free-floating. It separates from the concrete context of its productive geography. Money becomes in a second sense and to a second degree abstract (it was always abstract in the first and basic sense), as though somehow in the national moment money still had a content. It was cotton money, or wheat money, textile money, railroad money, and the like. Now, like the butterfly stirring within the chrysalis, it separates itself from that concrete breeding ground and prepares to take flight. (251)

The general equivalence of laundered money and legitimate funds generated through financial transactions can be registered by rewriting

Jameson's third sentence: "It was drug money, arms money, comprador money, and the like. Now . . . it separates itself . . . and prepares to take flight." No more than cotton money or wheat money is drug money or any other form of dirty money cleaned by its entry into the networks of global finance. In this context, it is instructive to remember, as Paul Smith (1997, 35) writes, "the activities of finance capital are scarcely as discrete from the processes of surplus labor extraction as they are usually depicted to be." First, the finance service industries "demand and command massive amounts of labor which waits upon and indeed carries on the processes of financial speculation" (35). Second, the shibboleth of the total technologization of finance capital conceals the labor involved in related activities "from data gathering and data processing, through office labor and janitoring, to the manufacture of computer and telecommunications instruments, and so on" (35). Finally, the informational production of services in wealthy capitalist regions relies on the labor of the periphery, which completes the tasks of manufacturing for the North even as these laboring processes are transformed by informatization.

In "Scattered Speculations on the Question of Value" (1987), Gayatri Spivak argues that this immanence of labor in the global financial system has important consequences for the theory of value. Pointing to the inadequacy of Antonio Negri's concept of immaterial labor for the analysis of the feminized labor practices of the South, she argues that the Marxist conception of value, based as it as on abstract labor power, can never fully represent labor as extant in the particular. Thus women's labor, "third world" labor, child domestic labor, and so forth, are supplements to value as we usually conceive it, traces of the value form as expressed in both use and exchange. Hardt and Negri (2000), who commend and absorb this analysis, build on Spivak's argument to reposition what they call affective labor (conceived in terms of women's work and the productivity of the corporeal) at the pinnacle of the immaterial labor practices that fuel the global capitalist economy. Affective labor, they argue, is immaterial insofar as its products are intangible, giving rise to "social networks, forms of community, biopower" (293). Whether involving direct bodily contact (as in the caring industries) or technological mediation (as in much entertainment), affective labor is central to capitalist postmodernization, functioning at the nexus where "the instrumental action of economic production has been united with the communicative action of human relations" (293). This creates an extremely open situation in which global capitalism relies on the constitution of communities and collective subjectivities that can turn against it, producing forms of life that potentially threaten the real subsumption of society under capital.

Although Hardt and Negri identify the interactive work of symbolic analysis and problem solving as another species of immaterial labor (separate from both the labor of industrial production and affective labor), the analysis of money laundering begs a direct confrontation with the question of biopower. Not only does such financial subterfuge push capitalism toward a limit where its tendencies to abstraction and deterritorialization begin to overpower it, but also, as the psychoanalytic formula shit = money suggests, money's relation to cleanliness and value cannot be thought in separation from affect and corporeality. For Freud, all values are bodily values, and the assimilation of money to excrement is the path by which extraneous things acquire significance for the body. He posits a distinction between the body's inside and outside, and maps this division over the split between cleanliness and pollution. To imagine the possibility of cleaning money is to interrupt this scheme, to contest the organic model of the body as a system of inclusion and exclusion and the correlate anthropological orthodoxy of purity and danger (Douglas 1966). Just as the launderer's practice disrupts the mapping systems of financial regulators and law enforcement agencies, so the business of money laundering questions the Freudian mapping of the body as a unified organic entity. Little wonder that Deleuze and Guattari (1983) seal their argument for the Oedipal limiting of capitalism by contesting the psychoanalytic dictum shit = money:

> It is not via a flow of shit or a wave of incest that Oedipus arrives, but via the decoded flows of capital-money.... Which explains the complex origin of the relation that is completely distorted in the psychoanalytic equation, shit = money; in reality, it is a question of encounters or conjunctions, or derivatives and resultants between decoded flows. (267)

At stake here is not the disarticulation of the relation shit = money but rather an attempt to trace its complex origin in the decoded flows of capitalism. The understanding of money laundering requires an antipsychoanalysis of corporeality, an attempt to delineate a disruptive topography that confounds the protocols of mapping, as oriented toward both the human body and the abstract mobility of capital. An interesting parallel here is the displacement of psychoanalysis effected by Nicolas Abraham and Maria Torok's rereading of Freud's Wolf

Man case history, itself a study of infantile neurosis (the very syndrome at stake in the fetishization of excrement). In *The Wolf Man's Magic Word: A Cryptonomy* (1986), Abraham and Torok discredit Freud's interpretation of the Wolf Man's neurosis, attributing the patient's disorder not to the trauma of the primal scene but to episodes of childhood sexual abuse. Derrida (1986) explains that Abraham and Torok install a "crypt" within the discourses of psychoanalysis, a strange locus that upsets the Freudian mapping of the body through the ego. A crypt is an unlocatable topography, hidden by being placeless, by being everywhere and nowhere. Just as Derrida understands the cryptonomy of Abraham and Torok to upset the logic of psychoanalysis, so the encryption methods of the money launderer (from secret words to complex systems of cybernetic coding) unsettle the workings of global capitalism. It is pointless to imagine the launderer's treasure buried beneath an identifiable point on the earth — X marks the spot! The money launderer's practice positions itself as a hidden interior to the global financial system, but at the same time outside it, external to the rules of regulation and equitable exchange. Behind the claim to launder money lies a complex geography of the unlocatable.

For all this, the business of money laundering would be impossible in the absence of modern geopolitical divisions, if only because these map out jurisdictions where the investment of illegally earned capital goes unpoliced. As Leyshon and Thrift (1997) argue, world finance remains dependent on geography, as spatial demarcations continue to structure monetary movements. There are dangers in the argument that the deterritorialization of abstract flows points to a transcendence of inherited borders and assumed divides, whether at the scale of the body or of the globe. Spivak (2000) worries that Deleuze and Guattari's understanding of capitalism conceals a last-ditch metaphysical longing: "Deleuze and Guattari's fantastic insight, that capital was...the abstract as such and capital*ism* codes it — is no longer sufficient....Finance capital cannot operate without interruption by the empirical" (30). For Spivak, the empirical stands for indigenous/rural land and the embodied female subject, while interruption is identified as "the 'irony' of the main text of global regularization...the systematic undoing, in other words, of the abstract" (31). My reading of the deabstracting of finance capital through money laundering, the emptying of the specularized world market on to the body and biopower, performs a similar ironic interruption. The money launderer produces a new abstraction, but this abstraction is at once doubled and concrete, free-floating and separated from its content but never cleansed of matter's dead weight, the very stuff of life.

Lee and LiPuma (2002, 208) argue that "capitalist social relations are no longer mediated only by labor, but also by risk" — an observation that acquires new meaning in light of the Enron bankruptcy, which demonstrates how risk and choice are unevenly distributed under global capitalism. (Those who were at risk made no real choice to be so, while the corporate managers who were aware of the risks acted to protect themselves.) But whatever the distribution of risk under global capitalism, it is in the last instance impossible to cleanse finance capital of its connections to the earth and the body. A focus on the global drug economy means that such a return to ground must center on a particular kind of indigenous/rural space and a particular kind of embodied subject: the indigenous/rural space of the Golden Triangle and the heroin-addicted body of the junky.

Earlier I argued that the Golden Triangle displaces the borders of contemporary geopower, disrupting the cartographic divisions of modern space through the combined effect of indigenous and global formations. By claiming that money laundering involves a rhetorical movement that questions inside/outside conceptions of the body, I suggest that this interruption of mapping protocols also disrupts organic notions of selfhood and corporeality. To trace the connection between the geographical displacements of the Golden Triangle and the bodily dislocations associated with money laundering it is necessary to refocus attention on drugs. While not all money laundering activity derives from drug trafficking, there is an indisputable link between the underground narcotics trade and the business of financial subterfuge. Both involve an attempt to evade official techniques of surveillance and mapping and both problematize unitary conceptions of the human body. In the case of money laundering, this renegotiation of corporeality is metaphorical, involving a contestation of the psychoanalytic identification of money with excrement. By contrast, the impact of drugs upon the body is physical and literal. The addict enters into a relationship of dependence upon the narcotic substance, flustering the inside/outside divisions that underlie dominant regimes of bodily hygiene. In this sense, the work of money laundering finds embodiment in the practices of the drug addict. For as the heroin addicted body requires a constant replenishment of the drug so global capitalism is hooked on the circulation of laundered money. There is no way to flush the system. Whatever objections governments or legal institutions may have to money laundering, the market itself has no interest in its control. Regulatory bodies can only do so much to prevent this practice without restricting the programs of trade liberalization and financial deregulation that are the hallmarks of capitalist globalization.

Trainspotting

"Ah'm just lettin it wash all over me, or wash through me ... clean me oot fae the inside. The internal sea. The problem is that this beautiful ocean carries with it loads ay poisonous flotsam and jetsam ... that poison diluted by the sea, but once the ocean rolls out, it leaves the shite behind, inside mae body" (Welsh 1993, 14). There is an undeniable link between heroin addiction, regimes of health, and the fear of contagion that surrounds contemporary epidemics. Drugs impact directly on the body, drawing it into the disposal systems of the postmodern age, promising pleasure, tranquilizing desire, and making repetition out of compulsion. Within seconds of heroin entering the body, it sends out alkaloids that attach themselves to neurotransmitter receptors in the brain. If the drug is injected, it causes a euphoric rush, often compared to a heightened sexual orgasm, which lasts a couple of minutes. Once the heroin has bathed the brain, it is distributed throughout the bloodstream and converted to the more usable form of morphine. In its molecular structure, morphine closely resembles that of the endorphins, naturally occurring feel-good chemicals manufactured by the brain. The activation of the neurotransmitter receptors by endorphins regulates many functions within the body, including pain perception, internal temperature, appetite, sexual behavior, and blood pressure. Because morphine molecules attach themselves to the same receptor sites as these endorphins, they can mimic their effects, suppressing the transmission of pain impulses within the nervous system, changing moods, and inducing a pleasant, drowsy state with a heightened sense of awareness. Over time, the repeated use of heroin changes the brain, producing an overabundance of endorphin receptors and causing the body to become physically dependent on an external supply of the drug. The user, who requires a daily dosage just to feel normal, enters the condition known as addiction.

While debate rages over the physiology of addiction and the politics of classifying it as a disease, there can be no doubt that the heroin users expose themselves to multiple dangers. Not least among these is the possibility of HIV infection — up to 50 percent of addicts in the Golden Triangle test HIV positive (Porter 1997). In recent years, advanced capitalist societies have attempted to manage this risk by policing the flow of fluids into and out of the body. Nowhere more than in the discourses of queer theory has there been an effort to expose and challenge these processes of regulation, which aim to protect the male heterosexual body from a series of perceived threats. For instance, the contributors to *Fluid Exchanges* (J. Miller 1992), a Canadian volume on AIDS, strive to imagine an alternative relation of fluids to the body, questioning the mapping of a clear demarcation between the body's inside and outside. But while much of the work in queer theory has sought to save sex, to reclaim the fluidity of *jouissance* in the face of this Foucauldian surveillance, there has been no correlative attempt to save drugs. The reasons for this are complex.

Drugs certainly do induce bodily pleasure, flowing into the bloodstream with a rush that might likewise question unitary notions of identity and corporeality. They also play a central role in acts of social transgression, offering instant and radical change from the doldrums of everyday life. Yet while drugs bring the addict immediate pleasure, they also produce dissatisfaction and craving. The temporality of addiction is radically discontinuous. As William Burroughs explains in *Junky* (1977, 87): "A junky runs on junk time. When his junk is cut off, the clock runs down and stops. All he can do is hang on and wait for non-junk time to start. A sick junky has no escape from external time." Drugs carry a utopian promise (it is important not to forget or discount this), but they also offer limited potential for transformative political action. The addict has no way of bridging between the ecstatic time of intoxication and the external time of historical narrativity, except by the privation of withdrawal. This does not mean that drugs cannot be the agents of resistance, the means by which users opt out of the temporality of work discipline and its attendant ethics of productivity and efficiency. Ultimately, however, the addict remains encased in capitalist rationality, even if she stretches this logic to its limit.

Heroin produces an economy of excess, an exorbitant expenditure without reserve. It inserts the user into a network of uncontrollable transactions, both capital and corporeal. Drugs foil the processes of economic and legal regulation, pushing capitalism to the outer reaches of its own fantasy and inducing a crash economy that threatens to destabilize the system as a whole. The addict, we might say, suffers a budget deficit. But this is not a problem that can be solved by tight fiscal policy. For financial constraints can be overcome, perhaps by theft or prostitution. From the viewpoint of prevention, the economics of addiction is distinctly supply-side. Stop the flow of heroin and the addict will withdraw; increase the flow and addiction will rapidly multiply. To raise the question of drugs is thus to raise the question of consumption.

The nexus of heroin and consumption is perhaps most neatly explored in Ann Marlowe's *How to Stop Time: Heroin from A to Z* (1999). Wall-Street-banker-cum-East-Village-junky, Marlowe understands her seven-year heroin habit not in the context of biochemical necessity but in relation to the large-scale transformations in capitalism since the 1970s. Noting that opiate addiction was not considered a social problem in the United States prior to the Vietnam War, she links the rising popularity of the drug to the arbitrariness of time under consumer capitalism. Digital culture, MTV, and video technology, she argues, have interrupted the unconscious assumption of time's linearity, enveloping the most trivial and the most tragic events in a banal timelessness that is always accessible, constantly flickering before our eyes. But biological rhythms remain constant, and thus people become anxious about the passing of time, seeking a means of arranging their days in the absence of an externally imposed social rhythm. Heroin supplies a solution. The drug induces a harsh chronology, providing the user with a compelling means of organizing her life on an hourly basis. Contrary to popular wisdom, Marlowe suggests that heroin does not make the user greedy and money-centered. Rather she contends that heroin addiction is a disease of those who are best suited to capitalist rationality. Using the drug may be the ultimate expression of rebellion, but it's still a purchase and the user is still a consumer. Centering a life on heroin addiction is not so different to centering a life on shopping or Wall Street dealing. The activity is the same, only the aesthetic is different.

Marlowe's antiabject account of recreational heroin use has received harsh criticism for its focus on the privileged urban recreational user, always in control and never short of a dollar. But it highlights a neglected link between the culture of heroin addiction and the culture of capitalist consumption. As Avital Ronnel (1992, 63) explains in *Crack Wars: Literature, Addiction, Mania*, her elegant poesis of addiction: "Drugs make us ask what it means to consume anything, anything at all." For Ronnel, drugs are to consumption as capital is to production. Just as the addict searches for heroin with a zealot's avidity, so capital scans the globe in search of ever-increasing opportunities for investment and return. This is the syndrome we call economic globalization. But if drugs give us special access to the question of consumption, surely they must reveal something about the formations of culture in the contemporary world. After all, as Daniel Miller argues in *Acknowledging Consumption* (1995), the issue of consumption opens cultural theory to the question of global/local relations, expunging a latent primitivism from its methodological assumptions. The threat of consumption to any mode of cultural inquiry that constructs its object as other is made clear in the famous comic strip that shows archetypal natives stowing away televisions and other conspicuous commodities because "the anthropologists are coming." What then can drugs tell us about the vital questions of globalization and transculturation?

The World on Drugs

The editors of the volume *Global Modernities* (Featherstone, Lash, and Robertson 1995) identify two schools of globalization theorists: the homogenizers or world-systems theorists (who understand the global capitalist system as a totality organized by center/periphery relations) and the heterogenizers (who refuse to recognize local particulars in relation to global universals, approaching globalization as a more chaotic process of cultural hybridization). World-systems theory, as classically elaborated in the work of Immanuel Wallerstein (1974), derives from a peculiar combination of *Annales* school historiography and that branch of Latin American political economy known as dependency theory. It traces the historical development of capitalism by dividing the international market into a dominant core, a dependent periphery, and a mediating semiperiphery. By this model, the workings of global capitalism drive the histories of classes and nation-states. Actors rarely appear to act on the system, but are acted on by it. Transferred to the debate about cultural consumption, as in the work of the anthropologist Jonathan Friedman (1995), this approach finds consumer identity to be constructed by the structural nature of core-periphery relations (via processes of integration, assimilation, and fragmentation). By contrast, the heterogenizers stress consumer activity and discrimination in the politics of cultural reception. Popular culture is made at the user's end, consumption and pleasure can be practices of resistance, and global audiences form hybrid identities by the local appropriation of transcultural forms. This mode of theorizing, which is readily associated with cultural studies, derives its impetus from a blend of poststructuralist theory, postcolonial studies, and psychoanalytic notions of desire (particularly as filtered through the project of feminist screen studies). There are thus two dominant approaches to globalization: the first rooted in a notion of consumer need or dependency and the second appealing to consumer desire, fantasy, or passion.

The shared assumptions of these homogenizing and heterogenizing theories are obvious in their means of describing the techniques of consumption. Behind the debate on consumption has lurked the question of drugs. For dependency theory the analogy has always been implicit, as in the title of Eduardo Galleano's classic study of Latin American neocolonialism, *Open Veins of Latin America* (1973). Similarly, communications scholars, who tend to subscribe to the heterogenizing position, characterize the theory of mass consumption (by which audiences passively receive media messages) as the "hypodermic needle theory of culture" (Fiske and Hartley 1978, 74–76). If one takes seriously the link between drugs and consumption, the divide between these homogenizing and heterogenizing theories begins to dissolve. Drugs expose the complex and contradictory nature of consumption under late capitalism. On the one hand, they produce bodily pleasures that can be transgressive and empowering. But on the other hand, they subject the addict to the most dominating, manipulative, and exploitative aspects of the market. As Ronnel (1992, 59) writes, drugs "have globalized a massive instance of destructive *jouissance.*" Reflecting on the addict's craving for external supplements, she claims "the distinction, so rigorously maintained in the Hegelian Lacan, between need and desire, may be the luxury of the sober" (135). If this is the case, there can no longer be a clear divide between homogenizing theories of globalization based on notions of need or dependency and heterogenizing theories that emphasize the hybridizing effects of consumer desire. Thinking about the relation of drugs to consumption implies a reassessment of contemporary theories of globalization and of the larger assumptions about space, culture, and power that underlie them.

To claim that drugs collapse homogenizing and heterogenizing models of globalization is to affirm a recent series of theoretical investigations that find transnational relations to be subject simultaneously to processes of integration and differentiation. By this view the global and the local are interdependent, mutually constitutive categories, which interrupt and amplify transnational flows of people, commodities, culture, and information (Robertson 1995; Hannerz 1996; Wilson and Dissanayake 1996). But to understand the workings of globalization in relation to the underground drug economy is also to question the ability of the local to reconcile homogenizing and heterogenizing perspectives. I have argued that the elusive mobility of drugs displaces familiar conceptions of the local, problematizing both scalar methods of cartographic projection and organic models of the human body. Whether the local is understood as geographical placement, bodily experience, or as a more complex charting of passages through the world, it requires a mapping of space. As Harvey (1996, 111–12) explains: "All talk about 'situatedness,' 'location' and 'positionality' is meaningless without a mapping of the space in which those situations, locations and positions occur." But the mapping of the Golden Triangle is continually interrupted by an encounter with the unmappable. After all if the drug economy could be clearly charted, it would not be an underground economy. Flows of drugs could be routinely interdicted and money laundering could be effectively controlled. The Golden Triangle flusters the logic of localization, interrupting the techniques of surveillance that isolate it as a source area for the global drug trade. While the work of demystification usually demands an engagement with local practices, this is a space that upsets the vogue for celebrating the local as the site of resistance and agency (Featherstone 1996).

Such a geographical indeterminacy does not obscure the Triangle's constitution through social processes. The Golden Triangle is not a purely discursive construct or what Lefebvre (1991) would call a "representational space," a space lived only through its association with symbols and signs. Unlike the unmappable loci identified by poststructuralist critics in literary and philosophical texts, it is at once real and imagined, material and metaphorical. As ephemeral as it may appear, the Golden Triangle maintains a concrete presence on the earth's surface, producing flows that cannot be conceived in separation from the body. But this concreteness is something other than an activity of mapping that might delineate the space of the local. The Golden Triangle represents a writing of global space — a geo-graphy that cannot be abstracted from its textuality but that at the same time encompasses realms of everyday life. The utility of this space for rethinking the workings of globality is that it introduces not an either/or but a both/and to the difficult articulation of poststructuralist theories of textuality to Marxist theories of socially produced space.

It is not a question of the Triangle providing a stable ground upon which to contest capital's reorganization of global space. Rather, the Triangle registers the constant removal of grounds, the sweeping away of foundational certainties upon which to construct alternatives to the dominant narrative of capitalist triumphalism. This lack of grounds should be understood as the condition of political action rather than as a retreat into rhetoric and discursivity. As Keenan (1997) argues, it is only when grounds are uncertain, temporary, or unstable that real political choices must be confronted. Far from licensing a retreat from politics, the removal of grounds forces a confrontation with the materiality of the world, an entry into the widening field of social struggles via the terrain of the imagination and desiring-production. At stake is not the endless repetition of deconstructive maneuvers that never completely displace the forms of power they contest, but the realization that deconstruction is, in effect, exhausted — providing not the endpoint but the precondition for any meaningful politics. In a world where deconstruction has been played out, it is necessary to identify new forms of resistance, practices of counterpower that make their geographical mark in nonnational, uncontainable spaces such as the Golden Triangle.

By characterizing the Golden Triangle as an attempt to map the unmappable, it becomes possible to question the received wisdom by which mapping is a conventional, nondialectical device that attempts to represent an independent reality. Such an approach draws attention to the potentially infinite variety of mapping systems and the relations of power that surround the decision to deploy one cartographic system rather than another. Yet by approaching different mapping systems as attempts to triangulate the same reality from different perspectives, this theory imputes complexity and structuration to the processes of cartographic representation alone. The extradiscursive ground of reality stands apart from writing technologies, essentially mute, the inert matter of fixity against which multiple cartographic projections are transformable into each other. The Golden Triangle cannot be assigned to such a nondifferentiated reality. One way of explaining this is to call upon the rhetorical or metaphorical agency of drugs, to highlight their capacity to distort reality or to produce a multitude of realities. As I have suggested, this brings the question of mapping back to the human body, displacing the inside/outside divisions that have traditionally constituted its integrity. Another means of explaining this situation is to highlight the incommensurability of the spatialities that surround the Golden Triangle (indigenous, modern, and global space), exploring their ability to set up radically different identifications of entities, places, and social relations. These incommensurate spatialities cannot be readily transformed into one another.

Indeed the preeminence of the Golden Triangle as a drug-producing area attests the continued instability of their relations. From this perspective, the attempt to institute a single, dominant cartography by drawing a triangle around the area is a power-laden attempt to contain this multiplicity. But how does this power relate to the complex topographies of contemporary capitalism?

Drug Wars

Not accidentally did the capitalist powers declare war on drugs in the wake of the systemic crises that swept the world economy in the early 1970s. U.S. President Richard Nixon set the agenda for the drug war, making the heroin boom that resulted from the Vietnam War a central issue in his 1972 election campaign. In *Agency of Fear* (1977), Edward Jay Epstein argues that Nixon's drug war was first and foremost an effort to establish a private security apparatus that would extend his power beyond democratic limits. Among the presidential aides who orchestrated the drug war were many of the same people involved in the Watergate scandal: G. Gordon Liddy, John Erlichman, John Mitchell, and Egil Krogh. Liddy suggested that the best way to set up a security organization that could gather intelligence on internal and external political opponents would be to found an agency with the mission of protecting U.S. families from the heroin plague. Nixon instructed Erlichman and Krogh to establish such an agency under the name of the Office of Drug Abuse Law Enforcement. As the preliminary version of this narcotics bureau set about turning drugs into an election issue, its key members were also involved in organizing the Watergate break-ins. The paradoxical thing is that long after the Watergate conspirators were found out and imprisoned, the rhetoric and imagery that they had pioneered in the manipulation of the drugs issue retained its power. The notion that drug addiction needed to be fought as a war between states and traffickers, rather than treated as a public health problem, took a hold that has yet to be relinquished.

In the United States, the war against drugs gained momentum in 1976 when two suburban Atlanta parents, Keith Schuchard and Sue Rusche, founded Families in Action, a nationwide parents movement to fight drug use among teenagers. Politicians became wary of the fact that white suburban swing voters were eager consumers of a tough-on-drugs message. By the time Reagan took power in 1980, no holder of public office could afford to equivocate on the drugs issue. Nancy Reagan launched a public antidrugs campaign under the slogan "Just

Say No" as her husband attributed the social problems in U.S. cities to an epidemic of foreign narcotics. Meanwhile the CIA escalated its operations in Latin America, militarizing the drug war and prompting an unprecedented flow of cocaine into U.S. markets. With the focus on Latin America and the Nicaraguan Contras, the heroin trade was rapidly escalating in the Golden Triangle after the drought of 1978–80. Attempts at suppression forced the concentration of the traffic into the hands of a single warlord, Khun Sa, who was powerful enough to overcome the barriers imposed by national governments and law enforcement agencies. By 1990, when the U.S. government, now under the leadership of George Bush, issued a warrant for Kuhn Sa's arrest, this single figure controlled as much as 60 percent of the world's illicit opium supply.

Although meaningless as a practical exercise of law enforcement, the indictment of Kuhn Sa marked a strategic shift in the U.S. war on drugs. On the domestic front, Bush appointed the academic William Bennett as chief administrator of the government's antidrug efforts. Bennett's self-styled proselytizing articulated the war against drugs to the culture wars that flourished during the first Bush presidency, making opposition to the administration's increasingly ineffective drug suppression measures appear as a betrayal of a supposedly consistent set of national values. Despite this moral emphasis, police powers were extended and prisons began to overflow with drug offenders, a large proportion of them young African American males. There was also a rethinking of antidrug strategies in the international sphere. With the end of the Cold War and heralding of a new world order, the U.S.'s self-appointed role as global drug policeman supplied an important precedent for the political and military activities it would undertake over the next decade. Nationalist forms of popular culture marked out a new set of enemies for demonization. In Tom Clancy's military thriller *Clear and Present Danger* (1989), Jack Ryan, the CIA hero, battles with Colombian drug cartels, whereas in previous novels his agonists had been Soviet operatives. Drugs emerged as the symbol of everything that was antithetical to U.S. health, prosperity, and security: the agents of a deadly menace that threatened not only to pollute but also to literally destroy the national body.

Nor did this rhetoric quell under baby-boomer president Clinton, who sought to live down his politically disastrous "I never inhaled" comment by outdoing the Republican stance against drugs on every front. While Clinton continued antidrug military intervention in Latin America, the DEA stepped up its crop eradication programs in the

Thai areas on the Golden Triangle. This only further concentrated the Southeast Asian heroin industry in the hands of Khun Sa, who opened new trading routes through China and India. With Khun Sa's putative surrender in 1996, the United States was left to deal directly with Burma's military regime, which now controlled the heroin trade due to cease-fire agreements with minority insurgent groups. Clinton's second term was marked by struggles between the U.S. State Department and the combined force of the DEA and CIA regarding drug suppression in Burma. While the State Department engineered an international arms embargo and the suspension of international aid to Burma, the DEA and CIA continued to supply antinarcotics assistance to the military government. Caught between the international protocol of economic sanctions and the need to maintain covert intelligence operations on the ground, the U.S. antidrug effort became gridlocked, failing to slow the flow of heroin from the Golden Triangle during the late 1990s (D. Russell 2001). Meanwhile opium production was booming in Taliban-controlled Afghanistan, leading to a flood of the drug on Western markets. On the home front, Clinton oversaw the expansion of mandatory sentencing laws to the point where nearly 60 percent of federal and 25 percent of state prisoners were nonviolent drug offenders (Akiba 1997). Military personnel were drawn into domestic drug suppression, while federal, state, and local drug squads were collapsed into paramilitary task forces that seemed to act without the oversight of any particular agency. Finally, Clinton refused funding for needle exchange and other harm-reduction programs, despite the fact that several major studies commissioned by his own government recommended such measures as the only viable means of reducing HIV infection among intravenous drug users (Gorman and Weinberg 2001).

While the line separating legal-military from public health approaches to drug use has been particularly stark in the United States, the war against drugs has by no means been restricted to that particular nation-state. Countries like Switzerland, the Netherlands, the United Kingdom, and Australia have had more progressive approaches to needle exchange and harm-reduction programs, but they also maintain harsh penalties for the dealing and use of heroin and other opium derivatives. Even the Netherlands, which tolerates the sale of small amounts of marijuana and has successfully experimented with medical maintenance programs for heroin addicts, is signatory to EU agreements that criminalize drug trafficking and aim to reduce supply through crop eradication in producer nations (Dorn, Jepsen,

and Savona 1996). In Australia, drug policy shifted toward harm min-
imization following the 1984 federal election, when Prime Minister
Bob Hawke cried on national television after being asked about the
heroin addiction of his daughter. But the subsequent social marketing
campaign, The Drug Offensive, deployed shock tactics that reinforced
the demonized image of drugs. More recently, conservative prime minister John Howard launched a Tough on Drugs policy that wound
back many of the harm-reduction measures introduced by Hawke
and his Labor Party successor Paul Keating, channeling funds into
customs and military services while flatly rejecting the possibility of
heroin-maintenance programs (Van den Boogert and Davidoff 1999).
Meanwhile, in the drug-producing nations, international pressure tied
the receipt of aid to a willingness to participate in crop eradication.
Since the 1980s, conditional aid packages, extradition treaties, the
financing and advising of police forces, and direct military pressure
have been the primary means by which producer nations are forced to
comply with drug war imperatives. Alongside these measures, there
has been a strengthening of informal ties between police, military,
and intelligence agencies (Anderson and den Boer 1994). While such
efforts attempt to limit the destabilizing effects of the drug economy, they also strengthen the coercive powers of state apparatuses,
restricting the sovereignty of individuals, peoples, and nations by subordinating them to a complex network of antidrug alliances that have
no clear center and no obvious end.

Whatever the relative merits of harm reduction as opposed to criminal and military approaches to the drug problem, the drug war has
strategic, biopolitical, and economic consequences that extend well
beyond its effects on individual users. As Noam Chomsky comments
in an interview with Veit (1998), what is at stake is an issue of population control. In the United States, the war against drugs stimulates
fear of the social underclass — those people who are superfluous to
the business of profit making and wealth creation. Zero-tolerance
policing and mandatory-sentencing legislation discriminate against
impoverished sections of the community, deepening ingrained racial
divides. Not only does this remove entire segments of the urban
population from public circulation, apparently alleviating the social
problems caused by an increasing inequality in wealth distribution,
but it also prompts further profit making in the crime-control and
security industry, a state-funded sector that feeds off the military
system. Attempts to oppose this biopolitical control can quickly be
written off as moral laxity, especially in the wake of the stringent

antidrug rhetoric spearheaded by Bennett and others during the first Bush presidency.

Concentrating on the arguments offered by Bennett in *The Devaluing of America* (1992), Connolly (1999) suggests that the war against drugs cannot be effectively understood if approached solely as an attempt to solve the problem of drug use. If that were the case, it would suffice to point to the increasing consumption of illicit drugs throughout the world to demonstrate the failure of the strategies deployed against traffickers and users. Rather the drug war "concentrates and defines a series of vague, shifting resentments and anxieties in everyday life" (106) — uncertainties associated with phenomena such as the loss of working-class jobs, shifting demographic and linguistic trends, the disempowerment of national workforces under globalization, and the reduced power of the state before transnational forces. According to Connolly, what is involved in the drug war is an effort to renationalize the United States in the face of internal and external forces that dislocate the spiritual vision of the nation as a macrocosm of moral individuals. Drugs provide an appropriate foil to anchor and contain these anxieties, not least because of their transnational mobility and demonstrable effects upon addicts. Thus the image of the regular citizen is lined up against a series of agents that supposedly devalue the national ethos: "university intellectuals, liberal journalists and politicians, moderate school administrators, poor black residents of the inner city, illicit-drug users, drug dealers, welfare recipients, philosophical police chiefs, and convicted felons" (102). Each of these constituencies is rhetorically associated with the others on the list — the most negatively marked (drug dealers and prisoners) casting suspicion upon everything said and done by the others in opposition to the war on drugs.

The pattern is repeated wherever the drug war thrives. Thus in Australia, the attempt to reclaim a lost nationalism through the war on drugs is articulated to longstanding historical fears of Asian invasion — instantiated for the first seventy-two years of the twentieth century in the White Australia policy (an immigration restriction act that selected migrants by race) and continued today with mandatory detention of asylum seekers from central and Southeast Asia (Burke 2001). Not only does nationalist antidrug rhetoric implicitly point to the Asian geographical origins of drugs like heroin and to stereotypical images of Asians as drug peddlers (a standard of xenophobic Australian nationalism since the early twentieth century), but it also reinforces racist opposition to Asian migration such as that promoted by the nationalist populist political organization One Nation in the late 1990s (Khoo 2000). Similarly in Europe, antidrug rhetoric often works in tandem with the Fortress Europa mentality. With the signing of antidrug protocols at the EU level, the figure of the drug runner has become increasingly identified with the non-EU citizen, *Ausländer,* or *extracomunitario:* Albanian clansmen, Kosovar fighters, Russian gangsters, or Nigerian couriers. Such an association finds official confirmation in the General Declaration accompanying the 1986 Single Europe Act, which asserts "the right of member states to take such measures as they consider necessary for the purpose of controlling immigration from third countries, crime, the traffic in drugs" (European Union Online 2001). Antidrug measures thus become strongly articulated to populist anti-immigration measures, whether of the more inflammatory variety promoted by far-right organizations like Jorg Haider's Freedom Party in Austria, Jean-Marie LePen's National Front in France, and Umberto Bossi's Lega Nord in Italy or the more run-of-the-mill variety (involving stringency against asylum seekers) practiced by almost every major political party in western Europe.

The war against drugs is a response to the problems faced by states in dealing with the loss of their authority in a globalizing world. The end of the Cold War, regional integration, and neoliberal market reforms have produced new patterns of hierarchy and dominance, leading to a more fragmented competition for power and wealth. Against this background, there has also occurred an internationalization of crime and law enforcement. States have been forced to expand their policing powers beyond national borders to match the transnational connections and technological capabilities of criminal organizations. For Van der Veen (1999), the mutual interactions between criminal networks and coercive state agencies are reminiscent of the way in which the superpowers exerted control over their spheres of influence during the Cold War, although in this case the parties are not separated by geographical boundaries. But if, as he suggests, the drug war involves the substitution of the red scare that spurred the Cold War with new agents of fear and corruption, there can be in this case no triumphant rhetoric of victory over evil. Central to the celebratory rhetoric of capitalist globalization is the claim that the defeat of communism in the Cold War opened new vistas of liberal democracy, free trade, and economic opportunity. The relation of the drug war to global capitalism is more complex and ambiguous, since while it is a war that cannot be won, the battle continues. At stake is a struggle over changing forms of sovereignty that cannot be understood in separation from the regimes of transnational mobility, trade liberalization, and financial exchange fostered by capitalist globalization. From the start, the war against drugs involved the extension of state police powers beyond national territorial jurisdictions. Thus Nixon's drug war occasioned the formation of the DEA, the first narcotics agency with responsibility not only for the enforcement of domestic drug laws but also for the global coordination and pursuit of U.S. antidrug operations. Today, the drug war is one of the main legitimation venues by which states strengthen and enhance their powers to intervene, both on the national and global scales.

While to date there exists no international criminal justice system to meet the challenge of drug trafficking, the drug war allows states to reinvent themselves as deterritorialized sovereign powers on a par with transnational corporations and criminal networks. To fight transnational trafficking organizations, law enforcement agencies enter into systematic and symbiotic networks with these same actors, often compromising their integrity and indirectly fueling the drug economy. When successful, drug suppression leads to the escalation of street prices, and with these increased rewards, more people are attracted into the drug trade. Effective repression also means that drug entrepreneurs must protect themselves from detection and prosecution. This leads to rises in the costs to hire protection, decentralize production, recruit money launderers, and bribe state officials. Consequently, the drug war fuels not only the growth of the global drug economy but also the redistribution of the wealth generated by that industry (with funds continually siphoned away from drug-producing nations and redirected to the economies of the wealthy capitalist world). The problem is exacerbated by the fact that many drug enforcement agencies are partly or entirely self-financing. Police are actively drawn into trafficking rings, setting up front stores for criminal organizations or conducting buy-and-bust operations that extend their powers beyond jurisdictional boundaries and democratic controls. Furthermore, in many countries, alliances between drug-trafficking organizations, intelligence agencies, and political parties serve in the suppression of domestic opposition, the destabilization of foreign governments, and the marshaling of support against geopolitical enemies (Block 1986; McCoy 1991; Scott and Marshall 1991). The line between drug industry operatives and drug enforcement agents thus becomes increasingly thin. These parties acquire mutual interests, as both are symptoms of a redistribution of wealth, power, and security that takes place on every geographical scale and through every possible technological medium.

In the wake of the September 2001 attacks on New York City and Washington, D.C., the drug war also provides the most immediate precedent for the new global struggle against terror. Encompassing intelligence and counterintelligence activities, global and domestic policing, overt and covert military operations, money-laundering control, and the strengthening of ties between all of the above, the so-called war on terror not only adopts the strategies of the drug war but also borrows its moral rhetoric, nationalist fervor, and strict speech codes. Indeed, in the Afghan theater of operations, the struggles coalesce, finding a common enemy in the remnants of Taliban resistance, even if U.S. officials have been hard pressed to connect the Al Qaeda network accused of planning the attacks with the heroin trade (Meier 2001). Both the drug war and the war on terror present themselves as crusades against a manifest evil that is at the same time secretive, an enemy given to strategies of hiding and subterfuge that supposedly attest both its cunning intelligence and uncivilized barbarity.

Clearly drug-trafficking and terrorist activities have devastating consequences for human life. But the struggles against them are part of a more general crisis of sovereignty and remapping of geopolitical power on the global scale. At one level, these battles reflect the efforts of territorial states to maintain their position of power in a world where sovereignty is increasingly manifest in flexible deterritorialized networks. While the disciplinary power of the modern state aimed to isolate and close off territories, postmodern security measures presume opening and globalization, seeking not to produce order so much as to regulate disorder. As Agamben (2001) argues, the gradual surrender of the state's traditional duties (the provision of public goods such as education, welfare, and health care) leaves security to emerge as the basic principle of state activity and the sole criterion of political legitimation. Locked into a struggle with drug-trafficking and terrorist networks, the state becomes ever more like these organizations, leading to the formation of a single deadly system in which the actors justify and legitimate each other. Thus the need for strict moralist rhetoric and biopolitical control to demonize the enemy and discredit all criticism as an attack upon the health, security, and prosperity of the nation.

At the outset of the war against terror, a struggle that promises to shape strategic, economic, and political transformations over the next decade, it would seem salutary to remember the failures of the drug war and its entanglement with capitalist globalization. If, as I have argued, capital is the abstraction to which the body of world capitalism is addicted, then the global drug economy cannot be neatly abstracted from the contemporary world-system. Drugs feed the desire for a truly global marketplace since their illegality protects them from state-based systems of economic regulation: tariffs, taxes, and the like. But they also register the impossibility of this realization, the danger posed to capitalism by its own thirst for profit, growth, and acceleration. The addicted body appears as a cipher of global capitalism, at once the register of an ecstatic time that strikes out against capitalist rationalization and an abject reminder of capital's capacity to corrupt; its rupturing of productive forms of communality and impeding of life's generative power. At stake in the mapping of the Golden Triangle is something more than an attempt to localize or isolate a source for the global drug economy. The indeterminacy of this space reveals something about the elusiveness of transnational capital itself, particularly in relation to moral and legal systems of regulation and biopolitical regimes of control. Within the processes of capitalist globalization lies a counterforce of addiction that challenges the assumptions of free agency and rational choice that underlie our dominant models of economic, political, and ethical behavior. The Golden Triangle stands as a cartographic reminder of capital's addictive capacity, an unmappable space that demonstrates why a capitalist world must also be a world on drugs.

Four

Outside Shangri-La:
The Lost Horizon of Tibet

> The *outside* is not another space that resides beyond a determi-
> nate space, but rather, it is the passage, the exteriority that gives
> it access — in a word, it is its face, its *eidos.*
> — Giorgio Agamben, *The Coming Community*

Toward the end of James Hilton's *Lost Horizon* (1933), the novel
that unleashes the Shangri-La myth into the space of Western popular
culture, the High Lama has a vision of a future global cataclysm:

> It will be such a one, my son, as the world has not seen be-
> fore. There will be no safety by arms, no help from authority,
> no answer in science. It will rage till every flower of culture is
> trampled, and all human things are leveled in a vast chaos (198).

Only places "either too secret to be found or too humble to be noticed," the High Lama declares, will be spared, and "Shangri-La may
hope to be both of these" (199). Death will come to the world's
great cities from above, leaving only those sanctuaries that deliberately exclude themselves from transnational connections free from the
scourge. The High Lama is quite certain as to the means of destruction
and exclusion: "The airman bearing loads of death to the great cities
will not pass our way, and if by chance he should he may not consider us worth a bomb" (199). If Shangri-La is not saved by its absence
from the maps of global power, it will simply be passed over due to its
lack of pretension and strategic import. Hilton's mountain hideout is
a kind of nonglobal city — a place inaccessible to transnational flows,
a security haven beyond the fallout of global terror and chaos. Here,
time passes sweetly, and the inhabitants enjoy prolonged youth and
happiness, partly because the society's surplus is channeled into the
system of monasticism, yielding not economic but spiritual growth.

Shangri-La is an outside to the inside of world trade, communication, and military might. Or is it?

From the start, Hilton's antiglobal allegory focuses on the logistics of air control and hijacking. Poised at the nexus of the jet-age and de-colonization, *Lost Horizon* begins with a conversation between three British travelers at Berlin's Tempelhof airport. They remember the disappearance of a high-altitude survey aircraft during the evacuation of Baskul, an imperial outpost in China, stormed by rebels the previous year. Almost immediately, the narrative cuts to the chase, as Hugh Conway, a cool-mannered diplomat marked to become British foreign secretary, and three other Westerners, board the plane. Instead of heading to Peshawar, the aircraft diverts north toward Tibet, making a precarious landing to refuel, and eventually depositing the asylum seekers at the gates of Shangri-La, a hidden city unknown to the world at large. Here, Conway and his associates gradually warm to life's simple pleasures. The diplomat enters a deep repose, and it becomes evident that his abduction has been meticulously planned, part of the High Lama's scheme to make him leader of the isolated utopian community. But Shangri-La is not quite so cut off from the world as initially appears. The city is really a vast repository of world culture or what Richards (1993) describes as an imperial archive state, a place where Buddhist monks safeguard "treasures that museums and millionaires alike would have bargained for" (Hilton 1933, 94). Structured by a strict hierarchy, the society functions at the command of a "central intelligence" (177) or, to adopt a phrase from Georges Bataille (1991), by a system of demilitarized totalitarianism. The High Lama turns out to be a Belgian cleric, Father Perrault, who has inhab-ited the city since the eighteenth century, instructing his functionaries to collect and preserve precious cultural artifacts from around the world, so as to protect them from an impending catastrophe. In this sense, Shangri-La contains the global in the local, even if the High Lama's vision is ultimately unable to captivate Conway, who cuts loose from the highland paradise, and is left to wander aimlessly, uncertain of nationality and incapable of settling down.

Inside the outside or outside the inside? Shangri-La exhibits an acute ambivalence as regards its positioning in global regimes of power, capital, and knowledge. Presenting itself both as a refuge un-tainted by the ways of the world and as a storehouse that safeguards the world's cultural treasures, Shangri-La and its myth cannot extract themselves from the complexities of globalism and globality. The situ-ation is even more perplexing if one considers the positioning of Tibet, the geographical entity most frequently associated with Shangri-La, on contemporary maps of geopower. Imagined as a pristine site of Buddhist spiritualism, Shangri-La provides a means of envisioning the pre-1959 Tibet, before the Chinese invasion and the subsequent repression of Tibetan cultural traditions. The myth thus bolsters the Free Tibet movement, suggesting not only that the Chinese have wrought ethnocide upon a minority national group but that they have also destroyed a way of life that provides a general panacea to the ills of the world. Clearly the Shangri-La myth perpetuates Orientalist visions of Tibetan innocence and peacefulness. But not all Tibetan nationalists discourage this stereotyping, partly because it marshals support among Western sympathizers and reflects their own cultural tradition, which speaks of a hidden city called Shambhala, accessible only to those who have accumulated spiritual merit. There is no easy way to disentangle the Shangri-La myth from this Tibetan cultural tradition. Nor is it possible to extricate the myth from world politics and economics, particularly those aspects of the global political economy that impact most directly upon Tibet — the growing importance of China as a market for consumer goods and the role of human rights politics in global trade negotiations. What are the risks and possibilities in imagining a space outside of globalization, and what do they tell us about the vexed geopolitical circumstances of contemporary Tibet?

The Hollywood-Lhasa Axis

Hilton's *Lost Horizon* is a landmark text in popular culture, since it marks the appearance of the mass-market paperback in the United States. In 1938, Pocket Books introduced its first twenty-five-cent book, Pearl Buck's *The Good Earth*, sold in an unnumbered test edition at Macy's in New York. The following year, Pocket released ten further titles in runs of ten thousand, beginning with *Lost Horizon*. Although paperback publishing dates back to the nineteenth century in Europe (editions such as Routledge's Railway Classics were available in Victorian Britain), it was not until 1935, when Allen Lane founded Penguin Books, that the medium emerged as a vehicle of mass publishing (Morpurgo 1979). Pocket's release of *Lost Horizon* was an attempt to replicate Penguin's success on the other side of the Atlantic, making affordable volumes of popular literature available in quotidian contexts where books had previously not been sold: newsstands, grocery stores, drugstores, railway stations. But the marketing success of *Lost Horizon* cannot be attributed solely to an imitation of the Penguin formula, since the product's popularity was linked to the release of a film version of Hilton's novel, Frank Capra's *Lost Horizon* (1937). In an important sense, *Lost Horizon* was the first movie tie-in novel, building on the uptake of Capra's film among cinema audiences. The film's message of social moderation had struck a chord with filmgoers who sought a release from the economic and cultural hardships of the 1930s. World depression, the rise of fascism, ethnic persecution in Europe — all led to a disillusion with the promises of secular modernity. Capra was one of the first big Hollywood directors to denounce fascism and its persecution of minorities, and *Lost Horizon* is generally supposed to embody his opposition to the unfolding events in Hitler's Germany (McBride 1992). Under his direction, Shangri-La becomes the space of Hollywood melodrama, complete with a soft-focus romance subplot, comic homophobic undertones, and a spectacular set that imitates the architectural style of Frank Lloyd Wright. But the film also has more sinister elements, relating to the racial and social hierarchy that structures the imagined utopian community. As in Hilton's novel, Shangri-La is an elitist art colony, where compliant Asian servants serve leisured whites. L. Russell (2001) is not alone in suggesting that Capra's classic implicitly endorses the reactionary ideology that the director publicly opposed.

Whatever the ideological complexities of Capra's *Lost Horizon*, the film marks Hollywood's colonization of the Shangri-La myth, its integration into the seemingly limitless reserve that comprises the popular cultural imagination. Although the film was shot on a Hollywood back lot, the studio dispatched a camera crew to get a process shot of the Ojai Valley, about two hours to the north of Los Angeles. From that time on the town of Ojai has advertised itself as the place where Hollywood imagined Shangri-La, producing guides that direct tourists to the spot where Ronald Coleman supposedly stared down on the mythical Tibetan hideaway, attracting spiritualist organizations like the Krotona Institute for Theosophy and the Krishnamurti Foundation, and even suggesting itself as the site for other popular cultural dramas such as the 1970s sci-fi/spy thrillers *The Six Million Dollar Man* and *The Bionic Woman*. But this perpetuation of the Shangri-La ethos is not restricted to the geographical sites where Capra shot his film. The myth is endlessly recycled within and between popular media, whether in the name of the 1960s girl group the Shangri-Las (singers of "Leader of the Pack") or in the advertising images for the Shangri-La group of hotels and resorts, the largest luxury hotel chain in the Asia-Pacific. By 1973, it is no surprise to find a nostalgic Hollywood remake of *Lost Horizon*. Directed by Charles Jarrott, this box-office bomb retooled Capra's Great Depression allegory for the oil crisis, setting it to a high camp soundtrack by Burt Bacharach and Hal David. Even today, the theme of a hidden Asian paradise haunts popular film: for example, Danny Boyle's 2000 production of Alex Garland's novel *The Beach* (1995), starring Leonardo DiCaprio, which deals with a hidden community of young European backpackers on a remote island in the Gulf of Thailand.

More specifically, the Shangri-La myth reemerges in popular cultural materials that engage the troubled history of modern Tibet. Exemplary in this regard is *Shangri-La: The Return to the World of "Lost Horizon"* (1996), written by Tibetan independence advocates Eleanor Cooney and Daniel Altieri. Set amid the Chinese Cultural Revolution, the novel supposes that Conway, who at the end of Hilton's narrative searches for a way back to Shangri-La, has become High Lama. Barely aged, he risks his life and health by leaving the city to stave off General Zhang of the People's Liberation Army, who is poised to attack Tibet and purge it of all things holy. Conway diverts Zhang with a series of false clues. But in so doing, he falls in love with the general's daughter, Ma Li, who is also the novel's narrator. The story ends with Ma Li embarking on her own search for Shangri-La, where she hopes to be reunited with her lost lover. Combining the fantasy element of Hilton's novel with a political allegory concerning China's occupation of Tibet, Cooney and Altieri articulate mythical notions of Shangri-La to the current political struggle over Tibet. In particular, they collapse Hilton's utopian vision with the historical reality of preinvasion Tibet, representing it as an untouched site of Buddhist authenticity and contrasting this view with a demonic anti-communist portrayal of the Chinese invaders (good Asians versus bad Asians).

There is a real need to understand the complexity of intercultural relations in contemporary Tibet without resorting to such stark moral contrasts. In *Virtual Tibet* (2000), Orville Schell contrasts the realities of life in Chinese-occupied Tibet with the utopian elements of the Shangri-La myth. Concentrating on pro-Tibetan Hollywood films, most prominently Jean-Jacques Annaud's *Seven Years in Tibet* (1997) and Martin Scorsese's *Kundun* (1997), Schell places these fantasies in a long line of Western representations of Tibet, dating back to the accounts of seventeenth-century Jesuits. He identifies three main historical figures responsible for perpetuating fantastic visions of Tibet. The first is the Theosophist Madame Helena Blavatsky, who claimed to have clairvoyant communications with ancient Tibetan spiritual leaders. Second is Sir Francis Younghusband, the British military commander who led an expeditionary force to Lhasa in 1904. And third is Heinrich Harrer, the Nazi mountaineer who spent seven years in Tibet after escaping from a British POW camp during World War II. In the case of Younghusband, who was bitterly disappointed upon his arrival in Lhasa, it was only upon return to Britain that he retreated into mysticism, profoundly changed by his experience in Tibet. Lhasa had long been imagined as an inaccessible and forbidden city, and Younghusband's success in reaching it fired the Western imagination. Similarly in the case of Harrer, whose *Seven Years in Tibet* (1953) provides the basis for Annaud's film, it was the geographical isolation of Tibet that made it a safe haven from the British. Only after two years of trekking did the mountaineer reach Lhasa, where he became mentor to the young Dalai Lama, undergoing a deep personal transformation before fleeing the Chinese invasion of 1951. Schell argues that the continued inaccessibility of Tibet under Chinese domination ensured that the fantasies of Harrer and others remained imprinted on the Western imagination until the area was opened to tourism in the late 1980s. With the opening of Tibet, however, the Shangri-La myth offered an irresistible means of contrasting the ethnocidal conditions of the Chinese occupation. Films such as *Seven Years in Tibet* and *Kundun* deliberately seek to build support for the Free Tibet movement in the wealthy capitalist world, contrasting a sentimental portrayal of traditional Tibetan life with a depiction of the Chinese invaders as the agents of a tyrannous modernity. To this extent, they counter the official Chinese vision of Tibet, equally a construction, as the site of a backward and corrupt theocracy.

These big budget Hollywood productions are only one link in what Van Biema (1997) calls the Hollywood-Lhasa axis. Among Hollywood celebrities, silver-haired poster boy Richard Gere pioneered the embrace of Tibetan Buddhism, making his most heavy-handed anti-Chinese performance in *Red Corner* (1997), where he plays a U.S. businessman wrongfully accused of murdering a Beijing club girl. Dozens of celebrities have followed in Gere's footsteps, including Harrison Ford, Tina Turner, Herbie Hancock, Courtney Love, and Beastie Boys punk-rapper Adam Yauch, architect of two Tibet Freedom concerts that sparked off a late 1990s fashion trend known as Tibet Chic. Perhaps most bizarre among Hollywood's Tibetan Buddhist converts is the action star Steven Segal, recognized in February 1997 as the reincarnated Tulku of the Nyingma line of Tibetan Buddhism, a school

Richard Gere attending Kalachakra Initiation in Ulan Bator, Mongolia, 1995.
Photograph by Keng Leck. Source: www.kalachakra.com.

older than the Dalai Lama's. Other prominent U.S. Buddha boosters
are Chicago Bulls coach Phil Jackson, author of *Sacred Hoops* (1995),
a spiritual guide for basketball players, and Robert Thurman, professor of Tibetan studies at Columbia University, translator of Padma
Sambhava's *Tibetan Book of the Dead* (1994), and father of the actress Uma Thurman. Like Hilton, these figures tend to view Tibet as
the cure for a corrupt and ever-dissolving Western civilization, a direct link to ancient Buddhist traditions. But they also remain painfully
aware that present-day Tibet is nothing like Shangri-La, having been

overrun by Han Chinese settlers, stripped of its religious institutions, and, as recently as October 1998, officially recognized by the Dalai Lama as part of China.

In theory, China tolerates Tibetan Buddhism, just as it tolerates the Islam practiced by the Uighurs in its northwest Xinjiang Province. But in practice, this tolerance restricts itself to the most superficial aspects of Tibetan culture like festivals and performances, which are highly scrutinized and disconnected from grassroots political and re-ligious movements. Since 1959, when the Chinese gained complete political control of Tibet and the Dalai Lama fled to Dharamsala in northeast India, Buddhist religious practice has been systematically repressed. At first this repression took the form of ideological legit-imation or "re-education," the dominant mode of coercion during the Cultural Revolution, but it quickly gave way to intimidation and the outright use of force (W. W. Smith 1994). The violence peaked in March 1988, when security forces crushed a riot involving over two thousand Tibetans in Lhasa, leaving an estimated sixteen dead. Today Tibetans form an ethnic minority in their own homeland. They have been outnumbered by Chinese soldiers, entrepreneurs, volunteer im-migrants, and unofficial settlers to whom the authorities turn a blind eye. China has invested heavily in Tibet's infrastructure, intensifying economic exploitation of the area's natural resources, including vast deposits of oil and uranium. But while many Tibetans welcome the modern conveniences that have come with the Chinese colonization, they also complain that this development has predominantly benefited the immigrant population. Nervous about potential revolt, Beijing has stepped up its policy of Sinicization, suppressing religious activity and interfering in the selection of religious representatives. Buddhist monks and nuns are now the activists and dissenters of Tibetan soci-ety, routinely imprisoned and tortured for their stance against Chinese domination. Under these circumstances, the interest of Hollywood celebrities in Tibetan Buddhism becomes the most powerful weapon in the struggle against the Chinese. By means of this alliance, Tibetan nationalists in exile have generated global publicity for their cause, albeit by assenting to a mode of representation that identifies their culture with Shangri-La.

What is the peculiar status of the geographical entity of Shangri-La that it can become a crucial signifier in the geopolitical dispute sur-rounding Tibet and China? In Hilton's *Lost Horizon,* Shangri-La is a place so isolated that it remains unaffected by the outside world, a site immune to the forces of global disorder that the High Lama predicts

A truck of Chinese soldiers passes prostrate Tibetan pilgrims in Lhasa. Photograph by Manuel Bauer. Reprinted by permission of Manuel Bauer and Lookat.

toward the end of the book. The myth projects a powerful utopian vision that, filtered through the lens of Hollywood representation, folds back on to Tibet itself, or at least on to an imagined version of Tibet, before or after the period of Chinese domination. *Lost Horizon* is an appropriate name for Hilton's novel, since the narrative implies a nostalgia for a utopianism that once appeared on the horizon of possibility but has now receded from sight, a version of what Jameson (1991) calls utopianism after the end of utopia.

At the present juncture of global capitalism, the possibility of an outside to globalization presents itself as a necessary fiction, at once a literal impossibility and a powerful tool of political imagination. If, as the term "global capitalism" implies, the market system spreads itself completely and uniformly across the earth's surface, then the prospect of an outside (of a site unmapped by global capital) not only contravenes the supposed totality of capitalist relations but also suggests an alternative. This is why the Shangri-La myth provides a privileged means of interrogating the political, economic, and cultural dimensions of capitalist globalization. Global forces undoubtedly impact upon the China-Tibet situation, but, at the same time, the projected vision of Tibet as a pristine site of spiritual-cultural authenticity shapes hopes and desires for the transformation of the contemporary world-system. The irony is that these desires cannot completely extricate themselves from capitalist rationality, since the dream of overcoming global capitalism from the outside must eventually run up against the realization that the system is most vulnerable from within.

Searching for the Outside

In an article titled "Sites of Resistance in the Global Economy" (1995), Masao Miyoshi argues for the importance of maintaining a belief in a space outside of globalization. Globalization, he contends, does not recognize an outside by definition, and, to this extent, it mirrors the claim that nothing exists outside of discourse attributed to poststructuralism by its critics. Theorists who draw on poststructuralist models argue that diasporic or transnational flows disrupt established systems of meaning, identity, and value. For Miyoshi, this disruptive capacity does nothing to destabilize the operations of global capitalism, which itself operates according to a flexible logic of differentiation. Thus the importance of maintaining a materiality outside of language or a space outside of globalization from which the work of resisting capitalism might begin.

> As discourse presumably enables all presences, and nothing exists outside discourse, so there would be nothing outside of the "global" economy. In other words, discursive inclusivity and political-economic integration would be both unbounded, leaving out nothing — or rather, leaving no "outside" space for any "other" idea/object to exist. Such a discursive and political-economic extension, however, can be no more than a sheer fantasy.... The "global" economy is, in fact, nothing but a strategy for exclusion. Exactly in the same way, the discourse is coextensive strictly with the discourser's interest. Despite Wittgenstein and Foucault, there is always an outside to language and discourse. And to the extent that the money and production flow is beneficial only to the privileged few and inaccessible to the rest, resistance is not only possible but inevitable. Discourse must acknowledge the idea of resistance and opposition (71).

Miyoshi identifies the claim for capitalism's unbounded geographical expansion as a "sheer fantasy," contrasting it with an extra-discursive reality that provides a basis for resistance and opposition.

Such an argument implicitly reproduces the theory of false representation, which recognizes the distortions of ideology only by positing an outside to language and discourse. The difficulty with this approach is its appeal to a strict division between discourse and reality, and its subsequent relegation of all resistance to a space that sits outside of and is protected from the global flows of capital. Such a strategy obscures and even negates the real alternatives and potentials for change that arise from within the transformative capacities of capitalism itself. Miyoshi's polemic is directed as much toward those who argue that the destabilization of capitalism will occur from within as it is toward the exclusionary operations of the capitalist world-system itself. Despite his argument, it is entirely possible to identify a space outside of globalization and to acknowledge the inevitability of resistance and opposition, without subscribing to the full positivity of an extradiscursive ground.

One reason for the decline of the theory of false representation is a loss of faith in scientific objectivism and a subsequent blurring of ideology and nonideology. Once the rhetorico-discursive operations of a text are recognized as irreducible, there can be no extradiscursive ground from which the critique of ideology might proceed. In "The Death and Resurrection of the Theory of Ideology" (1997), Ernesto Laclau redesigns the theory of ideology to accommodate this predicament. He argues that reality cannot speak without discursive mediations. But he also contends that the notion of an extra-ideological viewpoint is the ideological distortion par excellence. Consequently, the notion of ideological distortion becomes the cornerstone for dismantling any claim to stand outside of ideology and discourse. Laclau explains that this does not mean "that ideological critique is impossible — what is impossible is *a critique of ideology as such;* all critiques will be necessarily intra-ideological" (299). By this argument, the claim for an outside to globalization would be just as mythical or fantastic as the claim for capital's total domination of the earth, but no less capable of providing a strategy for resistance and opposition than the appeal to extradiscursive reality.

The approach that understands myth as a potential form of social resistance has a complex history, extending from Roland Barthes's (1972) semiotic readings of everyday cultural practices to more recent accounts of popular culture as a set of resistant reading strategies (Fiske 1989). Within this tradition, however, relatively little work has examined the way in which popular discourses map out spaces on the earth's surface. Such an investigation is crucial to a project that explores the significance of popular mythographies for an oppositional account of capitalist globalization. It is generally recognized that globalization involves a compression of space and time through such factors as technology, economics, political representations, and cultural influences. Following Lefebvre (1991), who understands space as both a social product and the most important matrix of social relations, globalization theorists have asked how capitalism remaps the earth's surface. The possibility of a space outside of globalization raises the prospect of an alternative mapping of the world that intersects the capitalist production of space while departing significantly from it. This is why the myth of Shangri-La must be understood as at once ideological and nonideological, mapping out a geographical space that is clearly imagined but whose reality can be denied only from an scientific-objectivist perspective that disavows the cultural legitimacy of popular belief, feeling, and religion.

The Shangri-La myth conjures up the task of imagining a space outside of globalization, and although it is the stuff of fiction and fantasy, it does this in an immediately material way, since, in its present cultural-political articulation, the myth is inseparable from the geopolitical conflict surrounding Tibet. This is not to claim that Tibet is Shangri-La or that Shangri-La is Tibet, since one of the key aspects of this remote spiritual refuge is its geographical indeterminacy or unlocatability. Hilton situates Shangri-La in the Kun-Lun Mountains in Tibet's desolate north, but the physical location of this highland paradise is less important than the fact that it is hidden, inaccessible to even the most advanced cartographic technologies. It is possible to account for this in topographical terms, pointing to the unnegotiability of mountainous terrain, the likelihood of hidden valleys, and so forth. Thus the myth's proponents recite numerous stories that suggest the existence of an undiscovered valley in the Tibetan highlands. The Orientalist Alexandra David-Neel, who dressed as a Tibetan to hide her true identity, relates one such story in *The Superhuman Life of Gesar of Ling* (1934). She recalls an encounter with a wandering bard in the eastern Tibetan town of Jyekundo. As the story goes, she asked this man, who regularly ventured into the mountains, to carry a small bunch of paper flowers as an offering to the gods. Upon his return, he presented her with a blue flower of the type found only in Southern Tibet during the summer. As the temperature in Jyekundo was twenty degrees below zero at the time, David-Neel suggests that the bard must have visited an unknown valley, perhaps the site of a secret society of spiritual initiates.

Narratives of this kind point to the physical existence of a fertile valley that remains unmapped by the contemporary regimes of geopower. But a more radical claim asserts that this hidden realm is accessible only to those with the appropriate spiritual disposition. By this argument, the location of Shangri-La is determined not by physical but by metaphysical principles and conditions. While it has a physical existence, the materiality of this mysterious realm is knowable only to a dedicated few, who commit themselves to a life of peace, simplicity, and meditation. As a consequence, Shangri-La can be detached from the physical territory of Tibet, becoming a sign of longevity, joy, and other stereotypical qualities associated with stereotypical ideals of Buddhist simplicity and antimodernity, even if these attributes are clearly lacking among Tibetan communities both at home and in the diaspora.

The name Shangri-La circulates as a label for numerous Chinese restaurants, apartment buildings, hotels, tour companies, shopping malls, and holiday resorts in a variety of geographical locations. At one time it even served as the name for Franklin D. Roosevelt's Maryland retreat, later renamed Camp David. But despite the term's dissemination as a moniker for hospitality enterprises and works of vernacular architecture, it maintains a privileged link with Tibet. The myth of Shangri-La's inaccessibility doubtless relates to the difficulties surrounding the initial geographical survey of Tibet, which during the nineteenth century remained closed to both British and Russian cartographers. To map this inaccessible highland area the British sent Indian spies dressed as Buddhist monks into Tibet, equipping them with miniaturized surveying instruments concealed in secret pockets, staffs, and false-bottomed chests. Captain Montgomerie, the official in charge of the expedition, instructed these so-called pundits to estimate distances using body-based units such as paces and to record their measurements by adjusting beads on a Buddhist rosary. Although the British forces that invaded Tibet with Younghusband in 1903–4 altered Montgomerie's maps, they represent an important turning point in modern cartography. Constructed by means of a mobile paradigm of surveillance, these early maps of Tibet displaced the dominant technique of cartographic projection that assumed the existence of a static, neutral, and panoptic point of observation. As Richards (1993, 17) explains, Montgomerie's methods raised the possibility of "a global system of domination through circulation, an apparatus for controlling territory" not by occupying it but "by producing, distributing, and controlling information about it." In this aspect, the Shangri-La myth foreshadows the current era of globalization, in which information itself becomes a commodity and source of power, both in the territorial and extraterritorial senses.

This historical detail appears more than fortuitous when one considers the present-day cultural-political situation of Tibet. It is easy to point to the ways in which the Shangri-La myth romanticizes and idealizes Tibet, particularly in the context of the Chinese invasion and ethnocide. Nonetheless, any attempt to demythologize Tibet, to debunk the Shangri-La myth with a catalog of facts, risks reproducing the imperialist fantasy of control through the production and dissemination of information. As Laclau argues of the theory of false representation, the search for the real Tibet, beyond representation, itself partakes in ideological distortions, which purport to transparently map an extradiscursive ground — an external reality beyond the grip of religion or popular sentiment. The important questions about the Shangri-La myth concern not its veracity or falsity (issues that might be resolved only at the level of belief) but its uses. These, I suggest, are highly ambiguous, leading both to dangerous stereotypes of Tibetan naiveté and to utopian dreams of an outside to globalization.

Tibetology and Orientalism

Scholars such as Peter Bishop in *The Myth of Shangri-La* (1989) and Donald Lopez in *Prisoners of Shangri-La* (1998) contend that the Shangri-La myth perpetuates a series of fantasies about Tibet as a site of secret mystical knowledge. These fantasies are common to both British imperial travel writing and contemporary New Age spiritualism. An important crossover point here is Madame Blavatsky and the late nineteenth-century Theosophists who understood Shangri-La (or Shambhala as they called it following Tibetan tradition) as the seat of universal knowledge and source of a pure Aryan culture. Madame Blavatsky claimed to have spent seven years in Tibet as an initiate of a secret order called the Great White Brotherhood. Throughout her career, she believed herself to be in esoteric communication with the Masters of this Brotherhood, whom she called the Mahatmas, sometimes through dreams and visions but also through mysterious letters that materialized in her cabinet. Supposedly written by the Grand Master of the Brotherhood, Mahatma Koot Hoomi, one of these letters, which reputedly appeared in her cabinet in 1880, describes Tibetans as "a moral, pure hearted, simple people, unblest with civilization" and their homeland as "the last corner of the globe not so entirely corrupted as to preclude the mingling together of the two atmospheres — the physical and the spiritual" (Barker 1948, 434). Clearly Blavatsky's vision of Tibet exerted a strong influence on subsequent generations of Theosophists. But Bishop and Lopez suggest that this sentimentalism also colored the less esoteric, more academic tradition of Tibetology. Both thinkers approach the Shangri-La myth under the rubric of Orientalism, claiming that the association of Tibet with Shangri-La serves to deny Tibetans their historical agency. This argument must be taken seriously, not least because it finds confirmation in the work of contemporary Tibetan intellectuals (Shakya 1991). The construction of Tibet as a site of ancient guarded wisdom buys into fantasies of spiritual patrimony that reinforce elitist notions of knowledge transmission. It also institutes a strict divide between Tibet and the West, understanding this split as a gulf between modernity and its others.

Perhaps the most influential twentieth-century figure to view Tibet as the seat of ancient spiritual knowledge was Nicholas Roerich, Russian-born painter, mystic, and initiator of the Roerich Pact, an international agreement obligating nations to respect monuments and cultural institutions during times of war. Roerich was a member of the League of Nations and was entrusted by that organization with a fragment of the so-called Chintamani Stone, which he believed to be part of a meteorite from a solar system in the constellation of Orion. In 1923, he set out on an expedition to find the hidden city of Shambhala with the hope of installing this stone at the center of the town. During this trek, which took him five years and traversed Xinjiang, Altai, Mongolia, and Tibet, he produced over five hundred paintings, the most prominent being a series of nineteen titled The Banners of the East, depicting the world's religious teachers (Mohammed, Christ, Moses, Confucius, Buddha) against spectacular mountain backgrounds. Roerich conceived his mission as a search for the common roots of human religious experience, recording his thoughts in works such as *Heart of Asia* (1929) and *Shambhala* (1990). Following Madame Blavatsky, whose *The Secret Doctrine* (1888) his wife had translated into Russian, he postulated that Shambhala was the headquarters of the Mahatmas, a secret brotherhood of spiritual masters who had access to the principles uniting all religious traditions. His travel diary, *Altai-Himalaya* (1929), relates an incident that supposedly took place in 1926, a few days after the consecration of a temple in Mongolia. High in the sky, Roerich spied a golden spherical body approaching rapidly from the north and then

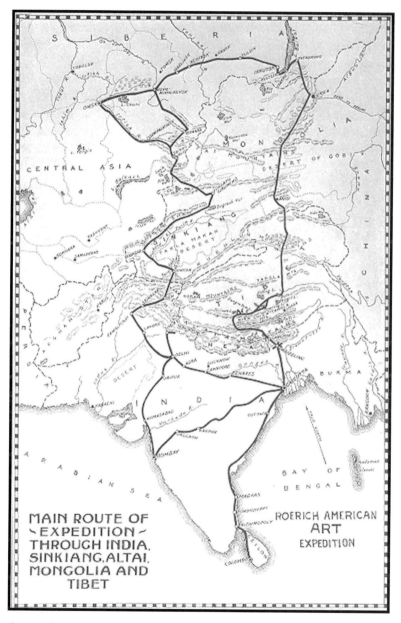

The search for Shambhala: the Roerich expedition of 1923–28. Reprinted by permission of the Nicholas Roerich Museum, Inc., New York.

suddenly veering southwest toward Tibet. Understanding this as a sign of Shambhala, he immediately struck camp and headed into Tibet's mountainous northwest. At a certain point, his guides refused to travel any further, but Roerich himself continued forward on a donkey. Reappearing after a few days, his escorts prostrated themselves before him, proclaiming that only a divine being could enter the kingdom of Shambhala. Although Roerich's account of this episode is cryptic and allegorical, followers have claimed to find hidden clues as to what happened to him during this time. One of the paintings produced during the expedition allegedly contains a cryptogram that shows Roerich's profile alongside a rocket or a wingless aircraft, suggesting that the artist's visit to Shambhala involved some form of advanced aerial travel.

Chief among the devotees to advance this version of Roerich's Shambhala experience is Andrew Tomas, author of *Shambhala: Oasis of Light* (1977). Following the theosophical tradition, Tomas posits the existence of the Brotherhood of the Wise, an international underground society of spiritual counselors, based in Shambhala and encompassing historical organizations such as the ancient Mystery cults and the Knights Templar. For Tomas, Shambhala is a sanctuary for initiate scientists and philosophers who have been forced to take refuge from societies that are unable to understand or tolerate their ideas. He explains that the work of this clandestine society becomes obvious in times of planetary crisis, when its adepts offer advice to world leaders on how to avoid destructive warfare, economic exploitation, and environmental disaster. In the final chapter of his book, "On the Threshold of the Cosmic Epoch," Tomas suggests that the most pressing task confronting the initiates of Shambhala is the formation of a world state that would pool all planetary resources, means of production, manpower, and scientific expertise. "The just distribution of planetary wealth," he writes, "must be vested in a world authority, not of demagogues but of scientists, scholars and philosophers, because science is essentially internationalistic while politics is nationalistic and religion is sectarian" (164). In this way, the Shangri-La myth provides the basis for a postnational scientific utopianism, which seeks to counter and prevent the kind of global disorder, inequality, and militarism foreshadowed by the High Lama in Hilton's *Lost Horizon*. Clearly, Tomas's cosmopolitan fantasy feeds dreams for a more peaceful, equitable, and environmentally sustainable world, even if it remains tied to statist modes of organization. But this ameliorative vision cannot be separated from stereotypical notions of Tibetan society and culture derived from Blavatsky, Roerich, and other esoteric sources. Consequently, it acquires a cultural-political meaning that works at cross-purposes to its utopian message. By associating Tibetan cultural practices with premodern spiritual traditions that supposedly offer salvation to the globalized world, Tomas effectively writes Tibet and the Tibetans out of modernity.

Lest this Orientalist rhetoric appear the inevitable price for the utopian appeal of the Shangri-La myth, it is worth remembering that the construction of Tibet as a pristinely preserved site of Buddhist authenticity corresponds only with a relatively recent stage of Western Buddhology. In the late nineteenth century, Buddhology was largely a philological discipline, based in the study of texts that documented the philosophy of reason and restraint spread by the Buddha in sixth-century BCE India. The leading British Orientalists of the late Victorian period sought to collect, edit, and translate texts originating in this so-called classical age of Buddhism. They imagined their task as the preservation of a tradition that had been long lost or corrupted, much like the ancient cultures of Greece, Rome, and Egypt. Almost all of these Victorian interpreters relied exclusively on a series of texts selected and edited by the Pali Text Society, an organization founded by Thomas W. Rhys Davids in 1881. Rhys Davids, the son of a Welsh Congregationalist Minister, advocated a mode of historicist exegesis that aimed to recover beliefs about the life of the Buddha as they had been at the time when these texts were composed. As Almond (1988, 3) explains, this involved a process of textualization by which "the essence of Buddhism came to be seen as expressed not 'out there' in the Orient, but in the West through the control of Buddhism's own textual past." Actually existing Buddhist beliefs and practices, particularly those associated with Tibet, were understood as degenerate offshoots of this original religion. Thus in his 1877 book *Buddhism*, Rhys Davids categorized Tibetan Buddhism as an altogether different belief system, giving it the name Lamaism and asserting that it was agonistic to the early Buddhist teachings. Central to his argument was the claim, elaborated by many before and after, that Lamaism resembled Roman Catholicism in its emphasis on ritual and sacerdotalism. By contrast, Rhys Davids suggested that the original Buddhism was akin to Protestantism, since it allowed rational intellectual inquiry without the mediation of the clergy. The philological approach to Buddhism thus served not only to establish textual control over a certain religious corpus, legitimating a sense of imperial ownership, but also to indirectly devalue Britain's European rivals and Irish subjects.

The parallel of Lamaism to Catholicism was developed further in the work of L. Austine Waddell. A British functionary in Sikkim from 1885 to 1895, Waddell learned about Tibetan Buddhism by purchasing a temple and then requiring its officiates to explain the rituals they performed. He also gained authority over his informants by leading them to believe that he was an incarnation of the Buddha, a deception that he willingly confided to his European readers. In *The Buddhism of Tibet, or Lamaism* (1895), Waddell followed Rhys Davids in describing Tibetan Buddhism as Lamaism. He argued that this religious practice resulted from the introduction of a corrupt Buddhism into Tibet and its subsequent melding with indigenous Bon traditions, including forms of demon worship. For him, Lamaism "is only thinly and imperfectly varnished over with Buddhist symbolism, beneath which the sinister growth of poly-demonist superstition darkly appears" (xi). But despite his rejection of Tibetan Buddhism as idolatry, Waddell was unable to dismiss it entirely, precisely because its existence legitimated his embrace of the original Buddhism. Having unsuccessfully tried to reach Lhasa in 1892, Waddell was evidently frustrated at his inability to penetrate the land whose religion the Tibetans themselves believed him to embody. Not until 1904 did he manage to enter the forbidden city. But on this occasion, he came not as a pilgrim but as chief medical officer with the Younghusband expedition, which left at least one thousand Tibetans dead in its wake. Apparently, Younghusband's securing of a trade agreement with Tibet raised Waddell's hopes for the British colonization of the territory. Needless to say, this colonization never occurred. But in his analysis of Lamaism, Waddell successfully constructed an ideological dominion over Tibet that might have served as the basis for such an imperial rule. As Lopez (1995, 263) observes, "many of the same characterizations of Tibetan Buddhism appear in Chinese discourse of the last four decades, serving as a justification to the west for the process of invasion, occupation, and colonization of Tibet by China."

Significantly, it was only with the Chinese occupation of Tibet that the dominant construction of Tibetan Buddhism as Lamaism began to shift. Following the Dalai Lama's flight to India in 1959, there arose widespread concern about the perilous condition of Tibetan religion and culture. This gave rise to a new understanding of Tibetan Buddhism as a particularly well-preserved variety of the religion. Unlike the other areas in which Buddhism had spread (India, China, Japan, and Southeast Asia), Tibet had never been colonized or opened to Western influence. For this reason, the preinvasion Tibet could be imagined as a closed society and Tibetan Buddhism as a form more authentic than any other. This viewpoint, which found confirmation in the discovery that Tibet preserved in translation the largest corpus of Indian Buddhist literature, readily echoed the colonialist fantasies of Tibetan exclusivism that ran throughout the theosophical tradition. A new generation of scholars, based largely in U.S. graduate schools, set about the task of rescuing Tibetan Buddhism from the ravages of history, translating texts and documenting the results of fieldwork in India. These researchers practiced a version of salvage ethnography, seeking to represent Tibetan Buddhist culture in the moment before its imminent loss. While often conducting their research among exiled Tibetan communities, their privileged objects of study were philosophical texts of the Tibetan scholastic curriculum. Having studied the Tibetan language, students would travel to India to receive instruction in these works from senior monks who had successfully completed the curriculum (about twenty years of study). Access to these scholars, who were usually old lamas trained in the monasteries of Tibet, was facilitated by making donations to the monks and supporting projects that were essential to the establishment of Tibetan religious institutions in India. The researchers were thus able to participate in Tibetan monastic life in a way that would have been impossible in the pre-1959 Tibet. The teaching of senior monks was deemed valuable as it carried the unspoken promise of transmitting the timeless and endangered knowledge imagined to have resided in Tibet prior to the Chinese invasion. The surviving elements of a disappearing cultural authenticity were thus located in terms of a spatial and temporal preserve, a vision of pre-1959 Tibet that reflected the remoteness and purity of Shangri-La.

Doubtless, this implicit appeal to the Shangri-La myth was a suppressed feature of academic Tibetology, relegated to the margins of acceptable scholarly discourse. Nonetheless, by approaching Tibetan Buddhism as an endangered practice unable to survive in the modern world, Buddhologists were effectively denying Tibetans a place in the emerging global system. Their work suffered from a compulsion to transcend the historical situatedness of both the observer and the observed, locking the researcher and his/her informants into an East/West binary that obscured the overlapping modernities that made their interaction possible. Not only did this fail to acknowledge the patterns of patronage that facilitated access to the teaching of senior monks, but it also usurped the authority of these monks, seeking to reclaim an endangered knowledge without recognizing that the researchers themselves had constructed this scenario of disappearing culture. The career of Donald Lopez is instructive in this regard since, among the U.S. Tibetologists trained during the Cold War era, he has been most critical of his own former practice.

In "Foreigner at the Lama's Feet" (1995), Lopez criticizes the chronopolitics of his earlier doctoral fieldwork, characterizing the tendency to view the pre-1959 Tibet as an atemporal civilization as New Age anthropology, no longer suited for serious academic discourse. This line of argument continues in *Prisoners of Shangri-La,* where Shangri-La becomes the prison that traps the Tibetan people, despite their willingness to accommodate and manipulate the myth to their own ends. Lopez asks what happens to Tibetans when they enter the diaspora, encountering in their everyday lives the modes of fantasy and invention that have led to the construction of their homeland as a timeless paradise. Exploring the Dalai Lama's denunciation of the worship of Shugden, a clan deity from eastern Tibet, he argues that it is only in the diaspora that Tibetans obtain a national consciousness. If the claim for an independent Tibet is to have any force, the Dalai Lama must suppress clan identities to forge a unified national culture. But because the Buddhism that enthuses Europeans and North Americans is represented as Tibet's universal inheritance to the world, the nationalist struggle must also deliberately cultivate the utopianism of the Shangri-La myth. Tibetan Buddhism thus begins to float "free from its site in a process of spiritual globalization that knows no national boundaries" (Lopez 1998, 200). Only through a complex process of doubling, by which the diasporic gaze on the homeland is reflected through Western fantasies, can the Tibetan nation be represented as unified, coherent, or complete.

It thus becomes incumbent upon the Tibetologist to counter the Shangri-La myth, asking how Western fantasies about Tibet have trapped Tibetan nationalists in a political paradox from which they are unable to escape. This is a task that Lopez pursues most succinctly in an article titled "New Age Orientalism: The Case of Tibet" (1994). Here he traces a direct line from late-nineteenth-century theosophical visions of Tibetan lamas as telepathic Mahatmas to contemporary New Age claims for Tibet as the center of an oppressed spiritual civilization. The underlying suggestion is that academic Tibetology must break free of its Orientalist illusions, which it is now its duty to expose. This is necessary not only for the sake of the Tibetans imprisoned by the Shangri-La myth but also for the preservation of Tibetology as an academic discipline. Rather than attempting to salvage the imperiled culture of Tibet, Tibetology must struggle to save itself, renouncing its former Orientalism, which can now be conveniently dismissed as New Age and dissociated from all worthwhile discussion of Tibet.

Lopez's argument must be commended for its self-critique, but, in offloading the formerly Orientalist elements of Tibetology on to the New Age movement, it neglects to analyze the politics of New Age culture itself. The article trades off the widespread academic distrust of New Age culture, as if the mobilization of this label alone were sufficient to disqualify it from serious consideration. Purged of its Orientalist elements, Tibetology enters the postcolonial moment, celebrating hybridity and diasporic movement as modes of destabilization that question former ethnographic certainties. Granted Lopez makes no claim to write from outside the prison of Shangri-La, but in exploring the confluence of scholarly and popular approaches to Tibet, he cannot help but evoke such an outside. Thus, while he offers no key to unlock language's prisonhouse, he hopes that "some may find a file with which to begin the slow work of sawing through the bars" (1998, 13). The question remains as to whether this outside is just another Shangri-La — the dream of a free and independent Tibet beyond discourse and outside the globalizing forces that keep the area under China's control. Lopez's argument effectively counters the romantic idealization of Tibet, seeking to build the case for Tibetan independence without falling prey to the Shangri-La romance. But in displacing the dialectic of same and other that structures Orientalist thought, he pays little attention to the dynamics of contemporary global power, which operate just as much through difference and disjuncture as through binary East/West oppositions.

It is insufficient to account for China's occupation of Tibet as a mode of colonization in the classical imperialist mode. Beijing's sovereign power is inseparable from the various population flows, military mobilizations, information vectors, and market forces that position China in the contemporary world-system. These transnational movements are complex and unpredictable, displaced from a single geographical center that, like the imperial metropolis of the nineteenth century, exerts disciplinary power over a sovereign territory. There are thus two axes of inquiry upon which it is necessary to interrogate the reduction of the Shangri-La myth to New Age Orientalism. First, there must be an attempt to understand the complex and contradictory politics of the New Age movement. For while New Age culture draws upon stereotypical ideals of Oriental wisdom and beneficence, it also represents a response to anxieties about official ideologies concerning growth and technology that have arisen, particularly in the wealthy capitalist world, over the past three decades. Second, it is necessary to ask how these anxieties articulate to transformations in the constitution of the world order, including the diminution of sovereign nation-state power and the globalization of the capitalist market. If, as I have suggested, Shangri-La represents the dream of an outside to globalization, then the prospect of escaping from Shangri-La raises the possibility that this outside is also an inside, not a determinate space outside the global system but a symptom of its passage, the mark of a transformation that arises from the heart of globalism itself.

New Age Politics

Ross (1991) argues that the New Age obsession with personal-spiritual expansion at once contests and reinforces dominant values concerning growth and development. This is to say that New Age culture questions the mainstream scientific-capitalist regime of knowledge while also deferring to its authority. For Ross, the New Age movement is at once alternative and middlebrow, attracting the derision of cultural intellectuals (who leap to discover resistance in more obviously popular cultural forms) while breeding the desire for "more democratic control of information and resources" (30). New Age practices produce a "cult of intelligence in a knowledge society" (35). Unlike science fiction, fantasy, or horror fans, whose reading practices teach them to perceive the appearance of a higher intelligence as a threat, New Agers understand such intelligence as a source of benign knowledge, necessary for both personal growth and the betterment of the world. The banality of this wisdom is a function of the movement's social constituency: non-expert, middle-class, economically comfortable, and predominantly white. But the New Age search for timeless knowledge is also a response to the uncertainties of life under global capitalism: the ever-growing culture of risk, the increasingly unmanageable turnover of information and technology, the chaotic patterning of global flows, and the growing instability of the environment. This opens the movement to a host of potentially critical positions: against centralized bureaucracies, against transnational business conglomerates, against environmentally destructive technologies, against strong nationalism, and against monolithic institutions in education, religion, and the family. In most cases, however, these radical impulses are contained at the level of personal transformation. Individual consciousness "becomes the source, rather than a major site, of socially oppressive structures, and the opportunities for a radical humanism are consequently lost" (71). But this emphasis on individualism also displays a certain inadequacy of the intellectual left — its inability to fashion a philosophy that would extend into a fully fledged ethics of action those elements of New Age personalism that arise from a critical response to technocratic society.

If one accepts this argument, it becomes necessary to examine the compromised cultural politics surrounding the New Age engagement with the Shangri-La myth, rather than simply dismissing it as Orientalist fantasy. A good place to start this project is with a consideration of a work by Australian Theosophist and mystic Victoria LePage, *Shambhala: The Fascinating Truth behind the Myth of Shangri-La* (1996). LePage's analysis of the Shangri-La myth reflects Ross's assessment of New Age politics, since she finds it to furnish the basis for an alternative science. Drawing on a wide range of popular and folkloric sources, including Nordic mythology, quantum physics, and UFO abduction narratives, she contends that "Shambhala is a real place with real geographical coordinates, but that it also contains a feature that by its very nature reveals itself only to mystical vision" (18). At stake is a "higher knowledge, a gnosis, that cannot be acquired from either organized religion or the current sciences," but that "opens up the possibility of acquiring a science that is, in brief, the knowledge of Reality itself" (238). LePage's primary source for this argument is René Guénon, a French scholar of Sufism whose 1927 book *Le Roi du Monde* proposes a remapping of the globe according to the chakric system of Kundalini yoga.

According to Guénon, Shambhala is a center of high evolutionary energies located somewhere in central Asia. This hidden city is a subtle accumulator of spiritual power, which is locked into the earth's center in the same way that Kundalini energy in its latent state is putatively locked into the root chakra at the base of the human spine. To validate this scheme of sacred geography or terrestrial Kundalini, LePage draws upon ancient Egyptian maps that locate what she calls a Heaven Pillar to the world's north. This Heaven Pillar supposedly corresponds with Mount Meru, the central peak of Shambhala and geographical pole of the World Axis, the supposed spiritual axis of the globe. As described by Guénon, the World Axis is a mobile stream of energy that extends from the earth's center into outer space, where it connects with a universal energy field by means of a giant spiritual

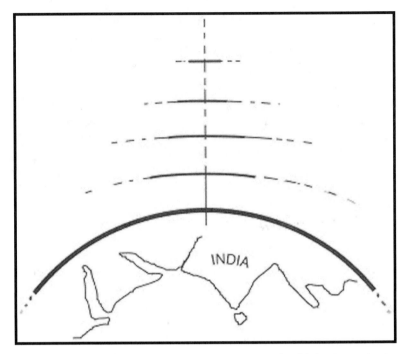

A clairvoyant view of the World Tree. From Victoria LePage, *Shambhala: The Fascinating Truth behind the Myth of Shangri-La* (Wheaton, Ill.: Quest Books, 1996); copyright 1996 Victoria LePage. Reprinted by permission of Quest Books and Victoria LePage.

antenna known as the World Tree. Despite the esoteric nature of this geographical scheme, LePage grounds her appeal to the Shangri-La myth in contemporary social, political, and environmental realities, announcing the need for a centering principle in a world of increasing global uncertainty:

Today we are aware that certitude has vanished. Now nothing is certain, and even the very concept of certainty is debatable. In a world in which all boundaries are dissolving, all values are becoming ambiguous, all sign-posts illegible; in which centrifugal forces of destruction are flinging us outward, unwinding civilization; and in which change and instability are endemic — in such a world as ours is today the need for a new centering principle is paramount. In every conceivable context — spiritual, ecological, political, social — our need is for a magnetic center, for a zone of order within the primeval chaos of possibilities. (3)

This invocation of global instability, dissolving boundaries, and centrifugal forces betrays a fundamental insecurity with the forces of globalization. LePage is not alone in viewing global transformations as productive of chaos and disorder. The tropes of unwinding civilization and unpredictable change are familiar from the High Lama's disquisition in Hilton's *Lost Horizon*. They also inform contemporary efforts to understand the global cultural economy. Thus Arjun Appadurai (1996, 47), the well-known theorist of transnational flows, explains that globalization relies on "images of flow and uncertainty, hence 'chaos,' rather than on older images of order, stability, and systemacity." LePage's response to this unstable predicament is to posit a zone of order, a space outside of globalization, which guarantees opportunities for personal-spiritual growth by offering shelter from the incertitude of political, ecological, and social change. It is easy to understand her argument in terms of Ross's (1991, 36) assessment of New Age culture as "a technology of therapeutic self-affirmation for people unsure about their place in the knowledge hierarchy, and who find a sense of communal purpose in responding to this teaching." LePage locates the possibility for social, political, and ecological betterment in a new definition of self and cosmos, buying into the New Age ethos of personal-spiritual development, by which changing the self provides a means of improving the world. As Ross observes, such a model of political transformation reflects a lack of available languages for linking subjectivity to larger social-structural change, attesting the need for the cultural left to articulate its analysis of the politics of everyday life to an analysis of the appeal of such social individualism. Nonetheless, the political meaning of LePage's encounter with the Shangri-La myth is not reducible to its Orientalist implications. Like other New Age mythologies, it acquires its political significance against a more finely grained network of conflicting ideological values, including a distrust of technical rationality, a commitment to personal-spiritual transformation, and a patronage of indigenous cultures.

To understand LePage's rewriting of the Shangri-La myth as an attempt to write the Tibetan people out of modernity is to misconstrue one of the book's fundamental structures of argument. For while her analysis examines the status of the myth within Tibetan Buddhism, it also attempts to ground its argument for the existence of Shangri-La in as wide a variety of cultural sources as possible. These include traditions often identified as Western (as inadequate a label as this may be), such as the myth of the tree of Yggdrasil, neo-Platonism, and Pythagorean esotericism. LePage refers freely to these traditions alongside Taoist philosophy, Australian Aboriginal dreamings, Sufi mysticism, Celtic druidism, and whatever other mythological sources from which she can infer the existence of a hidden spiritual realm. In general, the technique is one of induction (the more sources available, the more credible the existence of Shangri-La), feeding into the assumption of cultural universalism, in the manner of mythographers like Carl Jung or Joseph Campbell. Amid this slow accretion of evidence, the link between Tibet and Shangri-La is gradually diminished, if not eliminated. The point is that the concept of Orientalism is inadequate for analyzing the cultural politics surrounding LePage's construction of Shangri-La since the power differentials involved cannot be neatly mapped over an East/West divide.

The same is true of James Redfield's New Age adventure tale *The Secret of Shambhala* (1999). Building on previous allegories of spiritual growth, among them *The Celestine Prophecy* (1993), Redfield uses the narrative of a trip into Tibet's Kun-Lun Mountains as a vehicle to communicate various nuggets of New Age wisdom. Drawn to Tibet by the premonition of a friend's daughter, his search is both for the geographical site of Shambhala and for spiritual insights that might exceed and complement those achieved on previous adventures in the Andes and Appalachians. During the journey, a series of guides instruct him in a program of spiritual exercises known as The Four Extensions. These involve the cultivation of a personal energy and prayer field, the setting of this field to enhance the body's life flow, the utilization of these techniques to awaken the awareness of others, and the maintenance of a high-energy outflow that moves the human world toward a spiritual ideal. As Redfield masters these techniques and travels closer to Shambhala, he is pursued by the Chinese military. Much of his energy is devoted to defeating the anger he feels toward the Chinese for obstructing his passage and oppressing the spiritual civilization of Tibet. Indeed, overcoming his rage toward the Chinese becomes a precondition for his entry into Shambhala. When this finally occurs, he discovers it is an advanced society, which has moved beyond the global information economy to focus on purely spiritual matters. In the outer reaches of the kingdom, Redfield encounters new forms of thought-wave technology that allow individuals to create everything they need by the application of mental powers alone. He also meets an old man, the father of one of his guides, who lectures him about the misuse of technology in the contemporary world, including the genetic manipulation of food, the corporate control of the media, and the government monitoring of private activities. Like Father Perrault in Hilton's *Lost Horizon*, this would-be prophet forecasts an imminent global disorder:

> The growth toward a central, spiritless governmental authority, in a high-tech virtual world divorced from natural processes, where food, water, and the routines of living have been trivialized and distorted leads to disaster. When health is subverted into just one more commercial cycle of worsening food, new diseases, and more drugs, Armageddon is the result, and it has occurred several times in prehistory. It could happen again, only this time on a larger scale. (170)

At this point Redfield's narrative reaches a critical pitch. Not only is the high-tech virtual world held responsible for new forms of social control and surveillance, but it also allows the Chinese to track his presence in Shambhala. Ever since he sent an e-mail message before his departure from the United States, the Chinese have been on his case, and now it turns out that they plan to use his powers to appropriate the advanced spiritual technologies of Shambhala. But the society's elders have different ideas. As the Chinese attack, they establish a giant prayer field and the visitors are led into a monastery where they are placed before a spatial viewing window — a kind of spiritual computer screen that displays 3-D images with astounding verisimilitude. In this space, they see an image of the rotating globe, and in quick succession the scene shifts to various areas of the earth's surface. They zoom in on a conference where a couple cite the book of Revelation to sway delegates against security measures involving Internet tracking devices, retina and palm scans, and new alliances between computer corporations and intelligence services. Next, they witness a scene in which one teenage boy counsels another, convincing him not to commit a high school bombing. Subsequent scenes focus on problems related to the pharmaceutical industry, genetic engineering, political corruption, and religious conflict. Finally, the screen displays a fresh water spring near Redfield's suburban Florida home, and, as the Chinese attack, he steps back into familiar circumstances, joining with family, friends, and other white folks to pray for the liberation of Tibet.

With this transfer of Shambhala to suburban America, Redfield fabricates a spiritual authority to legitimate the various workshopping and marketing activities promoted on his Web site, CelestineVision.com. Visitors can enroll in seminars led by personalities such as Doreen

Virtue, angel therapist, and Carol Adrienne, numerologist and life coach. They can also purchase autographed books and CDs with the assurance that all profits go to forest-preservation charities. Trained as a counselor, Redfield's homegrown combination of adventure tale, self-help, and spiritual allegory has a vast middlebrow following. Every month, he publishes *The Celestine Journal,* an online magazine that comments on world events and counsels readers on how to cope with the traumas of global transformation. In the October 2001 edition, he writes an article titled "A Silver Lining: The Emergence of Worldwide Prayer Networks," dealing with the previous month's attacks on New York City and Washington, D.C.

These events, which Redfield understands to represent a global catastrophe of the order predicted by Hilton's High Lama, occasion a call for conscious intervention through prayerful communion and visualization. He advocates the raising of "a spiritual army devoted to peaceful intervention," a global prayer network "aimed at uplifting specific people and groups that world events suggest could be key players in the drama against terrorism." To this end, he links to a virtual prayer room, to which readers can click through and leave an online prayer. Redfield understands this prayer room as a specific technology of global transformation that, like the prayer network established by the inhabitants of Shambhala, will work by spiritual means to make the world a better place. Indeed, his call extends themes already present in *The Secret of Shambhala,* where one of his screen visions displays intelligence agents invoking the "fight against terrorism" to gain "access to every telephone line, including Internet communications, and secret identification devices in all computers" (212). The point is that Redfield's New Age voluntarism builds on the Internet and other existing digital technologies, which he believes have been misappropriated, to suggest an outside to capitalist globalization. Like LePage, he envisions an alternative science that wrests itself away from modern secularism to discover a transcendental domain that harbors fantasies and guarantees meaning. For him, the computer screen is nothing less than a window on to Shangri-La.

As Ross argues, technology supplies one of the primary arenas of the New Age struggle with conventional science. New Age culture is suspicious of any technology external to the body's holistic orbit. The life-energy of the mind-body-spirit continuum is supposedly self-sufficient, requiring no prosthetic intervention to maximize its evolutionary potential. In *The Secret of Shambhala,* Redfield explains, "technology has always been just a precursor for what could be done with the human mind alone" (143). People in the outer rings of Shambhala use technological prostheses only to amplify their prayer fields, while the adepts in the inner temples produce everything they need or want by prayer alone. With this claim for the body's intelligence and integration with the spiritual, social, and natural environments, there arises a discourse that parallels postmodern images of the cybernetic body. Life-energy becomes a conduit for information, and the technical fact of communication is celebrated as an inherent good. The New Age ethos thus affirms "features of modern corporate communications ideology," understanding "its will to wire up the world as if this were an evolutionary necessity" (Ross 1991, 35). For Redfield, the late capitalist shift toward the information and service economy is the evolutionary precondition for an increase in spiritual knowledge. The automatization of material production and provision of "just the right information at just the right time" means that everyone becomes "more intuitive and alert and focused on synchronistic perception as a way of life" (161). In this way, information technology supplies a gateway to the beyond, suggesting a means of piercing through the system of official science, which recognizes no outside. Thus as Redfield enters the inner sanctum of Shambhala, he encounters a kind of virtual space or screen without pixels, allowing both an instant global mobility and a spiritual escape from the uncertainties of militarism and world capitalism.

Numerous commentators have noted the spiritual investment that contemporary capitalism makes in information technology. Wertheim (1999) takes a skeptical approach to transcendent claims for cyberspace. She traces back to ancient Greek thinkers like Pythagoras and Plato the dualistic mentality that finds something unsatisfactory about this world and posits a better one elsewhere. According to her, Christianity deepens and legitimates this divide, making the other world the path to salvation and denouncing the living realm of the flesh as inherently fallen and sin-ridden. Wertheim thus views contemporary cyber-utopianism as a kind of religious revivalism, arguing that, like the Christian ethos to which it is indebted, it refuses to come to terms with the immanence of life on earth. Žižek (1997) builds a similar case. He claims that the current obsession with information technology is a function of a growing disenchantment with everyday life in the actually existing world. Cyberspace is a thoroughly technological-scientific phenomenon, but it involves the promise of a false opening, the spiritualist project of casting off the physical body to become a wholly virtual entity. Unlike Wertheim, for whom

Christianity provides the master logic of this fantasy, Žižek understands it in terms of the Shangri-La myth. In cyberspace, he writes, it
is as if "we encounter a Limit beyond which the mysterious domain
of phantasmic Otherness opens up, as if the screen of the interface is
today's version of the blank, of the unknown region in which we can
locate our own Shangri-las" (160). There is thus a certain resonance
between Žižek and Redfield, since both point to the equivalence of
the computer screen and the mythical realm of Shangri-La.

Where Žižek parts ways with Redfield is in his insistence that the
utopian allure of cyberspace reproduces the very structures of dominance from which it seeks an escape. Again, he explains this by
reference to the Shangri-La myth. According to Žižek, the Shangri-La
fantasy displays a basic paradox. The mystery of this hidden realm lies
in the fact that it delineates a space that has not yet been colonized, an
"imagined radical Otherness that forever eludes the colonizer's grasp"
(161). But at the heart of this phantasmic beyond, there lies another
form of imperial dominance — Hilton's Father Perrault, the white
master, who rules over compliant Asians as a benevolent theocratic
despot. Žižek contends that the utopianism of cyberspace becomes
caught in a similar conundrum. New Age storytellers like Redfield
imagine that cyberspace presages the next phase of evolution in which
each person will cut their substantial ties to their body and plug into
a new holistic mind. But this fantasy forecloses the social power relations that structure the way in which virtual communities actually
operate: the political decisions, institutional conditions, and market
mechanisms necessary for the functioning of a complex cybernetic system like the Internet. For Žižek, cyberspace, like Shangri-La, displays
the structure of the Moebius strip — "at the very heart of Otherness,
we encounter the other side of the Same, of our own structure of
masterhood" (161).

There can be little doubt that Redfield's spiritual-cybernetic vision also exhibits this Moebius strip structure. His screen memory of
Shambhala is ultimately inseparable from the commercial and institutional arrangements that allow a Web site like CelestineVision.com
to function both as a transnational marketing device and as the supposed hub of a global prayer network. Redfield's New Age vision of
Shambhala is not a function of the traditional open/closed universe,
with its structure of the limit and the phantasmic beyond (the place of
enchantment). Rather, his fantasy is a reaction to the disenchantment
inflicted by the global order of late capitalism, which by definition
recognizes no outside. It is not a matter of arguing that Shangri-La is

just another screen memory in a world in which all reality has become screen mediated. Nor is it a case of asserting that Redfield's virtual Tibet constructs a prison in which real Tibetans and their political struggles become entrapped. Neither of these positions captures the complexity of the New Age version of Shangri-La, which at once perpetuates dangerous stereotypes of Oriental peacefulness and wisdom and registers an ambivalent dissatisfaction with contemporary forms of technocracy, government, and capitalism. The difficulty with this New Age vision is its blindness to the contemporary geopolitical situation of Tibet, its inability to position the Tibet-China conflict within a wider global network. Such a project of contextualization must move beyond the mere critique of the Orientalist elements of New Age politics. To dismiss the New Age appropriation of Tibet on this basis alone is to risk substituting the Shangri-La myth with another equally problematic fantasy, no less rooted in an ideal of radical otherness — the vision of the Chinese invaders as agents of diabolical evil.

Free Tibet and Shambhala

Those who dismiss contemporary versions of the Shangri-La myth as New Age Orientalism need to account for the role of Tibetans in encouraging this fantastic vision of their homeland. Ever since the Dalai Lama fled to Dharamsala in 1959, the myth has been an important mediating point between Tibetan exile activists and their Western sympathizers. In the initial years of the diaspora, Tibetan exile communities were forced to rely on Western relief workers, travelers, and other sympathetic individuals for economic support. More recently, the establishment of centers for the teaching of Tibetan Buddhism in countries such as the United States, Switzerland, and Australia has resulted in the formation of a network of Western practitioners, a transnational *sangha* that offers financial support to Tibetan Buddhist institutions in exile. This cultivation of outside patrons, or *sbyin-bdags*, is consistent with the Tibetan cultural framework of *mchod-yon*, which involves the exchange of spiritual guidance for material and political support. As P. Christiaan Klieger explains in *Tibetan Nationalism: The Role of Patronage in the Accomplishment of a National Identity* (1992), a study involving extensive fieldwork in Dharamsala, there is no stigma for Tibetans in being the recipients of foreign patronage. Indeed, from the Buddhist perspective, there is honor in receiving patronage, since the client provides the patron with a vehicle by which the latter might accumulate spiritual merit. There has thus been a seemingly happy coincidence between the Buddhist practice of *mchod-yon* and the economic and political realities of Tibetan nationalism. Tibetan activists have obtained sufficient funding to build their struggle into a transnational political movement, employing strategies that involve computer-mediated communication, the fostering of alliances with NGOs, and the strategic positioning of the Dalai Lama to generate media stories. In return, Western supporters have received spiritual instruction, which many of them understand, in accordance with the Shangri-La myth, to embody timeless values that have disappeared in their own societies.

Whatever the circumstances surrounding the growth of the Free Tibet movement, its achievements must be balanced against the actual social, economic, and political conditions pertaining in Tibet. Since September 1987, when the Chinese military violently suppressed nationalist demonstrations in Lhasa, there has been a groundswell of support for Tibetan independence in the wealthy capitalist world, not only among Buddhist practitioners but also among well-heeled urban professionals with concerns about human rights, the environment, and other global issues. Despite this, the Tibetan government in exile has received official recognition from no Western government, and Tibetans remain unwelcome at the United Nations, not even having been granted observer status. This is largely due to the increasingly important role of China in world politics and the global economy. Western governments judge that official support for Tibetan independence would damage valuable trade agreements with China and restrict their access to growing markets. An additional concern is strategic. Too great an emphasis on human rights violations in Tibet would unbalance the delicate give-and-take of international relations, placing additional pressure on other areas of strategic concern, particularly the U.S. theater of operations in the western Pacific, centered on the island of Taiwan. The discourse of human rights, frequently evoked in relation to Tibet, thus emerges as a kind of bargaining chip in sensitive economic and strategic negotiations, with Western governments balancing their commitment to free market ideologies against domestic political pressure to assume a more interventionist role in Tibet. At stake in these bargaining processes is not only the Chinese ethnocide in Tibet (and other alleged infringements such as the treatment of political prisoners) but also a series of neoimperial relations by which Western powers seek to expand their economic and military influence over China. As Rey Chow (1991, 85) observes, "From the days of England's gunboat diplomacy to the present day, the question of human rights, when it is raised in relation to China's relation to the West, has never been separable from the privilege of extraterritoriality demanded by the Western diplomat, trader, or missionary." Given this state of affairs, it is inappropriate to consider the significance of the Shangri-La myth for the Tibetan nationalist struggle without also noting its relevance for anti-Chinese political agendas in which human rights become inseparable from the practicalities of world trade and strategic alliances.

If the mobilization of the Shangri-La myth by Free Tibet activists provides a means of attracting support in the advanced capitalist nations, it is not simply an opportunistic misrepresentation of Tibetan culture. The myth has strong precedents in the Tibetan Buddhist tradition. According to the *Kalachakra,* the most sacred text in Tibetan Buddhism, Shambhala (the original Sanskrit title from which Hilton adapted the name Shangri-La) is an actual place on this earth, although it is accessible only to those with the appropriate spiritual propensities (Bernbaum 1980; Sopa, Jackson, and Newman 1985). Reputedly shaped like a giant lotus flower, this mysterious land is filled with sandalwood forests and lakes, encircled by two ranges of snowy peaks. First mentioned in European chronicles by the seventeenth-century Jesuits Stephen Cacella and John Cabral, who heard about a country called Xembala in Bhutan, Tibetan accounts of this hidden paradise date back to the eleventh century, when the *Kalachakra* was first translated from Sanskrit. Indeed, the Shambhala myth is central to the *Kalachakra* tradition, since legend has it that the Buddha taught these sacred texts to the king of Shambhala. As the story goes, the king arranged for the texts to be preserved, and they remained in Shambhala for many centuries, before being returned to India, where they were eventually rediscovered and translated into Tibetan.

Kollmar-Paulenz (1992–93) surveys the prodigious Tibetan literature on Shambhala, including prayers, guidebooks, catalogs of kings, geographical works, and histories of religion. The most famous of these works is the *Shambhala Lam-yig,* written by the third Panchen Lama and first published in 1775. This text, ostensibly a guidebook, begins with physical directions for reaching Shambhala and gradually moves toward allegorical descriptions of spiritual and meditative practices that one must master to enter this land. By contrast, the most recent work on Kollmar-Paulenz's list, Gar-je K'am-trul Rinpoche's "A Geography and History of Shambhala" (1978), offers a direct physical description of the hidden kingdom. According to this account, Shambhala contains 960 million villages, distributed equally through the eight petals of the lotus flower. In the center is the capital of Ma-la-ya, which houses a giant three-dimensional Kalachakra mandala. Rinpoche reports that there is "not even a sign of nonvirtue or evil in these lands. Even the words 'war' and 'enmity' are unknown. The happiness and joy can compete with that of the gods" (7). But he also follows the allegorical history of Shambhala as developed in the *Kalachakra*. By this eschatological scheme, Shambhala has been invaded by barbarian troops (known as La-Los), who represent the temptations of the material world and will prevail until overcome by Buddhist forces in 2425 CE. In the Tibetan tradition, the myth of Shangri-La is thus articulated to a certain Buddhist triumphalism. This indigenous religious belief in Shambhala makes clearer the commitment of many Tibetans to peaceful methods of resistance (a territorial victory will eventually come) and their preparedness to negotiate, accommodate, or even perpetuate fantasies about Tibet as Shangri-La.

Even the Dalai Lama cannot speak of Tibet without a multitude of associations coming into play. In *My Tibet* (1990), he dreams that Tibet might become the world's largest national park or biosphere and a creative center for the promotion and development of peace. These proposals blend seamlessly into pre- and postdiaspora fantasies of Tibet as a zone of mystical compassion, free from harmful weapons and industries, an ecological and spiritual paradise. It is difficult to sustain the argument that the Shangri-La myth obscures the historical agency of Tibetans without recognizing that Tibetans themselves have been active in circulating fantastic stories about their homeland. Clearly it is possible and even necessary to develop an Orientalist analysis of the Shangri-La phenomenon, pointing out, for instance, that the construction of Tibetan culture as inherently peaceful obscures the military operations of the Tibetan resistance against the Chinese (Norbu 1994). One reason for the perpetuation of fantasies about Tibet as center for world peace is the prominence of the Dalai Lama in the global media spotlight. As the Tibetan media activist Tseten Samdup comments in an interview with McLagan (1996, 179), the Dalai Lama has become "more of a known entity than Tibet itself." Despite the lack of official recognition for the Tibetan government in exile, the Dalai Lama's self-deprecating humor and calls for nonviolent intervention continue to win over journalists and celebrities, eager to associate themselves with the mystique generated by this compassionate and charismatic spiritual leader.

The Dalai Lama has become a global celebrity, a political icon, and popular cultural saint, as well as more recently a computer salesman.

But not all Tibetans share his commitment to nonviolent resistance. Ganguly (2001) reports that Tibetan youth in Dharamsala are becoming increasingly warm to the possibility of armed resistance against the Chinese, looking to the seventeen-year-old Karmapa Lama for leadership. But despite their warlike rhetoric, these would-be freedom fighters cannot be identified as the representatives of the real Tibet, genuine Tibetans who expose the Orientalist distortions of the Shangri-La myth. The pacifist vision of the Dalai Lama remains official policy, while other young Tibetans in the diaspora mix into host cultures around the world, abandoning any intention of returning to the homeland even if conditions were drastically to change. Clearly the reality of Tibet is caught up with the way in which it is imagined, not only by the Tibetans themselves but also by the Chinese authorities and Tibetan sympathizers in the West.

What I am suggesting is that the Shangri-La myth acquires a significance beyond its Orientalist implications, a significance that cannot become apparent by means of an analysis that places an unbridgeable gulf between the real and the imagined. In other words, the Shangri-La myth can be reduced neither to a symbolic structure nor to an empirically verifiable set of geographical-physical features. While the myth is generated and transmitted through discursive forms (such as Hilton's novel or the Dalai Lama's speeches), it exists only in its links to social-spatial practices (the Chinese occupation of Tibet, for instance, or the establishment of Tibetan Buddhist centers in the West). These social-spatial practices, in turn, provide the material contexts that embed and embody the conceptual schemes against which the myth acquires meaning, schemes such as the triumphal predictions of the *Kalachakra* or the free trade ideology that underlies the capitalist push into China. To complicate things further, the myth circulates in different ways under different conceptual skies, confirming New Age dreams of an outside to globalization, for example, or corroborating human rights efforts that cut across Chinese ideals of suzerainty. This is why the Shangri-La myth cannot be anchored to a single scheme of false representation. As soon as one level of meaning is uncovered, its reliance on a particular social spatial context becomes evident and this, in turn, uncovers the possibility of other spatial practices or conceptual horizons against which the myth acquires different (and possibly contradictory) meanings.

To map these shifts in meaning, spatial context, and conceptual background is a complex task, which eludes the projection of distinct boundaries within established cartographic grids. In "The Tibetan

Tradition of Geography" (1965), Turrell V. Wylie notes that geography, as a scientific description of the physical world, did not develop in Tibet in a manner analogous to the mapping practices of the West. Tibetan geography was primarily a religious affair, since it pertained to the description of sacred sites and objects without reference to the physical features of the region such as flora and fauna. There was also a more fragmented tradition of political geography that traced the historical evolution of the Tibetan kingdom, although it was not until 1726, when the Chinese annexed Khams Province, that the idea of a border was recognized as a dividing line between discrete territories. Both religious and political geography in Tibet were based in written descriptions rather than visual representations. But the traditional Buddhist mandala also constitutes a type of map, which reputedly functions on both the spiritual and physical levels. Perhaps the most famous Tibetan Buddhist mandala is "The Land of Shambhala," which hangs in the Musée Guimet in Paris and depicts an oasis surrounded by two rings of snow-capped mountains. Intended primarily as a visual guide for meditation, the map is nonscalar and makes no reference to the earth's larger surface. Nonetheless, LePage (1996) suggests that it represents the ethnoreligious topography of central Asia, with the eight louts petals corresponding to eight separate ethnic-cultural areas: Siberia, Mongolia, China, Tibet, Kashmir, Afghanistan, Turkestan, and Kazakhstan. Such cartography clearly contrasts the rationalist (ocularcentric) procedures of observation and plotting by which mapmaking emerges, in the era of high imperialism, as a means of controlling territory. It thus suggests an alternative mapping of the world that, in the current context of globalization, questions the fantasy of capitalism's unbounded geographical command.

According to Paul Smith (1997), contemporary capitalism sustains itself by means of an ideological formation that asserts the existence of a single unified world market as if it were a fait accompli. If, as the Frankfurt school theorists argued, modern capitalism sought to master the natural world, post–Cold War capitalism seeks also to dominate the metaphysical dimensions of space and time. The Shangri-La myth disrupts this fantasy by raising the prospect of an outside to the processes of globalization: processes that, as the word globalization implies, are supposedly total or global, involving a system of mapping the relations between territory and capital that excludes no area of the earth's surface. Doubtless, the myth generates meanings and values that work at cross-purposes to capitalist regimes of accumulation: ideals of environmental sustainability, for example,

Representation of the Kingdom of Shambhala. Musée des arts asiatiques-Guimet, Paris. Courtesy of Réunion des Musées Nationaux/Art Resource, NY.

or notions of exchange that do not involve the production of surplus value (as in the practice of *mchod-yon*). Often cited as a classic of Buddhist economics, E. F. Schumacher's *Small Is Beautiful* (1973) is a popular text that appeared in the same year as Charles Jarrott's musical remake of *Lost Horizon*. Schumacher points to four major areas in which Buddhist economics differs from capitalist methods of accumulation: labor, consumption, peace, and environment. Whereas capitalism views labor a means to an end, the generation of value by means of abstract labor power, Buddhism purportedly understands labor as an end in itself, necessary for the development of character and the overcoming of the ego. For Buddhists, a higher level of consumption signals not a better life but an attachment to material goods that is ultimately a source of discontent. In addition, Buddhism supposedly promotes practices of economic simplicity and self-sufficiency, which minimize competition for scarce resources and thus serve the ends of peace. And finally, Buddhist economics favors the use of renewable resources, leading to more sustainable environmental practice.

Schumacher's economic vision is attached to a nostalgic localism that posits the small-scale human community as the basis for anti-capitalist reform. The invocation of values such as simplicity and self-sufficiency suggests a retreat from global complexity, an attempt to establish a society that, like Shangri-La, exists outside the circuits of capitalist valorization. Such a defensive localism, while well intentioned, offers no hope for overcoming capitalism on the wider scale, by pushing beyond its present limitations and instabilities. Nonetheless, it disrupts the global capitalist dream of exerting total control over space and time. Significantly, the Shangri-La myth points to the existence of a small-scale utopian community that maintains a terrestrial existence, a location in space and time that, although undisclosed, questions the possibility of capital's total engorgement of the earth. Due to the practical difficulties in locating this hidden land, the modes of transformation suggested by the Shangri-La myth cannot be anchored to a fixed goal, with an essential constitution or clear direction. Awkwardly, this means the myth offers no cast-iron guarantee of resistance to global capitalism, and that its oppositional meanings are linked to questionable ideals such as those associated with Orientalism, Theosophy, and New Age spiritual practices. For this reason, the critique of global capitalism implicit in the Shangri-La myth must be understood as an intra-ideological critique, involving not the debunking of capitalist ideology by scientific reality but the disruption of one mythography by another.

Mysticism and Ideology

The modes of desire embodied in the Shangri-La myth can be identified, with all rigor, as spiritual desires. As these desires tend to issue in mysticism rather than an encounter with the politics of everyday life, it is necessary to ask to what extent the myth harbors ideological elements that corroborate the operations of contemporary capitalism. In its most extreme form, mysticism is a claim for the transcendence of representation, the dissolution of corporeality, everydayness, and materiality into a mystical One that is strictly ineffable because it is incommensurable with everything existing. The mystic aspires to direct contact with this ineffable beyond, seeking a spiritual path that bridges the abyss between the Absolute and the empirical world. Thus the journey to Shangri-La is imagined not only as a passage in physical space but also as a process of spiritual enlightenment by which the traveler seeks communion with the mystical beyond. This kind of mysticism appears highly susceptible to the distortions of ideology. According to the traditional Marxist account of religion, the perfection of the world beyond is a form of compensation or, more precisely, an imaginary supplement for the uncertainties of life under capitalism. It thus makes sense that Capra should produce a film like *Lost Horizon* during the Great Depression, a period of great economic uncertainty for the work's most immediate audience. By this argument, the Shangri-La story would be simply an ideological fantasy. The positing of a paradise on earth would be nothing but a feel-good daydream that acquires particular force at times of economic and social hardship. To dislodge the myth all that is necessary is to highlight the oppressive effects of capitalism's economic, political, and social operations, since these provide the conditions under which the popular desire for such an escape becomes manifest.

The difficulty with this approach is its reliance upon the notion of extra-ideological closure: that is, the claim that capitalist exploitation provides some sort of irreducible truth against which the fantasies of mysticism can be measured and exposed. More recent theories of ideology abandon the claim for an extra-ideological ground that provides a neutral standard against which such distortions can be detected. As Laclau (1997) explains, the category of distortion makes sense only if something true and undistorted is considered to be within human reach. If one accepts that all truth is constructed and that an extra-ideological viewpoint is unobtainable, then the idea loses all meaning. This means that mysticism, with its claim for the transcendence of worldly differences, becomes something other than one ideological distortion among others (similar perhaps to the belief in individual social agency as the basis of market economics). Rather mysticism displays "the theoretical (and impossible) conditions under which the end of ideology could take place" (320). For the mystic, all material particularities are reduced to equivalents, insofar as they are transfigured by the mystical One that shines through them. Under these circumstances, there can be no hope of identifying an ideological distortion, because all differences are canceled out by a higher Unity that, by definition, stands outside of ideology. To maintain a notion of ideological distortion that remains free from the threat of dissolution, it is necessary to show that mysticism requires the appeal to something less than the Absolute. Žižek (1991) undertakes such a task, identifying the mystical One as what he calls a reflective signifier (the equivalent of the phallus in Lacanian psychoanalysis). The reflective signifier remains immanent within the ideological field but appears to transcend ideology by virtue of the fact that it unites or "quilts" all other signifiers into the space of ideological narration. To illustrate this argument, Žižek draws upon the paradox of the bodhisattva in Mahayana Buddhism. The bodhisattva is an adept who has attained enlightenment and can pass over into Nirvana, but is at the same time unable to do this, as it would constitute an act of selfishness unfitting of the enlightened state:

The basic experience of *bodhisattva* concerns precisely the *impossibility* of such an immediate withdrawal of the individual from the world of illusions — if an individual accomplishes it, he thereby asserts his difference from other human beings and thus falls prey to his selfishness in the very gesture of leaving it behind. The only escape from this deadlock is for the *bodhisattva* to postpone his own bliss until all mankind has reached the same point as he.... [T]he *bodhisattva* performs the act of supreme sacrifice by postponing his own entry into Nirvana for the sake of mankind. In relation to other, ordinary humans who are still victims of the veil of illusions, the *bodhisattva* functions as a "reflective" or "phallic" element: he does represent Liberation, stepping out of the world of illusions, but not immediately.... [R]ather, he embodies the very *impossibility* of the individual's immediate Liberation. In opposition to other, ordinary human beings, Liberation (the passage into Nirvana) is already present in him, but as *a pure possibility which must forever remain postponed.* (26)

By this logic, the possibility of a mystical transcendence of the material world remains immanent within the ideological field itself. There is no mystical outside to ideology, although the postponed possibility of such an outside provides the means by which the ideological field can be identified in the first place. In *The Coming Community* (1993), Giorgio Agamben develops a similar understanding of the outside. For him, the outside is delineated not by a limit that knows no exteriority, but by a threshold, "a point of contact with a space that must remain empty" (67). It is not a matter of identifying the outside as a transcendent space that eludes the immanence of everyday life or as a local site that remains untouched by capitalist globalization. In this sense, there is no longer any outside. What is at stake is rather a form of bordering. As Agamben explains, "the notion of the 'outside' in many European languages is expressed by a word that means 'at the door' (*fores* in Latin is the door of the house)" (68). To be at the door (or at the threshold) is to be "*within* an *outside*" (68), to occupy a position that borders on all possibility but that cannot be represented by a real condition, since it exists only in relation to an empty and indeterminate space.

Returning to the Tibetan Buddhist tradition, it is possible to situate Shangri-La within such an outside. Importantly, this utopian community maintains a terrestrial location. Although it is a spiritual paradise, accessible only to those with the appropriate religious learning, Shangri-La is also an actual place on the earth's surface, and thus it maintains an absolute immanence or materiality (unlike, say, the Christian heaven). This is why it can furnish the possibility of an outside to globalization (and the attendant ideology of global capitalism) without itself being positioned outside of space and time. The critique of global capitalism implicit in the Shangri-La myth is not a critique of ideology as such, delivered from an extra-ideological or extradiscursive standpoint. Rather it is an intra-ideological critique, which is to say that the Shangri-La myth remains precisely that, a myth, albeit one that sits uneasily with the mythographies of global capitalism.

Doubtless there are other powerful mythographies that can also provide a basis for the intra-ideological critique of global capitalism. Prominent among these is the Marxist eschatology of revolutionary progress toward communism, although this has been significantly discredited in the popular imagination by the decline of state socialism. If, as the celebrants of global capitalism contend, these events mark the possibility of an unlimited market economy and the worldwide spread of liberal democracy, they have also been accompanied by a reawakening of religious and mystical sensibilities potentially antithetical to global capitalism. These religious sensibilities can take many forms, from the New Age movement to the fundamentalisms that have struck religions as diverse as Christianity, Hinduism, and Islam. It is important to understand this moment of return not as an attempt to recover the premodern world but as a symptom of the very passage out of modernity marked by the transition to global capitalism. Even in its fundamentalist forms, where this return involves a call for the revival of premodern modes of social and cultural organization, what is at stake is a reaction to contemporary global conditions. Two important accounts of this return to religion come from Gianni Vattimo and William Connolly. Both shed light on the possibilities for imagining an outside to globalization without licensing a transcendentalism that eclipses the immanence of life on earth.

In *Belief* (1999), Vattimo argues that a worldwide return to religion has been made possible by the end of modernity, a loss of faith in scientific objectivity, and the bankruptcy of the ideal of rational human progress toward perfectibility. He writes: "We are all by now used to the fact that disenchantment has also produced a radical disenchantment with the idea of disenchantment itself; or, in other words, that demythification has finally turned against itself, recognizing that even the ideal of the elimination of myth is a myth" (29). Significantly, this return of religion and myth does not signal a recovery of the belief in the transcendent beyond. Seeking to reconcile his youthful Catholicism with his later embrace of Heidegger's critique of metaphysics, Vattimo claims that the Christian notion of *kenosis* (the incarnation of God in man) licenses the secularization of society and the rejection of the metaphysical view of God as a transcendent, omnipotent being. For the traditional Christian believer, the idea of recovery or return implies a search for the origin, namely, the creature's dependence on God. But for Vattimo, such a recovery implies the recognition of a necessarily fallen relation. This is where he draws upon his background as a Heideggerian philosopher. Heidegger argues that the recollection of Being does not involve an attempt to recover a forgotten origin by making it present again. Rather, such an origin is always already forgotten, and its existence can be inferred only from the experience of forgetfulness and distance. In a similar manner, Vattimo contends that contemporary religious experience consists in the recognition that a transcendental God is accessible only through his supposed worldly incarnation. The metaphysical is brought down to earth, where it remains active in a fallen, distorted version. As in the Shangri-La myth, the mystical One exists only in an immanent, embodied form, as a deferred or forgotten possibility that cannot escape the clutches of time and space.

William Connolly presents a similar argument in *Why I Am Not a Secularist* (1999). He claims that secular modes of social organization are insufficient to account for the visceral feelings aroused by religious belief, and that an effective political philosophy must acknowledge the impact of religious convictions upon political judgments. Secularism drains politics of metaphysics, but in so doing, it depreciates the affective dimension of human experience and hinders the elaboration of an expansive pluralism. A purely secular politics encounters difficulty in engaging a variety of contemporary issues, including "the legitimate variety of sexual orientations, the organization of gender, the question of doctor-assisted death, the practice of abortion, and the extent to which a uniform set of public virtues is needed" (37). Connolly argues that secularists are alone in leaving their religious and metaphysical convictions at home when discussing such issues, and that this makes their arguments weaker against participants who explicitly bring religious and metaphysical perspectives to such debates. Not only are secularists vulnerable to the charge that they secretly import metaphysics into their arguments, but they must also pretend that reason is sufficient to adjudicate the issues at hand, even as they recognize that cultural specificities shape the possibilities for discourse and judgment. The difficulty is to devise an ethics of publicity that allows for a plurality of metaphysical perspectives without reinstating a theologically centered politics that appeals to a transcendental source. Connolly suggests this can be accomplished by cultivating "little spaces of enchantment" (17), scattered pockets of commitment that cannot authorize a transcendental morality of command. For him, it is a matter not of reinstating the absolutism of transcendental judgment but of recognizing the insufficiency of any morality that claims to divorce itself completely from metaphysical legitimation. Once again, the metaphysical outside folds into the embodied world, paralleling the supposed grounding of Shangri-La in a real but unlocatable space.

If these arguments from Vattimo and Connolly at first seem remote from the problematic of globalization, it is important to remember that the spiritualist dream of a metaphysical outside promises an external standpoint from which the operations of global capitalism might be questioned and opposed. The issue is whether this questioning and

opposition can be reconciled with a materialist perspective that recognizes the immanence and the irreducibility of life on earth. Both
Vattimo and Connolly suggest that this can be achieved. If metaphysical transcendence is understood as a deferred or forgotten possibility,
the claim for an outside to globalization need not seek the certainty
of transcendental legitimation. This means the search for an external horizon can be compatible with globalization theories that stress
uncertainty, flow, and the immanence of space and time. Such approaches, which are often influenced by Deleuzean philosophy, tend
to combine Marxist historical materialism with an attention to disjunctures and multiplicities that question the totalizing aspects of the
Marxist tradition. But for Alain Badiou (2000), Deleuze's materialism does not altogether do away with the notion of transcendence.
Let me briefly explore Badiou's argument, since it demonstrates how
the possibility of deferred or forgotten transcendence resonates with
the Tibetan Buddhist claim for Shangri-La as a terrestrial paradise.

Contrary to the popular view of Deleuze as the prophet of multiple desires and flows, Badiou claims that Deleuze's philosophy submits
thinking to a new concept of the One. In *Difference and Repetition*
(1994, 35), Deleuze writes: "There has only ever been one ontological proposition: Being is univocal." Centering his argument on this
phrase, Badiou contends that such an emphasis on the One is fully
compatible with Deleuze's celebration of multiplicity. Indeed, he suggests that the One can only be identified in relation to the multiple.
He is careful to emphasize that Deleuze rejects the argument by which
the One inheres in the metaphysical realm. Rather than associating
the univocity of Being with the world beyond, Deleuze introduces
the category of the virtual, which he identifies as the dynamic agency
of the One. Badiou explains that the virtual maintains a transcendence that is transposed "beneath" the actual beings of the world,
in symmetrical relation to the "beyond" of classical transcendence.
This transcendence-in-reverse does not legitimate sovereign authority
or metaphysical certainty. But it does remain unavailable to representation, operating below and within culturally organized registers
of sensibility, appearance, and discourse. At stake is not the identification of the virtual as the site of disembodied spirituality, but a
vision of the outside as inseparable from the material world. The virtual remains part of the real. Like the hidden realm of Shangri-La,
which retains a terrestrial presence, it resists integration into established systems of navigation and empirical availability. The virtual is
too fast to be actual (like the photons that compose light rays) and/or

too small to be perceptible (like the quarks of particle physics, which display properties such as strangeness and charm). Little wonder that mythographers of Shangri-La often describe its existence as virtual. Whether in Redfield's screen visions or the literary and cinematic texts of Schell's *Virtual Tibet,* this little space of enchantment promises an alternative to the actually existing world while remaining anchored in space and time.

In pointing to an outside that resides within globalization, the Shangri-La myth posits the existence of a hidden paradise on the earth's surface, a geographical utopia, to recall the terminology of Ernst Bloch (1986). This contrasts with the argument of Miyoshi (1995), according to which the outside of globalization is simply given, nothing but an objective materiality that escapes capital's unbounded expansion. It also problematizes the New Age dream of a spiritual flight from the world's problems, whether imagined as a wholly supernatural phenomenon or, as in the case of Redfield, as an evolutionary extension of existing technologies. The critical potential of the Shangri-La myth must be understood against this lost transcendental horizon, which forever folds back into the banalities of everyday life. Rather than providing an Orientalist myth in need of demystification, it supplies a (compromised) political mythography that effectively contrasts the mythographies of global capitalism. If nothing else, Shangri-La describes a virtual outside to globalization. Virtual not in the sense that it generates possibilities, which remain devoid of reality, but in the sense that its actuality is accessible only through discursive elaborations — in books, films, paintings, and so forth. As soon as one tries to contextualize Shangri-La, it disappears or changes shape. The myth poses the challenge not of moving from texts, discourses, and metaphors to a socially constructed world where matter is merely a receptacle for projected fantasies, but of moving from a world pregnant with virtualities toward the domain of literature, discourse, and metaphors. In other words, it is a matter of inquiring into the functions of the Shangri-La myth in a globalized world that banishes utopia from the actual.

Highlighting the utopian dimensions of the Shangri-La fantasy does not mean ignoring the myth's perpetuation of dangerous cultural stereotypes, elitist models of knowledge transmission, or questionable attitudes toward Chinese expansionism. But an awareness of these difficulties need not obscure the fact that the Western enthusiasm for the Shangri-La myth and the related mobilization around Tibetan independence are woven into the crisis of late modernity. These fantasies are not simply the extension of an older imperialism. Rather they are the symptoms of anxieties that stem from the uncertainties of capitalist globalization. In an essay titled "Eurotaoism" (1997, 285–86), Peter Sloterdijk observes: "We have become so strangely unknown to ourselves through our modernization that the ancient unknown tones of the Far East begin to remind us of home, like an old, trustworthy idiom." According to Sloterdijk, North Atlantic capitalism is in the midst of an Asiatic renaissance that touches on the nerve of world processes: "Asia is for many the figure that offers shelter in a representation of what is unrepresentable" (284). In my analysis, the Shangri-La myth offers a means of imagining an outside to globalization, an outside that may be ultimately unrepresentable, that is to say, a space that resists localization and cannot be mapped within the fixed cartographic grids of the contemporary world order. At stake here is not merely a fashion or an episodic exoticism that can be dismissed under the label New Age Orientalism. As long as the relations between Tibet and the wealthy capitalist world are mediated by the Shangri-La myth, they will remain suspect and embattled. But this kind of mediation is not all bad news, which is probably just as well, since by now it is perhaps impossible to shake off.

Conclusion

Counterworlds:
Toward an Alternative Economy
of Global Space

In political thought and political theory, the category (or concept) of the "real" should not be permitted to obscure that of
the possible. Rather, it is the possible that should serve as the
theoretical instrument for exploring the real.
—Henri Lefebvre, "Comments on a New State Form"

Why popular geographies? The four sites studied in this book are
large-scale nonnational spaces that suggest alternative ways of understanding the manner in which the global, globalization, and globalism
have been constructed in mainstream geographical, ideological, and
political discourses. They are also popular formations, generated by
cartographic processes that embody the affective energies of everyday
life and contest dominant constructions of race, gender, and sexuality.
As such, they are anomalous sites that unsettle established theoretical
approaches to both globalization and popular culture. These popular geographical constructions cannot be pieced together to provide
a conclusive theoretical summa, a world-picture or overview that
extracts and offers a uniform epistemological yield. Each space produces singular disturbances in space and time. The Bermuda Triangle
is a vortex that detains transnational flows of transport and communication. Transylvania is an elastic territory in which vampiric
notions of sedition and excess mingle freely with postsocialist anxieties. The Golden Triangle is an outlaw zone that pumps out illicit
drug flows. And Shangri-La is a security haven, inaccessible to the
global circulation of capital and culture.

Each of these spaces expands to reproduce the world in its image.
But none is a world in the proper sense of the term, since all fail to
produce coherent totalizing visions of global processes. Rather these

popular geographies can be identified as counterworlds, which counter the all-encompassing representation of the contemporary world as a dynamic capitalist system. In each case, there is something that does not fit, something in excess of or beyond the workings of global capital, whether this falls under the label of the paranormal, the supernatural, the intoxicating, or the mystical. Disappearing ships and planes, vampires, opium addiction, inaccessible spiritual realms — all signal a desire for escape or destabilization, even as they are implicated in processes of production, distribution, and consumption that would go adrift without the guiding hand of the capitalist market. Like the wormholes of relativity physics, these popular geographies connect points distant in time and space, generating unexpected links, passages, and instabilities. But they are also sites of quotidian desire, cartographic emblems of popular fantasies that attain a complex geographical representation. How then to understand these contradictory spaces? How might the negotiation of their uneven topographies produce a terrain of critique upon which the global and the popular interact, displacing the orthodoxies of both popular cultural studies and critical geography?

One of the central features of contemporary globalization studies is the recognition that the geography of national boundaries is being replaced by a new geography of transnational connections. To discuss space in this context is to place emphasis upon social relations, material processes of production, and changing geographical contexts. As Appadurai (1996) notes, however, we know very little about the production of contexts, even as recent scholarship has bequeathed us a strong understanding of the relations between texts. To understand how the production, circulation, and reception of popular texts gives rise to geographical contexts that in turn affect our understanding of global capitalist processes requires not only an understanding of intertextual relations but also a sense of how contexts connect with other contexts, so that each context implies a global network of contexts. Only through an understanding of such *intercontextual* relations can we begin to grasp the contingent and contradictory interactions between geographical entities like the Bermuda Triangle, Transylvania, the Golden Triangle, and Shangri-La. The above chapters explore the complex interaction of discursive and nondiscursive practices in the imagination of these anomalous sites. Now it is time to ask how these geographical contexts relate to each other. How do they connect to produce an alternative economy of global space? What is the nature of these connections and how can they be mapped without subordinating them to an overarching or regularizing vision?

Such intercontextual relations cannot simply be read off the popular cultural texts associated with these various sites. For instance, a connection may be drawn between Transylvania and Shangri-La by noting that both involve a fantasy of longevity — the extended life of the vampire or the prolonged youth of the inhabitants of the Tibetan sanctuary. But this connection, which arises from the details of the popular texts in question (most immediately Stoker's *Dracula* and Hilton's *Lost Horizon*), is of a different order than the intercontextual relations that link, say, the Bermuda Triangle and Golden Triangle — manifest, for instance, in the money laundering systems that ply the global drug trade in the western Atlantic. Intercontextual relations cannot be separated from the operations of intertextuality (insofar as texts produce contexts and vice versa), but nor can they be completely subordinated to them. The challenge is to account for the intercontextual relations between these sites while also examining their intertextual connections. If their intertextual connections are left to run wild (without contextual restraint), the result is conspiracy theory — the anxious delight of clicking from one link to another as if in search of a lost totality. But if one attends only to their intercontextual relations (without linking these topographies to the corresponding intertextual networks), the result is a dry empiricism, which leaves the world exactly as it is, without room for change or variation. Only by examining the uneven and always unpredictable interactions between popular texts and geographical contexts is it possible to chart a passage between these extremes, situating popular geographical spaces within both intertextual and intercontextual networks. But this means entering a dangerous space in which the real and the imagined begin to intermingle, producing forms of sociality and circulation that fail to register on the paranoid radar screen of the sovereign state. To forge an alternative economy of global space is to leave behind epistemological certainties, to enter a domain in which the empirical repeatedly interrupts the abstract and the metaphorical indelibly corrupts the material.

What does this mean for the analysis of global capitalism? A materialist approach to culture entails vigilance against idealities, an attempt to analyze communication and other cultural practices in relation to the global political economy. But, as anyone who has read Marx's *Capital* will be aware, the workings of capital depend upon abstraction. Particularly in the era of informatization, when financial speculation seeks to withdraw itself from its productive geography, the fantasy of removing capital from the clutches of the earth (and the body) reigns supreme. For Deleuze and Guattari, this tendency to abstraction is implicit in the concept of deterritorialization, which describes capital's flight from all that is concrete. But the extent to which such a lift-off from the earth's surface is possible remains a point of contention. If capital operates in a new virtual realm, it also reserves the power to determine if and when the virtual becomes the actual. The world may be a fantastic place, but only insofar as capital actualizes the virtuality of fantasies. Thus the actuality of fantastic sites like the Bermuda Triangle, Transylvania, the Golden Triangle, and Shangri-La cannot be conceived in isolation from the workings of capital. Similarly the intercontextual links between these sites must be understood in relation to capitalism's coding of global flows, its motivation of transnational passages of people, information, commodities, and technologies. But capital can never fully extricate itself from the earth and the body in its virtual embrace, and this means that its fantasy of completely containing the world must remain unfulfilled. Remapping the earth's surface provides a series of interlinked contexts in which to question the triumphant narrative of capitalist globalization. These popular geographical contexts register the transnational circulation of vernacular sensibilities that demotivate the fantasy of free-floating capitalism, repeatedly interrupting it with the empirical and the corporeal. For Spivak (2000, 33), such an undoing of the abstract is necessarily ironic: "Triumphant global finance capital/world trade can only be resisted with irony." *Free Trade in the Bermuda Triangle* gives voice to such irony, offsetting the no-way-out rhetoric that haunts most studies of global culture/economy with analyses of popular realities that twist and fissure the processes of capitalist accumulation.

To be sure, the work of irony is never done. Reaching on the one hand toward an insubordinate refusal and on the other toward an unbearable lightness, irony necessarily holds forth a promise it cannot keep. As such, it provides no chart of programmatic action — no twelve-steps for the overcoming of global capital. Its tactics are inevitably polluted with ideological longings that can never quite be separated from utopian desires. But for all this, it is not an empty gesture. Irony refuses to abide the world as it is, pushing against the limits of the possible while constantly checking itself against the hard face of the real. To argue that popular geographies demotivate the triumphant narrative of capitalist globalization is to attribute them an ironic movement that charts new paths for the global, passages that suggest the potential for alternative circuits of production and valorization.

These counterworlds are at once discursive and nondiscursive realities, and as such they generate a multiplicity of possible and impossible futures. Like the unmappable topographies (J. H. Miller 1995) and geographical plots (Moretti 1998) traced out by philosophical and literary texts, they have a chronotopic dimension that exists in a purely imagined space. But their modes of intertextual patterning cannot be understood in isolation from real processes of production, distribution, and consumption responsible for the transnational dissemination of media messages and material artifacts that allow their mapping in the first place. The modes of imagination at stake are thoroughly imbricated in the real, constantly mapping and remapping the geographical contexts in which people act out their everyday lives. To chart the intercontextual relations between these topographies, it is necessary to reposition them in a general economy of global space. As Lefebvre (1991, 60) writes, it is a matter of surmounting "these oppositions by exploring the dialectical relationship between 'possible' and 'impossible,' and this both objectively and subjectively."

One productive domain for exploring the dialectic of the possible and the impossible is the field of utopian studies. Like other popular cultural materials, the mythographies that generate these geographical formations produce both ideological and utopian meanings and effects. The Bermuda Triangle myth is entangled with the celebration of U.S. military power even as it points to renewable energy sources and the destabilization of world capitalism. The vampire mythography of Transylvania has become inseparable from conservative programs of ethnonationalist politics, but it also generates excessive pleasures that override established epistemological and geographical boundaries. Similarly the drug flows that emanate from the Golden Triangle epitomize rapacious profiteering while producing instabilities that threaten global capitalism's routine functioning. And finally the Shangri-La fantasy reinstitutes imperial relations of patronage and power even as it produces a space that putatively sits outside global capitalist circuits of exchange. *Free Trade in the Bermuda Triangle* examines how the ideological and utopian dimensions of these popular mythographies interact, paying close attention to the potentially liberating elements within artifacts and practices that emerge from the fallen detritus of the capitalist system. But insofar as the sites of study suggest the possibility of reappropriating the spaces of global capitalism, questions are likely to arise regarding their geographical status. The prospect of a materially embodied utopia raises serious epistemological issues that also have important political implications. Ever since the publication of Ernst Bloch's *The Principle of Hope* (1986), theorists of utopia have argued about the possibility of what Bloch calls geographical utopias, spaces of human perfectibility that have an actual existence on the earth's surface.

Following Bloch, critics distinguish between abstract and concrete utopias. The former are cast purely at the level of fantasy and are thus disconnected from any future that might actually be realized, while the latter simultaneously anticipate and effect a possible future. Terry Eagleton (2000, 22) contrasts bad utopias, which consist simply in "a sort of wistful yearning," with good utopias, which construct "a bridge between the present and the future in the forces within the present that are potentially able to transform it." Popular geographical formations like the Bermuda Triangle, Transylvania, the Golden Triangle, and Shangri-La embody elements both of concrete and abstract, good and bad utopias. They arise from myths and fantasies that construct and interpret reality in unorthodox and defamiliarizing ways. These fantasies involve phenomena such as unexplained disappearances, the living dead, drug-induced intoxication, and secret spiritual rites. But the empirical verifiability of these fantasies bears no relation to the materiality of the media responsible for their production, distribution, and consumption. Nor does it obscure the reality of the audiences that rearticulate their meanings and effects. No matter how abstract or incredible these mythographies may appear, they map out concrete spatial realms, susceptible to all the transformations of physical, political, economic, and human geography. In this sense, they give rise to neither concrete nor abstract utopias. Indeed, their troubling of the division between the concrete and the abstract plays havoc with the epistemological distinction that informs Bloch's classificatory scheme. These anomalous spaces are not rightly utopias at all. Rather they are nonplaces articulated within and against the circuits of global capital.

One way of classifying these popular geographies is to compare them to the anomalous sites that Foucault (1986) calls heterotopias. Heterotopias are spaces of alternative ordering, actual geographical formations that organize part of the social world in a different way from the spaces that surround them. Unlike the classical utopia of literature and philosophy, they maintain a concrete existence in social space, but their materiality cannot be conceived in separation from a desiring-production that shapes them as sites of difference and otherness. Heterotopias "juxtapose in a single real place several spaces, several sites that are in themselves incompatible" (25). They also "presuppose a system of opening and closing that both isolates them and makes them penetrable" (26). Consequently, they are sites of incongruous intercontextual relations that challenge the dominant space of representation within a society. But heterotopias are more than the sum of their representations, consisting rather of the peculiarities that emerge from the relations between representations and the everydayness of life. For Foucault, they are predominantly local sites (cemeteries, brothels, gardens, dance clubs) in which deviant and transgressive behavior occurs. But they can also be mobile spaces that shift across the earth's surface. Thus Foucault explains, the "ship is the heterotopia par excellence" (27).

The susceptibility of heterotopias to movement and flow points to their capacity to partake in what Spivak (1987), following Heidegger, calls the "worlding of the world" — that is, the remaking of the world in their image. Such a process of worlding need not entail a roughshod riding over other spaces considered blank or uninscribed, as in the classic worlding processes of imperialism. Rather it registers the possibility of a counterglobalization, which shows that other temporalities and other forms of worlding coexist with, overlap, and in some cases overshadow capital's engorgement of the earth. Indeed, an emphasis on counterglobalization is implicit in Foucault's initial exploration of heterotopias. He explains that heterotopias function in relation to all the spaces that exist outside of them, that while they encompass a culturally defined space quite unlike any other, they can also act as microcosms that reflect larger cultural patterns or social orders. This is an important feature of heterotopias, especially for critical geographers who follow in Foucault's wake. If heterotopias reflect the nature of the spaces that exist outside them, they are not simply "other spaces" to be added to existing typologies of spatial forms. Rather they suggest different ways of thinking about space as such.

As Soja (1996) notes, there exist interesting similarities between Foucault's heterotopias and Lefebvre's reconceptualization of social space. For Lefebvre (1991, 33), the lived dimension of social space foregrounds relations of dominance and resistance, but it also remains mysterious and secretive, associated with "the clandestine or underground side of social life." As such, it comprises both real space and imagined space, transforming and collapsing the distinction between these two. Social space is "the dominated — and hence passively experienced — space which the imagination seeks to change and appropriate," but, at the same time, it "overlays physical space, making symbolic use of its objects" (39). It thus questions both *"the illusion of transparency"* (27), which makes space appear completely intelligible and open to the free play of the imagination, and *"the realistic illusion"* (29), which reduces space to its material or empirical substantiality. In this domain, spatial representations of power cannot be separated from the power of spatial representations. Social space thus becomes a terrain for struggle, generating sites of resistance that interpenetrate and superimpose themselves upon one another at all geographical scales, from the intensely localized space of the body to the global space produced by worldwide networks of communication, exchange, and information.

This jumping of scales, from the corporeal to the planetary, parallels Foucault's emphasis on the counterglobalizing tendency of heterotopias. Like Foucault, Lefebvre (1991, 60) declares that his project points "the way towards a different space, towards the space of a different (social) life and of a different mode of production," a space that "straddles the breach between science and utopia, reality and ideality, conceived and lived." *Free Trade in the Bermuda Triangle* also charts a different kind of space. By exploring four large-scale nonnational topographies that produce spatiotemporal disturbances in the operations of global capital, the book deliberately departs from works of critical geography that discover resistance in local enclaves of difference. The Bermuda Triangle, Transylvania, the Golden Triangle, and Shangri-La — all are global spaces that straddle multiple territories, networks of flow, and cultural localities. They are also subject to constant processes of remapping and recontextualization. As such, they cannot be understood as places that give rise to localized struggles against global capitalism. To be sure, these popular geographies encompass quotidian spaces in which people act out their everyday lives, but they are also constituted by plural mappings that muddle any attempt to pin them to a specific locality, whether constituted by territory or identity. In this way, they chart a path beyond the familiar argument by which the globalization of capital has allowed the reemergence of the local as a site of resistance.

Free Trade in the Bermuda Triangle remains fundamentally dissatisfied with the notion that resistance becomes increasingly manifest as the scale gets smaller, disappearing in the big picture like the pixels that make up an image on a computer screen. Lefebvre (1991, 86) declares *"the worldwide does not abolish the local,"* but this does not license the opposite view by which the local completely captures the global. Each of the sites I study embodies precategorical dimensions of lived experience that resist engulfment in wider geographical or interpretive systems. The Bermuda Triangle spans urban cultures in Florida as well as the complex island cultures of the Caribbean. Transylvania encompasses a fraught borderland of conflicting Romanian and Hungarian ethnonational claims. The Golden Triangle comprises overlapping indigenous spaces of opium cultivation. And Shangri-La remains inseparable from the privations of life in Chinese-occupied Tibet. But these local forms of uniqueness and heterogeneity do not exclude the construction of other forms of uniqueness and heterogeneity that stretch across more global networks of transport and communication. For instance, claims for unexplained disappearances in the Devil's Triangle off Japan suggest that such anomalies are not restricted to the Bermuda Triangle. Similarly the appearance of the Golden Crescent, a second area of opium production in central Asia, shows that the Golden Triangle forms part of a worldwide drug economy that generates its own specificities of addiction and exchange. By studying these expanding and self-replicating sites, *Free Trade in the Bermuda Triangle* refuses the argument by which a retreat to the local constitutes an effective resistance against global capital. This means taking seriously the proposition that capitalism must be contested at its own level of generalization, by pushing the processes it offers past their present limitations. The book remains dubious about the possibility of resisting capitalism from real or imagined spaces that putatively exist outside the global. Rather, it searches for mechanisms of counterglobalization that inhabit the global capitalist imaginary itself.

The critical geographical preoccupation with global/local relations stems from a more general concern with the politics of scale. Following the influential work of N. Smith (1984), critical geographical accounts of globalization have maintained that scale is a social construct. Numerous studies have explored the dynamics of re-scaling processes by which established scalar configurations are overridden and remade through intense sociopolitical struggles. As a consequence, traditional Euclidean, Cartesian, and Westphalian conceptions of scale have given way to processual notions that highlight the contested, continually evolving role of scale in reorganizing sociospatial practices under contemporary capitalism. But as Brenner (2001, 597) argues, geographical scale "is merely one *dimension* — albeit a particularly crucial one — of the multifaceted and polymorphic geographies of capitalist modernity."

Too exclusive a focus on scale can detract from other important dimensions of capitalist spatiality — such as territoriality, distanciation, and network formation — that may involve very different geographical properties: for example, embeddedness, immobility, dispersion, or connectivity. Furthermore there exists a tendency to understand scale as a boundary that delineates differentiated geographical units — such as localities, regions, or nations — without linking the substantive social content of these spatial units to their positioning within broader (and shifting) scalar hierarchies. Brenner notes that this use of scalar terms "to connote the substantive sociological content of particular social, political, and economic processes" is evident in "the equation of the local scale with contextual particularity" (602). Such an equation is crucial to the argument that identifies the local as the site of difference that interrupts the global capitalist striving toward totality. But the popular geographies examined in this book embody forms of contextual particularity that stretch across wide (and constantly resizing) geographical expanses. Indeed, these anomalous spaces are involved in complex processes of re-scaling or what might be termed — ironically reversing Harvey's (1989) well-known formula for the time-space effects of globalization — *time-space expansion*. Think of the Bermuda Triangle's ever-widening boundaries and purported reappearance in eleven other global sites, the so-called vile vortices. Ponder the border fluctuations of Transylvania and the restless cosmopolitan circulation of the vampire. Contemplate the addictive flows that emanate from the Golden Triangle and the massive financial subterfuge that shadows them. Or consider Shangri-La's supposed diffusion of spiritual energies on a planetary scale. These popular geographic formations generate overlapping intertextual and intercontextual networks that suggest the possibility of alternative forms of worldliness, processes of counterglobalization that like capital itself strive to encompass the entire earth's surface. At stake is not the totality of capital and the corollary forms of sovereignty that extend over the social, economic, and political relations of the planet but another form of totality — a rival and asymmetrical totality that is "open, as open as the world of possibility, the world of potential" (Hardt and Negri 2000, 196).

To take seriously Lefebvre's injunction to map the real through the possible is to submit neither to desperation nor hope, but to unflinchingly confront the mechanisms of global capitalist control while at the same time looking beyond them. Such a movement through and beyond the capitalist imaginary requires a remapping of global space that neither fetishizes the local nor celebrates too eagerly the disruptive effects of homelessness and dislocation. To chart an alternative economy of global space is not only to disrupt the dominant nation-state cartographies that divide the planet into discrete territories but also to contest the hegemony of the economic and cultural forces that shape the world at capital's command. By pointing to carto-graphic constructs that register the operations of popular affect at the transnational level, *Free Trade in the Bermuda Triangle* moves popular cultural studies beyond its entanglement with the national-popular. It is to be expected that this exercise of mapping will fall short of generating a transnational ethos of action-oriented solidarity, a kind of manual or "how to" for some future revolution. But it is also to be expected that, under current conditions, transnational forms of solidarity and even action will themselves fall similarly short — will be subject to the same sorts of ironic all-too-human interfer-ence that we have come to associate with these popular geographical formations. Hence the need to chart a new geography of globaliza-tion that sidesteps the global/local dynamic in which so many studies of transnational culture have become enmeshed. The challenge is to define an alternative that seeks emancipation neither in the specifici-ties of the local nor in the supposedly disruptive effects of large-scale transnational passages. Only in this way can we hope to devise tac-tics for living in the postutopian moment of global capitalism without losing sight of another time and space that arises from the limits and instabilities of this same globalizing system.

Works Cited

Abraham, Nicolas, and Maria Torok. 1986. *The Wolf Man's Magic Word: A Cryptonomy.* 1976. Trans. Nicholas Rand. Minneapolis: University of Minnesota Press.

Adorno, Theodor, and Max Horkheimer. 1979. *Dialectic of Enlightenment.* Trans. John Cumming. London: Verso.

Agamben, Giorgio. 1993. *The Coming Community.* Trans. Michael Hardt. Minneapolis: University of Minnesota Press.

———. 1998. *Homo Sacer: Sovereign Power and Bare Life.* Trans. Daniel Heller-Roazen. Stanford, Calif.: Stanford University Press.

———. 1999. "The Messiah and the Sovereign: The Problem of the Law in Walter Benjamin." In *Potentialities: Collected Essays in Philosophy,* ed. and trans. Daniel Heller-Roazen. Stanford, Calif.: Stanford University Press.

———. 2000. *Means without End: Notes on Politics.* Trans. Vincenzo Binetti and Cesare Casarino. Minneapolis: University of Minnesota Press.

———. 2001. "On Security and Terror." *Theory and Event* 5. http://muse .jhu.edu/journals/theory_and_event/v005/5.4agamben.html [26 May 2002].

Agence France Presse. 2001. "Northern Alliance Afghanistan's Main Opium Producer: UN." http://news.123india.com/full/05102001/regional/afp/ 011005173423rs02hjs4q4.html [20 October 2001].

Akiba, Okon. 1997. "International Trade in Narcotic Drugs: Implications for Global Security." *Futures* 29:605–16.

Alexi, Terrance. 2000. *Through the Vortex: Escape from the Bermuda Triangle.* Lincoln, Nebr.: iUniverse.com

Allman, T. D. 1971. "The Fortunes of War." *Far Eastern Economic Review* July 24:37.

Almond, Philip. 1988. *The British Discovery of Buddhism.* Cambridge: Cambridge University Press.

Altman, Dennis. 1996. "On Global Queering." *Australian Humanities Review.* www.lib.latrobe.edu.au/AHR/archive/Issue-July-1996/altman.html [20 December 2000].

Amin, Samir. 1997. *Capitalism in the Age of Globalization: The Management of Contemporary Society.* London: Zed Books.

Anderson, Benedict. 1991. *Imagined Communities: Reflections on the Origin and Spread of Nationalism.* Rev. ed. London: Verso.

Anderson, Edward. 1993. *Plants and People of the Golden Triangle: Ethnobotany of the Hill Tribes of Northern Thailand.* Portland: Dioscorides Press.

Anderson, Malcolm, and Monica Den Boer, eds. 1994. *Policing across National Boundaries*. London: Pinter Publishers.

Ang, Ien, and Jon Stratton. 1996. "On the Impossibility of a Global Cultural Studies: 'British' Cultural Studies in an 'International' Frame." In *Stuart Hall: Critical Dialogues*, ed. Kuan-hsing Chen and David Morley. London: Routledge.

Appadurai, Arjun. 1996. *Modernity at Large: Cultural Dimensions of Globalization*. Minneapolis: University of Minnesota Press.

———. 1998. "Dead Certainty: Ethnic Violence in the Era of Globalization." *Development and Change* 29:905–25.

Árápad, Varga E. 1999. "Hungarians in Transylvania between 1870 and 1995." In *Occasional Papers 12*, ed. Nándor Bárdi, László Diószegi, and András Gyertyánfy. Budapest: Teleki László Foundation.

Arata, Stephen. 1990. "The Occidental Tourist: Stoker and Reverse Colonization." *Victorian Studies* 33:621–45.

Arrighi, Giovanni. 1994. *The Long Twentieth Century: Money, Power, and the Origins of Our Times*. London: Verso.

Baban, Adriana. 2000. "Women's Sexuality and Reproductive Behavior in Post-Ceauşescu Romania: A Psychological Approach." In *Reproducing Gender: Politics, Publics, and Everyday Life after Socialism*, ed. Susan Gal and Gail Kligman. Princeton, N.J.: Princeton University Press.

Badiou, Alain. 2000. *Deleuze: The Clamor of Being*. Trans. Louise Burchill. Minneapolis: University of Minnesota Press.

Balibar, Etienne. 1998. "The Borders of Europe." In *Cosmopolitics: Thinking and Feeling beyond the Nation*, ed. Bruce Robbins and Pheng Cheah. Minneapolis: University of Minnesota Press.

Barker, Alfred Trevor. 1948. *The Mahatma Letters to A. P. Sinnett from the Mahatma M. and K. H.*, ed. Christmas Humphreys and Elsie Benjamin. New York: Rider and Company.

Barsamian, David. 1990. "An interview with Alfred McCoy." www.lycaeum .org/drugwar/DARKALLIANCE/ciah1.html [28 July 1998].

Barthes, Roland. 1972. *Mythologies*. Trans. Anne Lavers. London: J. Cape.

———. 1975. *The Pleasure of the Text*. Trans. Richard Miller. New York: Hill and Wang.

Bataille, Georges. 1991. "The Unarmed Society: Lamaism." In *The Accursed Share: An Essay on General Economy*. Trans. Robert Hurley. New York: Zone Books.

Beeching, Jack. 1975. *The Chinese Opium Wars*. New York: Harcourt Brace Jovanovich.

Behr, Edward. 1991. *Kiss the Hand You Cannot Bite: The Rise and Fall of the Ceauşescus*. New York: Villard Books.

Belanger, Francis W. 1989. *Drugs, the U.S., and Khun Sa*. Bangkok: Editions Duang Kamol.

Benítez-Rojo, Antonio. 1993. *The Repeating Island: The Caribbean and the Postmodern Perspective*. Trans. James Maraniss. Durham, N.C.: Duke University Press.

Benjamin, Walter. 1969. "Theses on the Philosophy of History." In *Illumina-tions*, ed. Harry Zohn. New York: Schocken Books.

———. 1982. "Exposé: Paris, Capital of the Nineteenth Century." In *Gesam-melte Schriften*, ed. Rolf Tiedemann and Herman Schweppenhauser. Vol. 5. Frankfurt-am-Main: Suhrkamp Verlag.

Bennett, Tony. 1992. "Putting Policy into Cultural Studies." In *Cultural Studies*, ed. Lawrence Grossberg, Cary Nelson, and Paula A. Treichler. London: Routledge.

Bennett, Tony, and Janet Woollacott. 1987. *Bond and Beyond: The Political Career of a Popular Hero*. Houndsmill, U.K.: Macmillan.

Bennett, William J. 1992. *The De-valuing of America: The Fight for Our Culture and Our Children*. New York: Simon and Schuster.

Bequai, August. 1979. *Organized Crime: The Fifth Estate*. Lexington, Mass.: Lexington Books.

Berlitz, Charles. 1974. *The Bermuda Triangle: An Incredible Saga of Unex-plained Disappearances*. New York: Doubleday.

———. 1977. *Without a Trace*. New York: Doubleday.

———. 1989. *The Dragon's Triangle*. New York: Wynwood Press.

Bernbaum, Edwin. 1980. *The Way to Shambhala: The Search for the Mythical Kingdom beyond the Himalayas*. New York: Anchor Books.

Berridge, Virginia, and Griffith Edwards. 1987. *Opium and the People*. New Haven: Yale University Press.

Beverley, John. 1997. "Does the Project of the Left Have a Future?" *boundary 2* 24:35–57.

Bhabha, Homi. 1994. *The Location of Culture*. London: Routledge.

Bishop, Peter. 1989. *The Myth of Shangri-La: Tibet, Travel Writing, and the Western Creation of a Sacred Landscape*. Berkeley: University of California Press.

Blavatsky, Helena. 1888. *The Secret Doctrine: The Synthesis of Science, Religion, and Philosophy*. Adyar, India: The Theosophical Press.

Bloch, Ernst. 1986. *The Principle of Hope*. Trans. Neville Plaice, Stephen Plaice, and Paul Knight. Oxford: Blackwell.

Block, Alan A. 1986. "A Modern Marriage of Convenience: A Collaboration between Organized Crime and U.S. Intelligence." In *Organized Crime: A Global Perspective*, ed. Robert J. Kelly. Totowa, N.J.: Rowman and Littlefield.

Boner, Charles. 1865. *Transylvania: Its Products and People*. London: Longmans, Green, Reader, and Dyer.

Bonnecarrère, Paul. 1977. *The Golden Triangle*. Trans. Oliver Coburn. Nuffield, Henley-on-Thames, U.K.: Aidan Ellis Publishing.

Booth, Martin. 1996. *Opium: A History*. London: Simon and Schuster.

Borton, Douglas. 1992. "Voivode." In *Dracula: Prince of Darkness*, ed. Martin Greenberg. New York: DAW Books.

Brah, Avtar. 1996. *Cartographies of Diaspora: Contesting Identities*. London: Routledge.

Braudel, Fernand. 1980. "History and the Social Sciences: The *Longue Durée.*" In *On History.* Trans. Sarah Matthews. Chicago: University of Chicago Press.

Brennan, Timothy. 1997. *At Home in the World: Cosmopolitanism Now.* Cambridge, Mass.: Harvard University Press.

Brenner, Neil. 2001. "The Limits to Scale? Methodological Reflections on Scalar Structuration." *Progress in Human Geography* 25:591–614.

Brown, Norman O. 1959. "Filthy Lucre." In *Life against Death: The Psychoanalytic Meaning of History.* Middletown, Conn.: Wesleyan University Press.

Browning, Frank, and Banning Garrett. 1971. "The New Opium War." *Ramparts* 9:32–39.

Buck, Pearl. 1938. *The Good Earth.* New York: Pocket Books.

Burke, Anthony. 2001. *In Fear of Security: Australia's Invasion Anxiety.* Sydney: Pluto Press.

"Burma Must Show It Deserves Drug Aid." 2002. *Bangkok Post.* 5 February. http://scoop.bangkokpost.co.th/bkkpost/2002/feb2002/bp20020205/news/05Feb2002_opin37.html [1 July 2002].

Burnett, Chistina Duffy, and Burke Marshall, eds. 2001. *Foreign in a Domestic Sense: Puerto Rico, American Expansionism, and the Constitution.* Durham, N.C.: Duke University Press.

Burroughs, William S. 1977. *Junky.* 1953. New York: Penguin.

Califia, Pat. 1988. "The Vampire." In *Macho Sluts: Erotic Fiction.* Los Angeles: Alyson Books.

Carroll, Lewis. 1974. *Alice's Adventures in Wonderland.* London: Bodley Head.

Case, Sue-Ellen. 1991. "Tracking the Vampire." *differences* 3:1–20.

Castells, Manuel. 1989. *The Informational City.* Oxford: Blackwell.

———. 1996. *The Rise of Network Society.* Oxford: Blackwell.

Chambers, Iain. 1986. *Popular Culture: The Metropolitan Experience.* London: Methuen.

Chaterjee, S. K. 1981. *Legal Aspects of International Drug Control.* The Hague: Martinus Nijhoff.

Chouvy, Pierre-Arnaud. 1999. "Drug Diversity in the Golden Triangle." *Crime and Justice International* 15:5, 6, 18.

———. 2001. "Les territoires de l'opium: Géopolitique dans les espaces du Triangle d'Or et du Croissant d'Or." Ph.D. diss., Panthéon-Sorbonne University, Paris.

Chow, Rey. 1991. "Violence in the Other Country: China as Crisis, Spectacle, and Woman." In *Third World Women and the Politics of Feminism,* ed. Chandra Talpade Mohanty, Ann Russo, and Lourdes Torres. Bloomington: Indiana University Press.

Clancy, Tom. 1989. *Clear and Present Danger.* London: HarperCollins.

Clifford, James. 1997. *Routes: Travel and Translation in the Late Twentieth Century.* Cambridge, Mass.: Harvard University Press.

Cohen, Jeffrey Jerome. 1996. "Monster Culture (Seven Theses)." In *Monster Theory: Reading Culture,* ed. Jeffrey Jerome Cohen. Minneapolis: University of Minnesota Press.

Collins, Jim. 1977. *The Bermuda Triangle.* London: Raintree Children's Books.

Coman, Julian. 2001. "Dracula Park Plan Gets Blood Boiling." 18 September. www.romania-gateway.ro/news/ViewDoc.asp?Document_Id=3266 [30 September 2001].

Connolly, William E. 1999. *Why I Am Not a Secularist.* Minneapolis: University of Minnesota Press.

Cooney, Eleanor, and Daniel Altieri. 1996. *Shangri-La: The Return to the World of "Lost Horizon."* New York: Morrow.

Copjec, Joan. 1991. "Vampires, Breast Feeding, and Anxiety." *October* 58: 25–43.

Cosgrove, Denis. 1994. "Contested Global Visions: One World, Whole Earth, and the Apollo Space Photographs." *Annals of the Association of American Geographers* 84:270–94.

Critchley, Simon. 2000. "Let's Stop Talking about Europe." *Signs of the Times.* www.signsofthetimes.org.uk/Critchley.html [3 April 2001].

Crosse, Andrew F. 1878. *Round about the Carpathians.* Edinburgh: William Blackwood and Sons.

Dalai Lama and Galen Rowell. 1990. *My Tibet.* Berkeley: University of California Press.

Davenant, Charles. 1771. "Discourses on the Public Revenue and on the Trade of England." 1698. In *Political and Commercial Works,* ed. Sir Charles Whitworth. Vol. 1. London: R. Horsfield.

David-Neel, Alexandra. 1934. *The Superhuman Life of Gesar of Ling.* New York: C. Kendall.

Dean, Jodi. 1998. *Aliens in America: Conspiracy Theory from Outer Space to Cyberspace.* Ithaca, N.Y.: Cornell University Press.

De Certeau, Michel. 1984. *The Practice of Everyday Life.* Trans. Steven F. Rendall. Berkeley: University of California Press.

Deletant, Dennis. 1995. "Ceauşescu's Appeal to National Sentiment: The Case of Transylvania." In *Ceauşescu and the Securitate: Coercion and Dissent in Romania, 1965–1989.* London: Hurst and Company.

Deleuze, Gilles. 1988. *Foucault.* Trans. Sean Hand. London: Athelone Press.

———. 1991. *Bergsonism.* Trans. Hugh Tomlinson and Barbara Habberjam. New York: Zone Books.

———. 1994. *Difference and Repetition.* Trans. Paul Patton. New York: Columbia University Press.

Deleuze, Gilles, and Félix Guattari. 1983. *Anti-Oedipus: Capitalism and Schizophrenia.* 1972. Trans. Robert Hurley, Mark Seem, and Helen R. Lane. Minneapolis: University of Minnesota Press.

Derrida, Jacques. 1986. "Fors." 1976. In Nicolas Abraham and Maria Torok, *The Wolf Man's Magic Word: A Cryptonomy.* Trans. Nicholas Rand. Minneapolis: University of Minnesota Press.

———. 1993. "The Rhetoric of Drugs." *differences* 5:1–25.

Dessaint, Alain Y. 1972. "The Poppies Are Beautiful This Year." *Natural History* 9:32–37.

Diehl, Andrea. 2000. "GoNomad Destination Mini Guide: Vieques Island, Puerto Rico." Available online at www.gonomad.com/destinations/0101/diehl_viequesminiguide.html [23 June 2001].

Dolar, Mladen. 1991. " 'I Shall Be with You on Your Wedding Night': Lacan and the Uncanny." *October* 58:5–23.

Donald, James. 1992. "What's at Stake in Vampire Films." In *Sentimental Education: Schooling, Popular Culture, and the Regulation of Liberty.* London: Verso.

Donegan, Greg. 2000. *Atlantis: The Bermuda Triangle.* New York: Berkley.

Dorn, Nicholas, Jorgen Jepsen, and Ernesto Savona, eds. 1996. *European Drug Policies and Enforcement.* Houndsmill, U.K.: Macmillan.

Douglas, Mary. 1966. *Purity and Danger.* London: Routledge and Kegan Paul.

Drake, Alvin W., Stan N. Finkelstein, and Harvey M. Sapolsky. 1982. *The American Blood Supply.* Cambridge, Mass.: MIT Press.

Dreamscapes. 2001. Bermuda Triangle Database. www.mysteries-megasite .com/main/bigsearch/bermuda-1.html [5 June 2001].

Drucker, Peter. 1993. *Post-capitalist Society.* New York: Harper Business.

Eagleton, Terry. 2000. *The Idea of Culture.* Oxford: Blackwell.

Ebon, Martin, ed. 1975. *The Riddle of the Bermuda Triangle.* New York: Signet.

Epstein, Edward Jay. 1977. *Agency of Fear: Opiates and Political Power in America.* New York: Putnam.

European Union Online. 2001. "General Declaration on Articles 13 to 19 of the Single Europe Act." http://europa.eu.int/abc/obj/treaties/en/entr14b .htm#Declaration_6 [20 September 2001].

Featherstone, Mike. 1996. "Localism, Globalism, and Cultural Identity." In *Global/Local: Cultural Production and the Transnational Imaginary,* ed. Rob Wilson and Wimal Dissanayake. Durham, N.C.: Duke University Press.

Featherstone, Mike, Scott Lash, and Roland Robertson, eds. 1995. *Global Modernities.* London: Sage.

Fiske, John. 1989. *Understanding Popular Culture.* Boston: Unwin and Hyman.

Fiske, John, and John Hartley. 1978. *Reading Television.* London: Routledge.

Foucault, Michel. 1973. *The Order of Things: An Archaeology of the Human Sciences.* New York: Vintage Books.

———. 1978. *The History of Sexuality.* Trans. Robert Hurley. New York: Pantheon Books.

———. 1986. "Of Other Spaces." *Diacritics* 16:22, 27.

Freud, Sigmund. 1908. "Character and Anal Eroticism." In *Works,* ed. James Strachey. London: Hogarth Press.

———. 1917. "On Transformation of Instinct as Exemplified in Anal Eroticism." In *Works,* ed. James Strachey. London: Hogarth Press.

Friedman, Jonathan. 1995. "Global System, Globalization, and the Parameters of Modernity." In *Global Modernities*, ed. Mike Featherstone, Scott Lash, and Roland Robertson. London: Sage.

Frow, John. 1997. "Gift and Commodity." In *Time and Commodity Capitalism: Essays in Cultural Theory and Postmodernity.* Oxford: Clarendon Press.

Fukuyama, Francis. 1992. *The End of History and the Last Man.* Harmondsworth, U.K.: Penguin.

Gaddis, Vincent H. 1964. "The Mystery of the Deadly Bermuda Triangle." (February).

———. 1965. *Invisible Horizons: True Mysteries of the Sea.* Philadelphia: Chilton.

Galleano, Eduardo. 1973. *Open Veins of Latin America: Five Centuries of the Pillage of a Continent.* Trans. Cedric Belfrage. New York: Monthly Review Press.

Ganguly, Meenakshi. 2001. "Generation Exile: Big Trouble in Tibet." *Transition* 87:4–25.

Garland, Alex. 1995. *The Beach.* New York: Riverhead.

Gelder, Ken. 1994. *Reading the Vampire.* London: Routledge.

Gerard, Emily. 1885. "Transylvanian Superstitions." *Nineteenth Century* (July): 130–50.

Gibson, Tobias. 1995. "The Dimensions of the Triangle." http://blindkat .tripod.com/triangle/gl.html [19 June 2001].

Gilroy, Paul. 1993. *The Black Atlantic: Modernity and Double Consciousness.* Cambridge, Mass.: Harvard University Press.

Glover, David. 1996. *Vampires, Mummies, and Liberals: Bram Stoker and the Politics of Popular Fiction.* Durham, N.C.: Duke University Press.

Godwin, John. 1968. *This Baffling World.* New York: Bantam.

Golden Triangle Park. 2001. www.goldentrianglepark.org [22 July 2001].

Gomez, Jewelle. 1991. *The Gilda Stories.* Ithaca, N.Y.: Firebrand Books.

Goodstone, Tony. 1970. *The Pulps.* New York: Chelsea House.

Gorman, Peter, and Bill Weinberg. 2001. "The Clinton Drug War Legacy." *High Times* 306 (February). www.hightimes.com/Magazine/2001/2001 _02/article2.tpl [1 September 2001].

Gramsci, Antonio. 1988. *Selected Writings, 1916–1935,* ed. David Forgacs. New York: Schocken Books.

Grosfeld, Frans. 1976. *Het mysterie van de Bermuda driehoek.* Amsterdam: Amsterdam Boek.

Gross, Peter. 1995. "Romania." In *Glasnost and After: Media and Change in Central and Eastern Europe,* ed. David L. Paletz, Karol Jakubowicz, and Pavao Novosel. Creskill, N.J.: Hampton Press.

Group, David. 1984. *The Evidence for the Bermuda Triangle.* Wellingborough, U.K.: Aquarian Press.

Guénon, René. 1983. *The Lord of the World.* 1927. Charlestown, W.Va.: Coombe Springs Press.

Halberstam, Judith. 1995. *Skin Shows: Gothic Horror and the Technology of Monsters.* Durham, N.C.: Duke University Press.

Hall, Stuart. 1988. "The Toad in the Garden: Thatcherism among the Theorists." In *Marxism and the Interpretation of Culture*, ed. Cary Nelson and Lawrence Grossberg. Urbana: University of Illinois Press.
———. 1995. "Negotiating Caribbean Identities." *New Left Review* 209: 3–14.
———. 1996. "The Problem of Ideology: Marxism without Guarantees." In *The Stuart Hall Reader*, ed. David Morley and Kuan-Hsing Chen. London: Routledge.
Halperin, David. 1996. A Response from David Halperin to Dennis Altman. *Australian Humanities Review*. www.lib.latrobe.edu.au/AHR/emuse/ Globalqueering/halperin.html [20 December 2000].
Hannerz, Ulf. 1996. "The Local and the Global: Community and Change." In *Transnational Connections: Culture, People, Places*. London: Routledge.
Haraway, Donna. 1997. *Modest_Witness@Second_Millennium.FemaleMan© _Meets_OncoMouse™: Feminism and Technoscience*. New York: Routledge.
Hardt, Michael, and Antonio Negri. 2000. *Empire*. Cambridge, Mass.: Harvard University Press.
Harrer, Heinrich. 1953. *Seven Years in Tibet*. London: Paladin.
Harvey, David. 1989. *The Condition of Postmodernity: An Enquiry into the Conditions of Cultural Change*. Oxford: Blackwell.
———. 1996. *Justice, Nature, and the Geography of Difference*. Oxford: Blackwell.
Hebdige, Dick. 1979. *Subculture: The Meaning of Style*. London: Methuen.
Hilton, James. 1933. *Lost Horizon*. London: Macmillan.
Hobbes, Thomas. 1651. *Leviathan*. Online at www.orst.edu/instruct/phl302/ texts/hobbes/leviathan-d.html#CHAPTER%20XXIV [21 March 2001].
Huntington, Samuel P. 1996. *The Clash of Civilizations and the Remaking of World Order*. New York: Simon and Schuster.
Hupchick, Dennis P. 1995. *Conflict and Chaos in Eastern Europe*. New York: St. Martins.
Inglis, Brian. 1976. *The Opium War*. London: Hodder and Staughton.
———. 1999. *The Bermuda Triangle*. Austin, Tex.: Raintree Steck-Vaughn.
Innes, Brian. 1999. *The Bermuda Triangle*. Austin, Tex.: Raintree/Steck Vaughn.
Jackson, Phil. 1995. *Sacred Hoops: Spiritual Lessons of a Hardwood Warrior*. New York: Hyperion.
Jameson, Fredric. 1979. "Reification and Utopia in Mass Culture." *Social Text* 1:130–48.
———. 1981. *The Political Unconscious: Narrative as a Socially Symbolic Act*. Ithaca, N.Y.: Cornell University Press.
———. 1991. *Postmodernism, or, the Cultural Logic of Late Capitalism*. Durham, N.C.: Duke University Press.
———. 1992. "Totality as Conspiracy." In *The Geopolitical Aesthetic: Cinema and Space in the World System*. Bloomington: Indiana University Press.
———. 1997. "Culture and Finance Capital." *Critical Inquiry* 24:246–65.

Jeffrey, Adi-Kent Thomas. 1973. *The Bermuda Triangle*. New York: Warner.

Johnson, Major E. C. 1885. *On the Track of the Crescent: Erratic Notes from the Pireus to Pesth*. London: Hurst and Blackett.

Joseph, May. 1999. *Nomadic Identities: The Performance of Citizenship*. Minneapolis: University of Minnesota Press.

Jungclaus, David G. 1985. *City Beneath the Bermuda Triangle*. Santa Barbara, Calif.: National Literary Guild.

Kant, Immanuel. 1991. "Perpetual Peace: A Philosophical Sketch." In *Kant: Political Writings*, ed. Hans Reiss. 1796. Cambridge: Cambridge University Press.

Kaplan, Caren. 1996. *Questions of Travel: Postmodern Discourses of Displacement*. Durham, N.C.: Duke University Press.

Keenan, Thomas. 1997. *Fables of Responsibility: Aberrations and Predicaments in Ethics and Politics*. Stanford, Calif.: Stanford University Press.

Khoo, Tseen. 2000. "(Dis)infecting Australia." *Amida Magazine*. www.amida .com.au/ident/1003disinfect.html [27 August, 2001].

King, Stephen. 1975. *'Salem's Lot*. Garden City, N.J.: Doubleday.

Klieger, P. Christiaan. 1992. *Tibetan Nationalism: The Role of Patronage in the Accomplishment of a National Identity*. Meerut, India: Archana Publications.

Kligman, Gail. 1988. *The Wedding of the Dead: Ritual, Poetics, and Popular Culture in Transylvania*. Berkeley: University of California Press.

———. 1998. *The Politics of Duplicity: Controlling Reproduction in Ceauşescu's Romania*. Berkeley: University of California Press.

Kollmar-Paulenz, Karénina. 1992–93. "Utopian Thought in Tibetan Buddhism: A Survey of the Sambhala Concept and Its Sources." *Studies in Central and East Asian Religion* 5/6:78–96.

Kurti, Laszlo. 1989. "Transylvania, Land beyond Reason: Toward an Anthropological Analysis of a Contested Terrain." *Dialectical Anthropology* 14:21–52.

Kusche, Lawrence. 1975. *The Bermuda Triangle Mystery — Solved*. New York: Harper and Row. Reprints, Amherst, N.Y.: Prometheus Books, 1986, 1995.

Laclau, Ernesto. 1997. "The Death and Resurrection of the Theory of Ideology." *Modern Language Notes* 112:297–321.

Laclau, Ernesto, and Chantal Mouffe. 1985. *Hegemony and Socialist Strategy: Toward a Radical Democratic Politics*. London: Verso.

Landsburg, Alan. 1978. *Secrets of the Bermuda Triangle*. New York: Warner.

Lavery, David. 1992. *Late for the Sky: The Mentality of the Space Age*. Carbondale: Southern Illinois University Press.

Leach, Edmund. 1960. "The Frontiers of Burma." *Comparative Studies in Society and History* 2:49–68.

Lee, Benjamin, and Edward LiPuma. 2002. "Cultures of Circulation: The Imaginations of Modernity." *Public Culture* 14:191–213.

Lefebvre, Henri. 1991. *The Production of Space*. Trans. David Nicholson-Smith. Oxford: Blackwell.

———. 2001. "Comments on a New State Form." Trans. Victoria Johnson and Neil Brenner. *Antipode* 33:769–82.

LePage, Victoria. 1996. *Shambhala: The Fascinating Truth behind the Myth of Shangri-La*. Wheaton, Ill.: Quest Books.

Lévesque, Jacques. 1997. *The Enigma of 1989: The USSR and the Liberation of Eastern Europe*. Trans. Keith Martin. Berkeley: University of California Press.

Lévi-Strauss, Claude. 1976. *Tristes Tropiques*. Trans. John and Doreen Weightman. Harmondsworth: Penguin.

Levy, Adrian, and Cathy Scott-Clark. 1997. "Burma's Opium King Recast as Business Man." *Guardian Weekly*, March 23, 8.

Lewis, Martin W., and Kären E. Wigen. 1997. *The Myth of Continents: A Critique of Metageography*. Berkeley: University of California Press.

Lewis, Paul, and Elaine Lewis. 1984. *People of the Golden Triangle: Six Tribes in Northern Thailand*. London: Thames and Hudson.

Leyshon, Andrew, and Nigel Thrift. 1997. *Money/Space: Geographies of Monetary Transformation*. London: Routledge.

Lintner, Bertil. 1991. *Cross-Border Drug Trade in the Golden Triangle*. Durham, N.C.: Boundaries Research Press.

———. 1993. *The Politics of the Drug Trade in Burma*. Nedlands, Western Australia: Indian Ocean Centre for Peace Studies.

———. 2001. "Taliban Turns to Drugs." *Far Eastern Economic Review*, 11 October. www.feer.com/2001/0110_11/p026region.html [20 October 2001].

Livezeanu, Irina. 1995. *Cultural Politics in Greater Romania: Regionalism, Nation Building, and Ethnic Struggle, 1918–1930*. Ithaca, N.Y.: Cornell University Press.

Lloyd, David, and Paul Thomas. 1998. *Culture and the State*. London: Routledge.

Lopez, Donald. 1994. "New Age Orientalism." *Tricycle: The Buddhist Review* 3:37–43.

———. 1995. "Foreigner at the Lama's Feet." In *Curators of the Buddha: The Study of Buddhism under Colonialism*, ed. Donald Lopez. Chicago: University of Chicago Press.

———. 1998. *Prisoners of Shangri-La: Tibetan Buddhism and the West*. Chicago: University of Chicago Press.

Lutz, Catherine, and Jane Collins. 1993. *Reading National Geographic*. Chicago: University of Chicago Press.

McBride, Joseph. 1992. *Frank Capra: The Catastrophe of Success*. London: Faber.

McCoy, Alfred W. 1972. *The Politics of Heroin in Southeast Asia*. New York: Harper and Row.

———. 1991. *The Politics of Heroin: CIA Complicity in the Global Drug Trade*. New York: Lawrence Hill.

McLagan, Meg. 1996. "Computing for Tibet: Virtual Politics in the Post-Cold War Era." In *Connected: Engagements with Media*, ed. George Marcus. Chicago: University of Chicago Press.

McNally, Raymond T., and Radu Florescu. 1972. *In Search of Dracula.* Greenwich, Conn: New York Graphic Society.

———. 1973. *Dracula: A Biography of Vlad the Impaler.* New York: Hawthorn Books.

Mandel, Ernest. 1975. *Late Capitalism.* Trans. Joris de Bres. London: New Left Books.

Marlowe, Ann. 1999. *How to Stop Time: Heroin from A to Z.* New York: Basic Books.

Marx, Karl. 1848. "On the Question of Free Trade." *Marx and Engels Internet Archive.* http://csf.colorado.edu/psn/marx/Archive/1848-FT/1848-ft.txt [20 October 2002].

———. 1976. *Capital,* Vol. 1. Trans. Ben Fowkes. 1867. Harmondsworth, U.K.: Penguin.

———. 1978. *Capital,* Vol.2. Trans. David Fernback. 1885. Harmondsworth, U.K.: Penguin.

Massey, Doreen. 1994. *Space, Place, and Gender.* Cambridge: Polity.

Mauss, Marcel. 1967. *The Gift: Forms and Functions of Exchange in Archaic Societies.* Trans. Ian Cunlinson. 1960. New York: Norton.

McGhee, Fletcher. 1998. *The Bermuda Triangle Subdued.* New York: Vantage Press.

Meier, Barry. 2001. " 'Super' Heroin Was Planned by Bin Laden, Reports Say." *New York Times.* www.nytimes.com/2001/10/04/international/04DRUG.html [20 October 2001].

Melton, Gordon J. 1994. *The Vampire Book: The Encyclopaedia of the Undead.* Detroit: Visible Ink Press.

Miller, Daniel. 1995. "Consumption as the Vanguard of History: A Polemic by Way of Introduction." In *Acknowledging Consumption: A Review of New Studies,* ed. Daniel Miller. London: Routledge.

Miller, Elizabeth. 1997. *Reflections on Dracula: Ten Essays.* White Rock, B.C.: Transylvania Press.

Miller, James, ed. 1992. *Fluid Exchanges: Artists and Critics in the AIDS Crisis.* Toronto: University of Toronto Press.

Miller, J. Hillis. 1995. *Topographies.* Stanford, Calif.: Stanford University Press.

Miller, Toby, et al. 2001. *Global Hollywood.* London: BFI Publishing.

Miyoshi, Masao. 1993. "A Borderless World? From Colonialism to Transnationalism and the Decline of the Nation-State." *Critical Inquiry* 19: 726–37.

———. 1995. "Sites of Resistance in the Global Economy." *boundary 2* 22:61–84.

Moretti, Franco. 1983. "Dialectic of Fear." In *Signs Taken for Wonders: Essays in the Sociology of Literary Form.* London: Verso.

———. 1998. *Atlas of the European Novel, 1800–1900.* London: Verso.

Morpurgo, John. 1979. *Allen Lane, King Penguin: A Biography.* London: Hutchinson.

Morris, Meaghan. 1990. "Banality in Cultural Studies." In *Logics of Television,* ed. Patricia Mellencamp. Bloomington: Indiana University Press.

Morton, David. 1996. "The Crisis of Queer Theory and/in Altman's 'Globalism.'" *Australian Humanities Review.* www.lib.latrobe.edu.au/AHR/emuse/Globalqueering/morton.html [20 December 2000].

Mungiu-Pippidi, Alina. 1999. *Subjective Transylvania: A Case Study of Post Communist Nationalism.* www.osi.hu/ipf/publications/AlinaPP-nation.html [14 March 2001].

Norbu, Jamyang. 1994. "The Tibetan Resistance Movement and the Role of the CIA." In *Resistance and Reform in Tibet,* ed. Robert Barnett. London: Hurst.

OGD (Observatoire Géopolitique des Drogues/Geopolitical Drug Watch). 1996. *The Geopolitics of Drugs: 1996 Edition.* Boston: Northeastern University Press.

Ohmae, Kenichi. 1990. *The Borderless World: Power and Strategy in the Interlinked Economy.* New York: Harper Business.

———. 1995. *The Decline of the Nation-State: The Rise of Regional Economies.* London: Harper Collins.

Orth, Maureen. 2002. "Afghanistan's Deadly Habit." *Vanity Fair* 499 (March): 64–72.

Osborne, Peter. 1995. *The Politics of Time: Modernity and Avant-Garde.* London: Verso.

Ó Tuathail, Gearóid. 1996. *Critical Geopolitics: The Politics of Writing Global Space.* London: Routledge.

Oxlade, Chris. 1999. *The Mystery of the Bermuda Triangle.* Oxford: Heinemann Library.

Paterniti, Michael. 2002. "Florida: America *In Extremis.*" *New York Times Magazine,* 21 April. Available online at www.nytimes.com/2002/04/21/magazine/21FLORIDA.html [24 April 2002].

Petras, James. 2001. "'Dirty Money' Foundation of U.S. Growth and Empire." *Centre for Research on Globalisation.* http://globalresearch.ca/articles/PET108A.html [11 July 2002].

Phongpaichit, Pasuk, Sungsidh Piriyarangsan, and Nualnoi Treerat. 1998. *Guns, Girls, Gambling, Ganja: Thailand's Illegal Economy and Public Policy.* Chiang Mai, Thailand: Silkworm Books.

Porter, Doug J. 1997. "A Plague on the Borders: HIV, Development, and Traveling Identities in the Golden Triangle." In *Economies of Pleasure: Sexualities in Asia and the Pacific,* ed. Lenore Manderson and Margaret Jolly. Chicago: University of Chicago Press.

Portes, Alejandro, and Alex Stepick. 1993. *City on the Edge: The Transformation of Miami.* Berkeley: University of California Press.

Prachan, Jean. 1978. *Le triangle des Bermudes: Base secrète des OVNI.* Paris: Belfond.

Proud, Franklin M. 1976. *The Golden Triangle.* London: Sphere Books.

Quasar, Gian. 2001. bermuda-triangle.org. http://www.bermuda-triangle.org [5 June 2001].

Radway, Janice. 1984. *Reading the Romance: Women, Patriarchy, and Popular Literature.* Chapel Hill: University of North Carolina Press.

Ratesh, Nestor. 1991. *Romania: The Entangled Revolution.* New York: Praeger.

Rausa, Rosario. 1980. *Gold Wings, Blue Sea: A Naval Aviator's Story.* Annapolis, Md.: Naval Institute Press.

Redfield, James. 1993. *The Celestine Prophecy: An Adventure.* New York: Warner Books.

———. 1999. *The Secret of Shambhala: In Search of the Eleventh Insight.* New York: Bantam.

———. 2001. "A Silver Lining: The Emergence of Worldwide Prayer Networks." *Celestine Journal* (October). Online at www.celestinevision.com/ 01october.html [15 October 2001].

Reid, Jim. 2001. "We Were Not Lost, . . . or, I Believe in the Bermuda Triangle." *Wings of Gold.* www.abledogs.com/DogPattern/DogPattern.htm [26 April 2002].

Rhys Davids, Thomas William. 1877. *Buddhism: Being a Sketch of the Life and Teachings of Gautama, the Buddha.* London: Society for Promoting Christian Knowledge.

Renard, Ronald D. 1996. *The Burmese Connection: Illegal Drugs and the Making of the Golden Triangle.* Boulder, Colo.: Lynne Rienner.

Rice, Anne. 1976. *Interview with the Vampire.* London: Raven Books.

Richards, Thomas. 1993. *The Imperial Archive: Knowledge and the Fantasy of Empire.* London: Verso.

Rickels, Laurence A. 1999. *The Vampire Lectures.* Minneapolis: University of Minnesota Press.

Rider, Barry, and Michael Ashe, eds. 1996. *Money Laundering Control.* Dublin: Round Hall.

Rinpoche, Gar-je K'am-trul. 1978. "A Geography and History of Shambhala." *The Tibet Journal* 3:3–11.

Robbins, Bruce. 1999. *Feeling Global: Internationalism in Distress.* New York: New York University Press.

Robertson, Roland. 1995. "Glocalization: Time-Space and Homogeneity-Heterogeneity." In *Global Modernities,* ed. Mike Featherstone, Scott Lash, and Roland Robertson. London: Sage.

Roerich, Nicholas. 1929. *Altai-Himalaya: A Travel Diary.* New York: Frederick A. Stokes.

———. 1929. *The Heart of Asia.* Southbury, U.K.: Alatas.

———. 1990. *Shambhala.* 1930. Rochester, Vt.: Inner Traditions.

Ronay, Gabriel. 1972. *The Dracula Myth.* London: W. H. Allen.

Ronnel, Avital. 1992. *Crack Wars: Literature, Addiction, Mania.* Lincoln: University of Nebraska Press.

Rose, Gillian. 1996. "As If the Mirrors Had Bled: Masculine Dwelling, Masculinist Theory and Feminist Masquerade." In *Body Space: Destabilizing Geographies of Gender and Sexuality,* ed. Nancy Duncan. London: Routledge.

Ross, Andrew. 1991. *Strange Weather: Culture, Science, and Technology in the Age of Limits.* London: Verso.

————. 1999. *The Celebration Chronicles: Life, Liberty, and the Pursuit of Property Value in Disney's New Town*. New York: Ballantine.

Rumsfeld, Donald. 2002. News Transcript. 27 January. www.defenselink.mil/news/Jan2002/t01282002_t0127enr.html [17 June 2002].

Russell, Dan. 2001. "Drug War: Burma." *disinformation*. www.disinfo.com/pages/article/id871/pg2/ [1 September 2001].

Russell, Lawrence. 2001. "Modernism and Idealism: *Lost Horizon*, Frank Capra's Classic Restored." *Film Court*. http://www.culturecourt.com/F/Hollywood/LostHorizon.htm [8 September 2001].

Salecl, Renata. 1994. *The Spoils of Freedom: Psychoanalysis and Feminism after the Fall of Socialism*. London: Routledge.

Sambhava, Padma. 1994. *The Tibetan Book of the Dead*. Trans. Robert A. Thurman. New York: Bantam.

Sand, George X. 1952. "Sea Mystery at Our Back Door." *Fate* (October).

Sanderson, Ivan. 1975. "Worldwide Seas of Mystery." In *The Riddle of the Bermuda Triangle*, ed. Martin Ebon. New York: Signet.

Sassen, Saskia. 1991. *The Global City: New York, London, Tokyo*. Princeton, N.J.: Princeton University Press.

————. 2000. "Digital Networks and the State: Some Governance Questions." *Theory, Culture, and Society* 17:19–33.

Schell, Orville. 2000. *Virtual Tibet: Searching for Shangri-La from the Himalayas to Hollywood*. New York: Henry Holt.

Schmid, Justin. 1998. *The Bermuda Triangle: Secrets of the Devil's Triangle (Call of Cthulhu Roleplaying Game)*. Oakland, Calif.: Wizard's Attic.

Schumacher, Ernst Fritz. 1973. *Small Is Beautiful: Economics as if People Mattered*. London: Harper Collins.

Schwartz, Peter, and Peter Leyden. 1997. "The Long Boom: A History of the Future, 1980–2020." *Wired* 5, no. 7. www.wired.com/wired/archive/5.07/longboom.html [14 June 2001].

Scott, Peter Dale, and Jonathan Marshall. 1991. *Cocaine Politics: Drugs, Armies, and the CIA in Central America*. Berkeley: University of California Press.

Sharp, Joanne P. 1993. "Publishing American Identity: Popular Geopolitics, Myth, and *The Reader's Digest*." *Political Geography* 12:491–504.

Simmel, Georg. 1978. *The Philosophy of Money*. Trans. Tom Bottomore and David Frisby. London: Routledge.

Simmons, Dan. 1992. *Children of the Night*. New York: Putnam Books.

Senn, Harry. 1982. *Were-Wolf and Vampire in Romania*. New York: Columbia University Press.

Shakya, Tsering. 1991. "Tibet and the Occident: The Myth of Shangri-La." *Lungta* 5:21–23.

Skal, David. 1990. *Hollywood Gothic: The Tangled Web of Dracula from Novel to Stage to Screen*. New York: Norton.

Sloterdijk, Peter. 1997. "Eurotaoism." In *Cultural Politics and Political Culture in Postmodern Europe*, ed. J. Peter Burgess. Amsterdam: Rodolphi.

————. 2001. *Die letzte Kugel: Zu einer philosophischen Geschichte der terrestrischen Globalisierung*. Frankfurt: Suhrkamp Verlag.

Smith, Martin. 1991. *Burma: Insurgency and the Politics of Ethnicity.* London: Zed Books.

Smith, Neil. 1984. *Uneven Development: Nature, Capital, and the Production of Space.* New York: Blackwell.

Smith, Paul. 1997. *Millennial Dreams: Contemporary Culture and Capital in the North.* London: Verso.

Smith, Warren. 1975. *The Triangle of the Lost: The Bermuda Triangle Explored and Explained.* New York: Zebra.

Smith, Warren W. 1994. "The Nationalities Policy of the Chinese Communist Party and the Socialist Transformation of Tibet." In *Resistance and Reform in Tibet,* ed. Robert Barnett. London: Hurst.

Sofia, Zoë. 2000. "Container Technologies." *Hypatia.* 15:181–201.

Soja, Edward. 1996. *Thirdspace: Journeys to Los Angeles and Other "Real-and-Imagined" Places.* Cambridge, Mass.: Blackwell.

Solomon, Jon. 2001. "Taiwan Incorporated: A Survey of Biopolitics in the Sovereign Police's Pacific Theater of Operations." *Cultural Studies Monthly.* www.ncu.edu.tw/ eng/csa/journal/journal_park19.htm [12 July 2001].

Sopa, Geshe Lundub, Roger Jackson, and John Newman, eds. 1985. *The Wheel of Time: The Kalachakra in Context.* Madison, Wis.: Deer Park Books.

Spencer, John Wallace. 1969. *The Limbo of the Lost.* New York: Bantam.

———. . 1991. *The Bermuda Triangle — UFO Connection.* Potomac, Md.: Phillips Publishing Company.

Spivak, Gayatri Chakravorty. 1987. *In Other Worlds: Essays in Cultural Politics.* London: Methuen.

———. 2000. "From Haverstock Hill Flat to U.S. Classroom, What's Left of Theory?" In *What's Left of Theory?* ed. Judith Butler, John Guillory, and Kendall Thomas. New York: Routledge.

Stares, Paul. 1996. *Global Habit: The Drug Problem in a Borderless World.* Washington, D.C.: Brookings Institution.

Stoker, Bram. 1983. *Dracula.* 1897. Oxford: Oxford University Press.

Summers, Montague. 1968. *The Vampire in Europe.* 1929. New Hyde Park, N.Y.: University Books.

Sweeney, John. 1991. *The Life and Evil Times of Nicolae Ceaușescu.* London: Hutchinson.

Synovitz, Ron. 2002. "Afghanistan: Kabul Continues to Struggle with Poppy Cultivation, Drug Trade." Radio Free Europe. www.rferl.org/nca/features/ 2002/06/26062002165825.asp [1 July 2002].

Tanzi, Vito. 1996. "Money Laundering and the International Financial System." *IMF Working Paper.* Washington, D.C.: International Monetary Fund.

Thorne, Ian. 1978. *The Bermuda Triangle (Search for the Unknown).* Mankato, Minn.: Crestwood House.

Titler, Dale. 1962. *Wings of Mystery: True Stories of Aviation History.* New York: Dodd Mead.

Titmuss, Richard. 1970. *The Gift Relationship: From Human Blood to Social Policy.* London: Allen and Unwin.

Tomas, Andrew. 1977. *Shambhala: Oasis of Light.* London: Sphere Books.

UNDCP (United Nations Office for Drug Control and Crime Prevention). 2001. *Global Illicit Drug Trends 2001.* www.odccp.org [30 July, 2001].

———. 2002. *Global Illicit Drug Trends 2002.* www.odccp.org [1 July, 2002].

U.S. Department of State. 1972. *Report of the Cabinet Committee on International Narcotics Control Task Force on Air and Sea Smuggling.* Washington, D.C. 21 February.

———. 2001. *Narcotics Control Reports—2000.* Washington, D.C. 5 March.

Van Biema, David. 1997. "America's Fascination with Buddhism." *Time* 150, 13 October. Online at www.time.com/time/magazine/1997/dom/971013/cover1.html [23 October 2001].

Van der Boogert, Kate, and Nadine Davidoff. 1999. *Heroin Crisis: Key Commentators Discuss the Issues and Debate Solutions to Heroin Abuse in Australia.* Melbourne: Bookman Press.

Van der Veen, Hans T. 1999. *The International Drug Complex.* Amsterdam: Centre for Drug Research, Universiteit van Amsterdam.

Vattimo, Gianni. 1999. *Belief.* Trans. Luca D'Isanto and David Webb. Stanford, Calif.: Stanford University Press.

Veit, John. 1998. "The Drug War Industrial Complex: The *High Times* Interview: Noam Chomsky." *High Times* 272 (April). www.tfy.drugsense.org/chomsky.htm [19 August, 2001].

Verdery, Katherine. 1996. *What Was Socialism, and What Comes Next?* Princeton, N.J.: Princeton University Press.

———. 1999. *The Political Lives of Dead Bodies: Reburial and Postsocialist Change.* New York: Columbia University Press.

Vignati, Alejandro. 1975. *El triángulo motal de las Bermudas.* Barcelona: ATE.

Viliers, Alan. 1974. *Posted Missing.* 1956. New York: Charles Scribners.

Virilio, Paul. 1998. "Military Space." In *The Virilio Reader,* ed. James Der Derian. Malden, Mass.: Blackwell.

Waddell, Laurence Austine. 1895. *The Buddhism of Tibet, or Lamaism.* London: W. H. Allen.

Wallerstein, Immanuel. 1974. *The Modern World System.* New York: Academic Press.

———. 1979. *The Capitalist World Economy: Essays.* Cambridge: Cambridge University Press.

Wasson, Richard. 1966. "The Politics of Dracula." *English Literature in Transition* 9:24–27.

Weller, Bob. 1999. *Salvaging Spanish Sunken Treasure.* Lake Worth, Fla.: Crossed Anchors Salvage.

Welsh, Irvine. 1993. *Trainspotting.* London: Minerva.

Wertheim, Margaret. 1999. *The Pearly Gates of Cyberspace: A History of Space from Dante to the Internet.* New York: Norton.

Wicke, Jennifer. 1992. "Vampiric Typewriting: *Dracula* and Its Media." *English Literary History* 59:467–93.

Wild and Exotic Thailand. 2001. "Mystery of the Golden Triangle." www
.wild-exotic-thailand.com/tour/triangle [20 July 2001].

Williams, Raymond. 1958. *Culture and Society, 1780–1950.* London: Chatto
and Windus.

Wilson, Rob, and Wimal Dissanayake, eds. 1996. *Global/Local: Cultural
Production and the Transnational Imaginary.* Durham, N.C.: Duke
University Press.

Winer, Richard. 1974. *The Devil's Triangle.* New York: Bantam.

Winichakul, Thongchai. 1994. *Siam Mapped: A History of the Geo-Body of
a Nation.* Honolulu: University of Hawaii Press.

Wolfe, James Raymond. 1975. "Of Time and the Triangle." In *The Riddle of
the Bermuda Triangle,* ed. Martin Ebon. New York: Signet.

"The Wonderland of Opium." 1971. *Far Eastern Economic Review,* July
24, 37.

Wylie, Turrell V. 1965. "The Tibetan Tradition of Geography." *Bulletin of
Tibetology* 2:17–25.

Yang, Bo. 1987. *The Golden Triangle: Frontier and Wilderness.* Hong Kong:
Joint Publishing Company.

Yarbro, Chelsea Quinn. 1978. *Hotel Transylvania.* New York: St. Martins.

Zathureczky, Gyula. 1967. *Transylvania: Citadel of the West.* Astor, Fla.:
Danubian Press.

Žižek, Slavoj. 1991. *For They Know Not What They Do: Enjoyment as a
Political Factor.* London: Verso.

———. 1993. *Tarrying with the Negative: Kant, Hegel, and the Critique of
Ideology.* Durham, N.C.: Duke University Press.

———. 1997. "Cyberspace, or, The Unbearable Closure of Being." In *The
Plague of Fantasies.* London: Verso.

Filmography

Annaud, Jean-Jacques. 1997. *Seven Years in Tibet.* TriStar Pictures.

Badham, John. 1979. *Dracula.* Universal.

Barba, Norberto. 1998. *Lost in the Bermuda Triangle.* Columbia Pictures.

Brittain, Donald. 1978. *Secrets of the Bermuda Triangle.* Questar Video.

Browning, Tod. 1931. *Dracula.* Universal.

Bunnag, Rome. 1980. *The Golden Triangle.* NM Video (Hong Kong).

Campbell, Doug. 1995. *The UFO Diaries: The Bermuda Triangle/Area 51.* Video One (Canada).

Capra, Frank. 1937. *Lost Horizon.* Columbia TriStar Home Video.

Cardona, René, Jr. 1978. *The Bermuda Triangle (Devil's Triangle of Bermuda).* MGM.

Carter, Chris. 1998. *Triangle.* The X-Files Episode. Fox Television.

Coppola, Francis Ford. 1978. *Apocalypse Now.* Malofilm Group.

———. 1992. *Bram Stoker's Dracula.* Columbia TriStar Home Video.

Crain, William. 1972. *Blacula.* Metromedia Home Video.

Craven, Wes. 2000. *Wes Craven Presents: Dracula 2000.* Dimension Films.

De Luca, Rudy. 1985. *Transylvania 6-5000.* Starmaker Entertainment.

Dragoti, Stan. 1979. *Love at First Bite.* Metromedia.

Ferarra, Abel. 1995. *The Addiction.* Polygram Video.

Fisher, Terence. 1956. *Dracula.* Matinee Theatre Episode. NBC Television.

———. 1958. *Horror of Dracula.* Hammer.

———. 1960. *The Brides of Dracula.* Hammer.

Franco, Jess. 1978. *Count Dracula.* Facets Video. BBC.

Friedenberg, Richard. 1979. *The Bermuda Triangle.* United Entertainment.

Gordon, Stuart. 1989. *Daughter of Darkness.* Vidmark Entertainment.

Graham, William A. 1975. *Beyond the Bermuda Triangle.* Vidmark Entertainment.

Herzog, Werner. 1979. *Nosferatu, the Vampyre.* Warner Home Video Ltd.

Hillyer, Lambert. 1936. *Dracula's Daughter.* Universal.

Jarrott, Charles. 1973. *Lost Horizon.* Columbia Pictures.

Jordan, Neil. 1994. *Interview with the Vampire.* Warner Home Video.

Lajthay, Karoly. 1921. *Drakula.* Filmnagy (Hungary).

Le, Bruce. 1991. *Black Spot.* Tai Seng Video Marketing (Hong Kong).

Lee, Yongmin. 1961. *Ahkea Kkots.* Sunglin Films (Korea).

Levy, Scott P. 1998. *Beneath the Bermuda Triangle.* Royal Oaks Entertainment.

Marshak, Philip. 1969. *Dracula and the Boys (Dracula Sucks).* First International Pictures.

Merhige, E. Elias. 2000. *Shadow of the Vampire*. Lions Gate Films.
Merrick, Laurence. 1969. *Dracula and the Boys*. Laurence Merrick Productions.
Misumi, Kenji. 1972. *Lone Wolf and Club: Sword of Vengeance*. Taho Films (Japan).
Moss, James. 1973. *Dragula*. Moss Productions.
Muhtar, Mehmet. 1953. *Drakula Istanbul'da*. Demiraf (Turkey).
Murnau, Friedrich Wilhelm. 1922. *Nosferatu, eines Symphonie des Grauens*. (Germany).
Nakagawa, Nobuo. 1956. *Kyuketsuki Ga (Vampire Moth)*. Shintoho (Japan).
Nicolaou, Ted. 1991. *Subspecies*. Malofilm Ltd.
Polanski, Roman. 1967. *The Fearless Vampire Killers*. MGM.
Reid, Alastair. 1989. *Traffik*. Channel 4 (U.K.).
Saichur, Sumat. 1985. *Raiders of the Golden Triangle*. Hong Kong/Thailand.
Saville, Philip. 1977. *Count Dracula*. BBC.
Schumacker, Joel. 1987. *The Lost Boys*. Warner.
Scorsese, Martin. 1997. *Kundun*. Touchstone Pictures.
Scott, Tony. 1983. *The Hunger*. MGM.
Seaton, George. 1970. *Airport*. Universal.
Sharman, Jim. 1975. *The Rocky Horror Picture Show*. Trimark.
Simmon, John. 1993. *Equinox: The Bermuda Triangle*. Columbia.
Siodmak, Robert. 1943. *Son of Dracula*. Universal.
Siu-ho, Chin. 1991. *Challenge to Devil Area*. Tai Seng Video Marketing (Hong Kong).
Soderbergh, Stephen. 2000. *Traffic*. Gramercy Pictures.
Sonnenfeld, Barry. 1997. *Men in Black*. Columbia.
Speilberg, Steven. 1977. *Close Encounters of the Third Kind*. Columbia.
Toynton, Ian. 1996. *The Bermuda Triangle*. Columbia.
Wecksberg, Peter. 1974. *Deafula*. Signscope.
Wilcox, John. 1996. *The Bermuda Triangle: Secrets Revealed*. Questar Video.
Woo, John. 1986. *Heroes Shed No Tears*. Da-Wei Films Unlimited (Hong Kong).

Index

Abortion, 33, 61, 96–97, 195
Abraham, N., 134
Addiction, xiv, xv, 102, 104, 136–38, 143, 151, 200, 207
Addiction, The, 100
Adorno, T., xxii, 58
Affect, xiii, xxi, xxii, 95, 100, 195, 199, 209
affective labor, 132–33
flows of, xxviii
and media, xvii, xxx
and national belonging, xxiv
Afghanistan, xv, 16, 42, 107–11, 145, 188
Agamben, G., xxvi, 16, 37, 58, 150, 152, 193
AIDS, xxvi, 15, 76, 96, 99, 137
Allman, T. D., 113
Al Qaeda, 16, 42, 110, 150
Altman, D., 98
Amin, S., xxvi
Anderson, B., xxi, xxviii, 63, 117, 122
Ang, I., xxiii
Appadurai, A., xxi, xxviii, 46–47, 83, 177, 200
Arata, S., 55
Argosy magazine, 1, 20–21, 44
Arrighi, G., xxvi, 35
Asylum seekers, 2, 14–17, 42, 147, 153
Cambodian, 41
Cuban, 3
Haitian, 3, 14
Sino-Vietnamese, 41
Vietnamese, 41
See also refugees

Badiou, A., 196
Balibar, E., 82
Barthes, R., xxv, 162
Bataille, G., 153
Beach, The, 156
Belief, 165
popular, xx, 59, 73, 76, 163
religious, 15, 169, 186, 194–95
Benítez-Rojo, A., 13
Benjamin, W., xxii, 36, 37

Bennett, T., xxiii
Bennett, W., 144, 147
Bergson, H., 39
Berlitz, C., 1, 4, 8, 12, 22–23, 27, 31, 37, 44, 49
Bermuda, 9
Bermuda Triangle, The, 21
akin to Dragon's Triangle, 40–41, 43–44
and capitalism, 26
and globalization, 45–52
mythography, xi–xii, 1–4, 22, 48
paranormal theories, 18, 32–35
psychoanalytic and feminist reading, 27–31
publications on, 20–22, 24–25
in relation to history, spatiality, and temporality, 35–38
as space of flows, 38–40
Beverley, J., xxiv
Bhabha, H., 36, 37
Biopolitics, xxvi, 95, 100, 146
Bishop, P., 165
Blavatsky, H., 156, 165–66, 169
Bloch, E., 197, 204
Blood, xiv, 60, 95
banking, 99–100
circulation of, 90
transfusions, 74–76
Body, xxvi, 105, 206
control/regulation of, 4, 137
and drugs, xxix, 105, 135–36, 151
ethnic, 83
Freudian conception of, 131–33, 134
national, 61, 95, 97, 144
New Age conceptions of, 180–81, 182
Borderlands, xiii, xiv, 55, 80, 104, 106, 118, 207
Borderless world, 3, 123
Borders, xx, 2, 18, 30–31, 122–23, 125, 135
of Burma, xv, 109
control of, xvi, 16, 17
cultural, 46
of Europe, 80
fixed, 14

Borders (*continued*)
flows across, 46
of the Golden Triangle, 102, 104, 124
guards of, 60
national, xix, xxi, xxiv, 16, 99, 123,
148
between need and desire, xiv
redrawing of, 89
of Thailand, 116, 122–23
of Tibet, 188
of Transylvania, 62, 67
unstable (indeterminate), 2, 4, 51–52,
82, 88, 103, 107, 208
violation/transcendence of, 20, 104,
134
See also Geography: boundaries
Brah, A., xxv
Braudel, F., 35
Brennan, T., 13
Brenner, N., 207–8
Brothers to the Rescue, 14
Brown, N. O., 131
Burke, A., 147
Burma (Myanmar), xv, 106, 109, 111,
114, 116, 118–19, 122, 145
Burroughs, W., 137
Bush, G. H. W., 12, 14, 24, 32, 41, 43,
144, 147
Bush, G. W., 12
Bush, J., 13

Califia, P., 96
Camp X-Ray, 16–17, 42
Capitalism, xiv, xxv, xxvi, 20, 46, 89,
203
center/periphery, 139
disruption of, 22, 25–26
interaction with globalization and
socialism, 92
new wave, 2–4
post–Cold War, 56
postsocialist order, 56
processes and effects, xx
versus socialism, 89, 91
Caribbean, 13–17
Cartography, xii, 38, 39, 81, 120, 125,
135, 164, 187–88
of the Bermuda Triangle, 7, 20
of dispersion, xxv
of global capitalism, xxviii
and indeterminacy, 88
postnational, xxi
scalar methods of, 141
technologies of, 163
virtual, xxvii

Case, S.-E., 55, 95
Castells, M., xxi, 38
Cayce, E., 23, 33
Ceauşescu, N., 57–58, 67–68, 71, 74–77,
83, 91, 93, 96, 100
Challenger space shuttle, 24
Chambers, I., xxii
Chomsky, N., 146
Chouvy, P.-A., 107, 109
Chow, R., 184–85
CIA (Central Intelligence Agency), 106–
7, 112, 113, 114, 115, 117, 126,
144, 145
Circulation, xiv, 90, 95, 99, 131, 135,
199
of capital, 2, 39, 52, 89, 199
of people and products, xxvii, 3, 4, 72,
93, 105, 112, 146, 164, 200, 201
of vernacular sensibilities, xxii, 202
Citizenship, 98
double (Hungarian/Romanian), 80
global, 48
Clancy, T., 144
Class, xxii, xxiii, 54, 60, 139
comprador, 127
conflict, 66
dominant, 25, 29
entrepreneurial, 77
middle, 106, 174
peasant, 63
underclass, 146
white leisure, 10, 27
working, 106, 147
Clifford, J., xxv, 117
Clinton, W. J., 14, 25, 41, 144–45
Cohen, J., 84, 89
Collins, J., 113
Connolly, W., 147, 194, 195
Conspiracy theory, xii, 47, 51–52, 57,
201
Consumption, xxvi, xxvii, 104, 105,
138–40. See also drugs; popular
culture
Copjec, J., 55, 84
Cosgrove, D., 47–48
Cosmopolitanism, xxiv, 66, 73, 92, 117,
168, 208
Critchley, S., 80
Cuba, 10, 13, 14, 15, 16, 32

Daks, 64, 65, 68
Dalai Lama, xvii, xviii, 157–59, 170,
172, 183–84, 186–87
Davenant, C., 90

DEA (Drug Enforcement Agency), 115, 127, 144, 145, 149
Dean, J., 18, 33, 48
De Certeau, M., 104
Deletant, D., 67
Deleuze, G., xxi, xxvi, xxviii, 3, 4, 30, 39, 133, 196, 202
Dependency theory, 45, 139, 140
Derrida, J., 104, 134
Desiring-production, xxvi–xxvii, xxviii, xxix, 3, 37, 40, 51, 142, 204
Dessaint, A., 113
Deterritorialization, 3–4, 46. See also reterritorialization
Diaspora, xxiv, 161, 173
  in Caribbean, 13–14
  and drug smuggling, 125–26
  in former eastern bloc, 89
  Indian, 127
  space, xxv
  and vampire culture, 127
Disaster films, 2, 23
Dissanayake, W., xxi, 140
Dolar, M., 55, 84
Donald, J., 55, 83–84
Douglas, M., 133
Dracula, xiii, 53, 54, 55, 60, 64, 73, 74
  and capitalist order, 55, 101
  feminist reading of, 95–96
  and intellectual property, 53–55
  as national narrative, 87
  in popular film and fiction, 69–72
  poststructuralist and psychoanalytic readings, 84–87
  and Transylvanian history, 60
Drucker, P., 56
Drugs, xiv, xvi
  consumption of, 138
  cultivation of, 120–22
  and global capital, 105, 151
  heroin addiction, 136
  in history, 105–11
  trafficking, 102, 124, 125, 135, 149–50
  war on, 143–51
  See also money-laundering

Eagleton, T., 204
Epstein, E. J., 143
Ethnic nationalism, 55
  Romanian-Hungarian conflict, 66–67, 78–79, 89
  in Transylvania, 61

European Union, xiii, xx, 18, 80, 82, 92, 128, 148
Everyday life, 29, 85, 99, 137, 141, 147, 197, 199
  politics of, 177, 191
  practices of, xxviii, 92
Exiles
  Cuban, 14
  Tibetan, xvii, 159, 171, 183, 184, 186
Extraterrestrials, xviii, 23, 29, 32, 33, 35, 47–48

Featherstone, M., 139, 141
Finkelstein, S., 99
Fiske, J., xxii, 140, 162
Florescu, R., 75
Florida, xi, 5, 8–9, 12–14, 24, 27, 179, 207
Foucault, M., xxvi, 90, 204–6
Frankfurt School, xxii, xxiii, 56, 188
Freud, S., 130
Friedman, J., 139
Frow, J., 99
Fukuyama, F., 56

Gaddis, V., 1, 7
Galleano, E., 140
Gelder, K., 55, 73, 76
Gender, xix, xxvi, 22, 26, 27, 61, 195, 199
  codes, 96
  domination, 3, 4, 95
  in psychoanalysis, 30
  roles, 56, 96
  and space, 29
Geographers, xviii, 47, 112
  critical, 205
Geography, xviii, 37, 204
  of Bermuda Triangle, 11, 16
  boundaries, xii, 26, 50, 102, 112, 148, 200, 203
  centers, 12, 49, 173
  critical, 200, 207
  and decentralization, 89
  and displacement, 135
  of globalization, xxx, 40, 200
  human, xviii, 204
  and identity, 102
  imaginary, 112
  and indeterminacy, 141, 163
  of money, 50, 130–34
  plural, 30, 80
  popular, xi–xxxi, 61, 199–00, 202
  monstrous, 55, 82–89
  metageography, 81

Geography (*continued*)
  and representation, 200
  sacred, 175
  scale in, 150, 206–8
  of Shambhala, 175
  and space, xx, xxiv, 51, 55, 98, 163
  Tibetan, 188
  See also Borders; Scale
Gilroy, P., 18
Globalism, 199
Globalization, xii, xviii, xix, xx, 45–47,
  193, 199
  antiglobalization, xix, 153
  counterglobalization, xix, xxviii, 208
  and homogenization, 45, 139–41
  and hybridization, 139–41
  interaction with capitalism and
    socialism, 92
  localization, 141, 198
  outside to, xviii, 160, 162, 165, 174,
    180, 187, 188, 193, 194, 196, 197,
    198
  and queer sexuality, 98–99
  wild, 4, 38, 45
Global cities, 49, 50
Global-local links, xii, xxi, 46, 55, 139,
  140, 153, 207–9
Glocalization, xxi
Golden Crescent, xv, 107–8, 109, 111,
  207
Golden Triangle, xv–xvi, xxi
  in anthropological accounts, 117–18
  and global drug economy, 102
  as global space, 123–24, 141
  as indigenous space, 122, 124
  Park, xv, 119–20
  in popular cultural fantasy, fiction, and
    film, 112–17
  in relation to national borders, 122
  resisting globalization, 142
  and tourism, 119
Golden Triangle, The (Proud, F. M.),
  113, 114, 115
Golden Triangle: Wilderness and Frontier
  (Yang, B.), 116–17
González, Elián, 15
Gramsci, A., xxiii
Greater Romania Party (PRM), 77, 80
Guantánamo Bay, 14, 15, 16–17, 41, 42
Guattari, F., xxi, xxvi, 3, 4, 30, 39, 133,
  202
Guénon, R., 175–76

Haiti, 10, 13, 14
Halberstam, J., 72, 95

Hall, S., xxiii, xxvii, 13
Halperin, D., 98
Hannerz, U., 140
Hapsburg Empire, xiii, 63, 64, 88
Haraway, D., 95
Hardt, M., xxiv, xxvi, 48, 51, 90–91,
  132, 208
Hartley, J., 140
Harvey, D., xxvi, 2, 208
Hawala/Hundi banking, 127. *See also*
  money laundering
Hebdige, D., xxii
Heroes Shed No Tears, 116
Heterogenization, 105, 139, 140, 141
Heterotopias, 204–6
Hill tribes, 103, 113, 114, 120, 121, 122,
  123
  and ethnobotany, 117
Hilton, J., 152–53, 179
History
  Annales school of, 45, 139
  anticolonial, 13
  of Atlantic, 3, 18
  of Cold War, 32
  and colonialism, 9, 10
  end of, 56
  of Florida, 14
  of global capitalism, xxvi
  of opium, 105–6, 119
  of Shambhala, 185–86
  of Tibet, 156, 164–65, 186, 188
  and time, 31, 33, 35–37, 46
  of Transylvania, xiii–xiv, 53, 57, 60,
    61–66, 68, 75, 83, 85
Homogenization, xxiii, 67, 45, 98
  as theory of globalization, 105, 139,
    140, 141
Horkheimer, M., xxii
Hungarian Alliance (DAHR), 78, 79, 80
Hungarians (in Transylvania), Magyars,
  63, 65, 66
Huntington, S., 80, 82
Hupchick, D., 61
Hybrid
  identities, 91, 139
  reproduction, 33
Hybridity, 173
Hybridization, 3, 105, 139, 140

Ideology, 97, 155, 191–93
  of the marketplace, 56, 187, 190
  and representation, 160, 162
Imagination, xxviii–xxix
  popular, 72

Immanence, 52
  absolute, 193
  of desire, xxxi
  of ideological field, 192–93
  of labor, 132
  of life on earth, 48, 181, 193, 194, 196
  and mystical One, 195
  plane of, 91
  of space and time, 196
Imperialism, 10, 106, 153, 165, 168–70,
  182, 188, 198, 205
  and China, 173, 184
  power differentials of, 36
  and territory, ix, 13
Intellectual property, xxvii, 48, 53–55
Intercontextuality, 200–203, 205, 208
Interview with the Vampire, 71, 72, 97
Irony, xxvii, 20, 26, 134, 161, 202

Jameson, F., xxii, 2, 25, 35, 47, 131–32,
  160
Joseph, M., xxiv
Just war, 17, 49

Kalachakra, 185–87
Kaplan, C., xxiv
Karzai, H., 111
Keenan, T., 142
Khun Sa, 109, 119, 144, 145
Klieger, C., 183
Kligman, G., 59, 96
Kollmar-Paulenz, K., 185
Kundun, 156, 157
Kuomintang (KMT), 106, 116, 117
Kusche, L., 7–8

Laclau, E., xxiii, 162, 165, 191–92
Lamaism, 169–70. See also Religion,
  Tibetan Buddhism; Tibetology
Lash, S., 139
Lavery, D., 24
Leach, E., 122
Lee, B., 135
Lefebvre, H. xx, 36, 37, 38, 141, 163,
  199, 203, 205–6
LePage, V., 175–78, 188
Lévesque, J., 57
Levi-Strauss, C., 8
Lewis, M. W., 81
Leyshon, A., 50, 134
Lintner, B., 104, 110, 122
LiPuma, E., 135
Livezeanu, I., 83
Lloyd, D., xxiv
Locality, 46, 206, 208

Lopez, D., 165, 170, 172–73
Lost Horizon
  Capra film, xvi, 155–56, 191
  Hilton novel, xvi, 152–54, 159–60,
    177, 179, 190, 201
Lost in the Bermuda Triangle, 25, 34–35
Lugosi, B., 54, 69, 70
Lutz, C., 113

Magic, 2, 71, 131
  secular, xiii
Mandel, E., 2
Mariel boat lift, 14
Markets, xiv, xix, xxvii, 2, 26, 48, 104,
  140, 200
  Chinese, xviii, 44, 154, 173, 184
  clandestine, 105
  fall of, 24
  financial, xvi, 2, 128, 129
  free, 23, 100
  global, 2, 21, 24, 48, 56, 130, 151
  of Hollywood, 54
  international, 96, 102, 139
  and Internet, 182
  national, 77
  for opium, 106–7, 110, 125, 126,
    145
  for popular fiction, 154
  property, 128
  world, 25, 49, 115, 134, 188
Marlowe, A., 138
Marx, K., xi, xxv, xxvi, 90, 91
Massey, D., 29
Mauss, M., 99
McBride, J., 155
McCoy, A., 111, 126, 149
McLagan, M., 186
Men in Black, 33
Methamphetamines, xv, 109, 111, 119
Micu, I., 59, 63–64, 65
Miller, D., 139
Miller, E., 73, 93
Miller, J. H., 38, 137, 203
Miller, T., 54
Miyoshi, M., 123, 161, 197
Modernity, xii, xxvi
  capitalist, 207
  crisis of, 197
  and ethnography, 118
  and national imagining, 31, 66
  passage out of, 194
  secular, 155
  and Tibet, 166, 169, 177
  time-consciousness of, 36

Money-laundering, 126, 135
significance to theories of value,
130–34
stages of, 127–29
Moretti, F., 55, 203
Morris, M., xxiii
Morton, D., 98
Mouffe, C., xxiii
Multiculturalism, 10
Multitude, the, xx, xxiv, 91
Mungiu-Pippidi, A., 79, 85
Murnau, F. W., xiii, 54, 69, 71, 72, 74
Mysticism, xxix, 157, 178, 192
and Shangri-La, 191
Myth, 162–63, 177. See also Bermuda
Triangle; Dracula; Shangri-La

NAFTA, 20, 128
Nationalism, xx, xxi, 23, 25, 63, 100,
174
Australian, 147
economic, 2
ethnic, 55, 56
ethnic violence and, 83
and Free Tibet movement, 184–85
gender and reproduction, 96–97
Hungarian, 63, 67–68, 74
postsocialist, xii, 60, 92, 97
Romanian, 63–65, 67–68, 77–78
and sexual deviance, 98
Tibetan, 159, 184
Nation-state, xxi, xxiv, 33, 48, 122, 174
Hungarian and Romanian narratives
of, 85–86
policing of borders, 148
territoriality, 14–15
See also Nationalism
Negri, A., xxiv, xxvi, 48, 51, 90–91, 132,
208
New Age, xvii, xxix, 172–75, 177,
180–83, 197
and anthropology, 172
movement, 173, 174, 194
and Orientalism, 173, 183, 198
and spiritualism, 165, 190
See also Lamaism; Religion, Tibetan
Buddhism; Tibetology
Nosferatu, xiii, xiv, 54, 69, 71, 74
Nugan Hand Bank, 126–27

Observatoire Géopolitique des Drogues
(OGD), 124, 126
Ohmae, K., 56, 123
Oil crisis, 1, 23, 25, 29
Ojai, xvii, 155

Okinawa, 40, 43–44
Opium, xv–xvi, 200
cultivation/production of, 102, 104,
120–22, 145, 207
history of, 105–11
in popular fantasy, literature, and film,
112–17
tourism, 119–20
trade/trafficking of, 113, 123, 125, 144
wars, 106, 117
See also Drugs; Golden Crescent;
Golden Triangle
Orientalism, 166, 172–73, 178
and construction of Romanian culture,
75
and East-West divide, 81–82, 171,
173, 178
and fantasy, 175
and narratives of Transylvania, 74
See also New Age
Osborne, P., 37
Ó Tuathail, G., 124

Party of Romanian National Unity
(PUNR), 77
Party for Social Democracy (PDSR), 77,
79, 80
Paterniti, M., 9
Pleasure/enjoyment, 84, 86, 153
of drugs, xiv, 104, 136, 137, 139, 140
of popular culture, xxii–xxv, 13
and vampirism, 95, 97, 100, 203
Pocket books, 154
Popular culture, xx, xxii, xxiii, 139, 154,
162, 199
comic heroes, 20
and the Golden Triangle, 112–17
and the national-popular, xxiii
and Shangri-La myth, 156, 173,
182–83, 187
studies of, xxii, xxiv
western, 152
See also Shangri-La
Portes, A., 18
Post-Fordist capitalism, 22, 107
Postmodernism, xvi
and anomie, 56
and capitalism, 132
and economic activities, 120
theory, 36
Postsocialism, 58, 92
the living and the dead, 58–60
and nationalism, 60
and social memory, 59
as transition to capitalism, 56

Power, xiv, xxv, xxvi, 2, 100, 140, 142, 143
biopolitical paradigm of (biopower), 100, 132, 133, 134, 151
body as theater of, 105
of capital, 50
constitutive, xxiv
and control, xxvi
counterpower, xxviii, 142
geopower, 125, 135, 150, 154, 164
global regimes of, xvii, 56, 153, 173
labor, 131, 132, 190
of longevity, 76
military, 29, 82, 203
police, 144, 148, 149
relations/differentials, xiv, xxiii, xxx, 36, 142, 178, 182, 203
reproductive, 69
sovereign, xix, 16, 40, 149, 173
state, 33, 96, 120, 146, 147, 150, 174
transcendental, xix, 91
of U.S., 10, 12, 13, 17, 43
Production of space, xix, xxvii, 2, 30, 36, 38, 102, 108, 163
Pronatalism, 76, 96–97, 99, 100
Puerto Rico, 1, 4, 5, 7–11, 20, 43

Quasar, G., 6–7, 27
Queer sexuality, 61, 95, 96, 100
Queer theory, xxv, 55, 98–99, 137

Race, xix, xvi, 3–4, 22, 26, 29, 55, 60, 95, 199
Radway, J., xxii
Reagan, R., xxiii, 23, 24, 43, 143
Reburial rituals, 59–60, 68
Redfield, J., 178–82, 197
Refugees, 3, 33, 38, 41, 117
Australian government response to, 41–42
Cuban, 14–16, 27
Haitian, 27
See also asylum seekers
Religion
Buddhism, 169, 170, 172, 190
Christianity, 63, 66, 80, 82, 181–82, 194
Greek Catholicism, 59, 63, 79, 87
Hinduism, 194
Islam, 80, 107, 109, 110, 159, 194
Mahayana Buddhism, 192
Roman Catholicism, 63, 169, 170, 194
Tibetan Buddhism, 157, 159, 169–72, 177, 183, 185, 193
See also Lamaism, Tibetology

Renard, R., 112
Resistance, xxv, xxvii, xxviii, 137, 139, 142
to globalization, 161–62
Reterritorialization, 3–4, 40, 46. See also deterritorialization
Rhys David, T., 169–70
Rice, A., 72
Richards, T., 153, 164
Rickels, L., 89
Robbins, B., xxi
Robertson, R. xxi, 139, 140
Roerich, N., 166–69
Romanian Hearth, 77
Romanian revolution (Christmas revolution), 56–58
Ronnel, A., 138, 140
Ross, A., 9, 32, 174–75, 177, 180–81
Rumsfeld, D., 42

Salecl, R., 96
Sanderson, I., 20, 44–45
Sassen, S., 50, 128
Scale, 150, 206–8
of body, 134
global, xxvi, 23, 98, 110, 134, 149, 150
local, 190
national, 149
transatlantic, 17
transnational, xxi
See also Geography: scale in
Schmitt, C., 16
Schumacher, E. F., 190
Secularism, 66, 155, 180, 194, 195
Security, xvi, xvii, 18, 33, 150, 152, 177, 179, 199
border, 17
and drug wars, 143–44
industry, 146
state systems of, xiv
Senn, H., 74
September 11 attacks, 12, 16, 17, 110, 150, 180
Seven Years in Tibet, 156, 157
Shangri-La, xviii, 152, 178, 180, 199
myth, xvi, xvii, xxix, 160, 163, 165, 168, 175, 182–83, 190, 193
and Orientalism, 154, 165–66, 175, 187
as outside to globalization, 163, 174, 197
in popular fiction and films, 152–59
as popular geographic space, xii, xix, xxii, xxv, xxx, 200, 202, 204, 206

Shangri-La (*continued*)
and Shambhala, 168, 175, 178–81
and spirituality, 164, 165, 166
and Tibetan Buddhism, 169–73, 196
and Tibetan nationalism, 159, 184–87
See also Tibetology
Simmel, G., 130
Simmons, D., 76
Slavery, xxv, 105
African trade in, 18, 37
in Caribbean, 13
and colonialism, 9–10
Sloterdijk, P., xviii, 1, 198
Smith, N., 207
Smith, P., 48, 56, 132, 188
Sofia, Z., 29
Soja, E., xxix, 38, 205
Solomon, J., 43
Soros, G., 77
Sovereignty
capitalist, 48, 208
and centers, 13, 14
changing forms of, 149–50
of global finance, 129
imperial, 91
of nation-states, 48, 98, 122, 128, 146, 174, 201
and police, xvii, 43
and power, xix, 17, 40, 173
and state of emergency, 16–17
of Taiwan, 43
Spencer, J. W., 5, 6, 7, 17, 21, 24
Spivak, G., 132, 134, 202, 205
Stares, P., 123
Stepick, A., 18
Stratton, J. xxiii
Stoker, B., xiii, 53–55, 60, 69–77, 84, 87, 90, 93, 95, 201
Subjectivity, 39, 91, 98–99, 105, 177
Subspecies, 71, 76
Superstition, xx, 64, 170

Taiwan, xxiii, 40, 43, 44, 116, 117, 184
Taliban, 16, 42, 109–11, 145, 150
Tanzi, V., 129
Technology, 44, 72, 163, 174, 178, 180
biotechnology, xvii
cultural, 71
information, 25, 181
military, 12
New Age, 177, 178, 180
Tesla coils, 34
Video, 138
Thatcher, M., xxiii, 23, 24
Thomas, P., xxiv

Thrift, N., 50, 134
Tibetology, 165–66, 171, 172–73. *See also* Lamaism; Religion: Tibetan Buddhism
Timişoara massacre, 57–58, 68
Titmuss, R., 99
Tökes, L., 57
Tomas, A., 168
Topographies, xxx, 143, 163, 201, 203
disruptive, 133
ethnoreligious, 182
global/local, 55
imperial, 10
nonnational, 206
overlapping, 120
spatial, xxvii
uneven, 200
unlocatable, 134
unmappable, 38, 203
virtual, xix, 51
Torok, M., 134
Tourism
in Bermuda Triangle, 3, 8, 9, 10, 38
ethnotourism, xv
in Golden Triangle, xv–xvi, 105, 118–20, 123
Ojai, 155
resorts, xvii
in Tibet, 157
in Transylvania, 53–55, 71, 92–93, 99
Traffic, 125
Traffik, 125
Transcendence
of boundaries, 26, 50, 134
and cyberspace, 181
deferred, 196
of global forces, 47, 48
of history, 171
of ideology, 192
mystical, 193
in reverse, 196
of space and time, 49, 180
Transcendentalism, 192–96
and God, 194
and power, xix, 91
Transnationalism, 18
Atlantic, 18
critical, xxi
and cultural flows, xiii, xx, 140, 177
Transylvania, xiii, xiv, 53, 76, 87, 99, 100, 101, 201
association with the super-natural/vampire culture, xxix, 55, 56–57, 59, 72–73, 89, 92, 208

Transylvania (*continued*)
  ethnic history/ethnonationalist politics
    of, 61–68, 77–80, 82, 83, 85, 203,
    207
  ethnographic study of, 59
  mortuary practices in, 58–59
  orientalist construction of, 74, 75
  as popular geographic formation, xii,
    xix, xxii, xxv, xxx, 200, 202, 204,
    206
  and postsocialism, 88, 199
  as tourist site, 93
Transylvania University, 73

UFOs, xii, 18, 23, 25, 33, 175
Utopianism, xvii, 197, 203, 206
  and Bermuda Triangle myth, 8, 22,
    36
  and drugs, 137
  geographical utopias, 197, 204
  and irony, 202
  and Shangri-La myth, 157, 160, 165,
    168, 169, 172, 190, 193
  and Transylvania, 101

Valentine, J. M., 22
Vampires, xiii–xiv, xvii, xxx, 201
  biopolitics of, 95–96, 100
  and Ceauşescu, 75
  in films, 69–71
  as metaphor for capital, 91, 101
  in novels, 71, 76–77
  and othering, 72
  and tourism, 53–55, 92–93
  and Transylvania, 55–56, 66, 69, 72,
    73
  vampire culture, 59–60, 69, 73, 83–84,
    203
Van Biema, D., 157
Van der Veen, H., 148
Vattimo, G., 194

Verdery, K., 58–60, 67, 88
Vieques Island, 10–11, 16, 33, 43
Vietnam war, xv, 106–7, 112, 113, 115,
    126, 138, 143
Violence, 116
  of capitalist hegemony, 18
  drug-related, 114, 116
  ethnic, 78, 79, 83, 84, 87
  in film, 116
  of Romanian revolution, 57
  in Tibet, 159, 184
Virilio, P., 49
Vlad the Impaler (or Vlad Ţepeş), 53,
    74–76, 93

Waddell, L. A., 170
Wallerstein, I., xxvi, 45
War against terror, 16, 111, 180
  parallel with drug wars, 150–51
Weller, B., 50
Welsh, I., 136
Wertheim, M., 181
Wicke, J., 55, 72
Wigen, K., 81
Williams, R., xxiii
Wilson, R., xxi, 140
Winichakul, T., 122
Wired magazine, 25
Wolfe, J. R. 33
Wolfowitz, P., xvii
Woollacott, J., xxiii
World-systems theory, xxvi, 45, 139
Worlding, 205
Wylie, T. V., 188

X-Files, The, 25

Yunnan province, China, 103, 121

Žižek, S., 53, 84–85, 87, 91, 97, 181–82,
    192

Brett Neilson is senior lecturer in the School of Humanities at the University of Western Sydney, where he is also a member of the Centre for Cultural Research.